Praise for *Neurogiving*

"Prepare to feel your neurons firing! *Neurogiving: The Science of Donor Decision-Making* is a book I wish I had read 20 years ago. A compelling combination of first hand accounts, emerging research and storytelling, it will help newer and seasoned fundraisers understand how to respect and respond to the intricate gift of donor generosity. It does so with wisdom and heart, and thankfully avoids the 'secret revealed—just purchase our 12 step program' cliché of so many books today. I confess a deep admiration for the author and strongly recommend *Neurogiving* for practitioners and educators alike."

—Ken Mayhew
President & CEO, William Osler Health System Foundation

"Take the time to level up and learn how to replace stale fundraising strategies with game changing insights. Each chapter offers interesting yet actionable ideas that are guaranteed to help you nurture trusted lifetime connections with people who are passionate about your mission. Cherian masterfully knows and shows the way to increased fundraising success—grab your copy today & pick up all the good thinking he puts down."

—Tycely Williams
CEO, Liberty Fellowship

"Koshy has accomplished something rare: making the science of generosity not only accessible, but actionable. This book turns evidence into empathy and data into direction for anyone serious about understanding why people give and how to encourage generosity."

—Russell N. James III, J.D., Ph.D., CFP®
Professor & CH Foundation Chair in Personal Financial Planning;
Director of Graduate Studies in Charitable Planning

"Every fundraiser needs to read this book. *Neurogiving* finally puts words to what we've felt but couldn't always articulate: generosity is human, messy, emotional, wired into us and ultimately beautiful. This book will change how you work—and how you see your donors."

—H. Art Taylor
President & Chief Executive Officer, Association of Fundraising Professionals

"Koshy provides a roadmap to unlocking both the potential of philanthropy and the joy of giving. In a time when private support is more critical than ever, Koshy provides a guide to exceptional fundraising by understanding the minds of donors. Sometimes innovation does not require technology. Koshy shows the mind may be the next frontier for fundraising."

—Joshua Birkholz
CEO of BWF and author of *Fundraising Analytics and Benefactors*

"As an experienced fundraiser and fundraising coach, I've followed the research. I learned that in our asks, we were creating a lot of unnecessary friction for our donors. In *Neurogiving*, Koshy literally goes into the minds of our donors. He clearly explains how our brains work and why what seems to make sense in fundraising is actually hindering our work. And how to present the need so donors can make decisions more easily. Brilliantly, this isn't about manipulation or hacking. This is about respecting our donors, respecting our program staff, and respecting those we serve. I highly recommend every nonprofit purchase copies for everyone on their fundraising teams."

—Marc A. Pitman, CSP
The Concord Leadership Group

"*Neurogiving* is well researched, well written, and exactly what modern fundraising needs. Cherian Koshy doesn't just bring brain science into philanthropy—he uses it to illuminate the emotional core of giving. His work reminds us that generosity is a deeply human act, and that neuroscience and behavioral economics can help us connect with donors in more ethical, empathetic, and effective ways. I wouldn't expect anything less from Koshy, a true leader with a gift for clarity and connection. This is required reading for anyone serious about philanthropy."

—Paul Gravley
CEO, Didlake, Inc.

"This book beautifully captures a truth that resonates deeply with Japanese values: the act of releasing what we have gained in life for the benefit of others reflects the spirit of altruism long cherished in our culture. That's why legacy giving—an act that transcends the self—holds unique power to inspire cultural resonance in Japan. It is not just a fundraising strategy; it is a reflection of who we are."

—Mitsuhiko Yamazaki
Senior Researcher, Will for Japan

"*Neurogiving* is essential reading for every fundraiser. It gives voice to what we've all experienced but struggled to name: that our work isn't about asking but about facilitating the joy of mutual benefit between donors and causes. This approach moves us beyond the conversation of transactional vs relational to truly understanding generosity as something intrinsic to humanity, transforming how we see, our donors, the act of giving and the honor fundraisers have when we facilitate the process well."

—Nicola Lawrence MSc, MSFP, Pgc, CFRE, CAP
Vice President, Individual Giving

"This amazing book reminds us that fundraising isn't about persuasion. It is about honoring the innate generosity found within each person. *Neurogiving* shows us how."

—Dzenan Berberovic
Chief Philanthropy Officer at Avera Health

"This is not just a book about fundraising—it's a blueprint for rethinking human connection. With sharp academic insight and grounded empathy, Koshy uncovers the neuroscience behind real-world decisions. He shows us how to move past assumptions, connect with what truly matters, and design giving experiences that resonate deeply. This is precision meets purpose—science in service of generosity."

—Marina Jones
Executive Director Development & Public Affairs,
English National Opera

"*Neurogiving* couldn't be more timely. As AI and data-driven tools reshape how higher ed institutions, healthcare systems, and non-profits engage their supporters, this book offers a much-needed reminder: fundraising intelligence is about more than information—it's about understanding the people behind the data. Cherian Koshy offers a compelling framework that blends neuroscience, behavioral insight, and ethical design to help organizations build trust and lasting generosity in an increasingly digital world. It's a thoughtful, practical read—and one I'd recommend to anyone navigating the future of fundraising."

—Ross Beattie
CEO, Kindsight

"This groundbreaking book by Cherian Koshy offers an unprecedented exploration of neurogiving, a vital new insight that illuminates the intricate dance between the brain and the heart in philanthropic decision-making. With remarkable precision and profound compassion, he not only unveils the fascinating neural processes at play beneath the surface of giving but also offers a transformative framework for designing fundraising strategies that truly honor the complexity of the human brain and the inherent beauty of generosity. This book is an essential read for anyone seeking to understand and harness the power of altruism."

—Brenda Asare
President & CEO, Alford Group Chair, The Giving Institute

"Centered in empathy, compassion, and humanitarianism, this book charts new territory, delving into how the brain guides, navigates, and shapes our donors' most personal philanthropic decisions. The author even creates a new word for that magical moment when donors are 'their genuine generous selves': neurogiving! The ever thoughtful, thought-provoking, and thorough Cherian Koshy opens new pathways to implement a whole cloth, holistic approach with your philanthropic mission partners. In a time when change is the only constant, read this groundbreaking book to learn how to build trust by prioritizing transparency, authenticity, and consistency; create a storytelling-universe mindset; increase meaningful engagement; foster long-term loyalty; and much, much more."

—Martha Schumacher CFRE, ACFRE, MInstF
President, Hazen Inc. and HILT * @MarthaMaven, Global Strategies
Elevating Social Impact and Philanthropy

"In a time when we're seeing chronic decline of donors to nonprofits but surging generosity in many other ways, it's clear that giving is an act that is deeply rooted in our brains. Fundraisers need to understand the neuroscience that explains the complexity of the brain and the beauty of giving. *Neurogiving* does exactly that. It's an essential resource fundraisers and board leaders to understand how to design fundraising that is grounded in the kind of research that matters most: how real people actually make decisions. This isn't a how-to book. It's a why-we-do book—and that makes all the difference."

—Barbara O'Reilly, CFRE
Founder and Principal, Windmill Hill Consulting

"Every fundraising team should consider reading this book. *Neurogiving* offers valuable insights into donor psychology and outlines strategies for developing effective donor engagement that will transform your perspective on your donors."

—Roger D. Ali, MBA, C.Dir., CFRE
Social Sector Consultant | Executive Leader | AFP Global Chair

"For years, Cherian Koshy has espoused the need for nonprofits to provide donors with a 'joy of philanthropy' experience. In this well researched, well thought out and well written book, Cherian brilliantly provides not only the neuroscience and behavioral theories behind why people want to do good but offers a blueprint for organizations to follow so supporters will joyfully participate in the act of giving. If you're a nonprofit CEO and/or fundraiser, run—not walk, RUN!—to get this book, read it and implement what Cherian suggests. The results will be: Higher donor retention, more effective fundraising, organizational growth, more people served and more impact in the community."

—Ephraim Gopin
Founder, 1832 Communications
(Former nonprofit CEO and fundraiser)

"As a very small nonprofit, communication that resonates with our core supporters is critical to our success. In today's attention economy, this connection is both more difficult and more important than ever. *Neurogiving* is more than just another fundraising playbook—it's a deep dive into the emotional and biological signals that make humans uniquely generous, so that you can truly understand your donors' hearts and connect with them as committed, lasting Friends."

—Audra Wood
Executive Director, Fresh Water Friends

"I've often heard that fundraising is art and science. Koshy invites and compels us to reimagine fundraising as art driven by science, equipping us with the tools and knowledge to build stronger connections with donors."

—Marco Corona
Director of Individual Giving,
Southern Environmental Law Center

"In *Neurogiving: The Science of Donor Decision Making*, Cherian Koshy unlocks what motivates generous action and how fundraisers can truly help people be their most generous selves. His book is a fundraising guide meant to be revisited, again and again, as we chart our own journeys in fundraising, 'touching hearts and engaging the brain.' This book is a gift that, indeed, will keep giving."

—Rachel Hutchisson
CEO and Social Impact Leader, Common Impact

"Cherian is an experienced fundraiser who shares my belief that fundraising is about people. In *Neurogiving*, he combines what is known through scientific study with what he knows about working with donors to describe ethical and effective pathways to generosity."

—Heather Riddle
Senior Vice President and Chief Development Officer,
Minnesota Public Radio | American Public Media

"Cherian has reframed giving not as a mechanical ask, but as a deeply human response shaped by trust, identity, and emotion. *Neurogiving* brings behavioral science out of the lab and into the real world—reminding us that ethical, effective fundraising starts with understanding how people actually think and feel."

—Brantley Boyett
President, Giving Docs

"Koshy's *Neurogiving* brilliantly reframes giving as a deeply human act—something we're wired for, not tricked into. It's the kind of book that changes how you lead. In a world chasing clicks and conversions, *Neurogiving* is a reminder that the most powerful fundraising tools are empathy, identity, and trust. A must read for every person vested in the future of generosity."

—Nathan Chappell
Author of *The Generosity Crisis and Nonprofit AI*

"Amid the flood of books promising revolutions in fundraising and re-purposed, tired tactics, every once in a while one comes along that makes you sit up, grab your highlighter and notepad and say. 'Wait, why aren't we all talking about this?!?" *Neurogiving* IS that book. It's smart, practical, and grounded in real research that's easy to understand and implement. If you've ever wondered why donors—real-life human, caring, generous people—do what they do, this book finally gives us the science to back up what our instincts have been telling us for years - and it might just give you some insight into how fundraisers think and work, too."

—T. Clay Buck, CFRE
Founder and Principal, Next River Fundraising Strategies

"*Neurogiving* is a breakthrough for our field. Cherian brings together neuroscience, behavioral insight, and lived fundraising experience to reframe how we understand donor decision-making. It's not about tactics—it's about trust, identity, and the human experience behind every gift. This book is smart, practical, and deeply grounded in what really drives generosity."

—Carlo Laurore, CFP,CHFC,CLU,RICP,AEP,CAP
Senior Vice President of Development, Scouting America

"Fundraisers have consistently emphasized the significance of being donor-centered. This book takes that concept to the next level by providing strategies rooted in identity, memory, and meaning. It goes beyond being a guide; it's a transformative shift in how we approach philanthropy."

—Pamela Perkins-Dwyer
Director of Major Gifts, Los Angeles Master Chorale

"Cherian Koshy goes beyond the buzzwords of 'donor-centered' practices. He offers a transformative framework rooted in the science of human identity, memory, and meaning. Koshy's strategies will empower nonprofit-sector practitioners to build genuine, lasting relationships with donors by aligning fundraising with what truly drives human behaviour. This book is essential reading to help us embrace a deeper, more sustainable approach to philanthropy."

—Usha Menon
Founder, Usha Menon Management Consultancy (Asia)

"*Neurogiving* arrives at a pivotal moment for the nonprofit sector and the fundraising profession—an era demanding profound self-examination after years of inadvertent complacency and, at times, oppressive practices. Drawing on cutting-edge insights from neuroscience and behavioral science, this book challenges us to elevate our thinking, refine our methods, and embrace a more enlightened, ethical approach to philanthropy. It's not merely a timely read; it's a clarion call to reimagine how—and why—we inspire generosity, offering us the intellectual tools to do better by those we serve."

—Rochelle Jerry, CFRM

CEO & Co-Founder, Jerry Consulting Group; Adjunct Faculty, Indiana University, Lilly Family School of Philanthropy, The Fund Raising School

"*Neurogiving* is a pioneering exploration of how neuroscience and behavioral psychology shape the way donors think, feel, and act. Cherian Koshy offers fundraisers a scientifically grounded and deeply ethical framework for aligning with donors' natural generosity rather than manipulating it. This book is essential reading for anyone serious about transforming donor relationships and advancing meaningful philanthropy."

—Ken Miller, CFRE

President, Denali FSP Fundraising Consultants

"The best fundraising books give you new tools. The rare ones give you a new lens. *Neurogiving* does both. It belongs on every fundraiser's bookshelf."

—Megan Spranger, JD, CFRE

Regional Development Director

"Most books on donor behavior skim the surface, but Cherian Koshy goes deeper. Neurogiving: The Science of Donor Decision-Making unpacks not just why people give, but how our brains interpret need, identity, and connection. Koshy translates complex neuroscience into practical and ethical strategies that can make appeals more resonant and more human. This isn't just a guide for fundraisers; it's a roadmap for anyone seeking to understand the emotional architecture of generosity and build deeper, lasting donor relationships."

—Ashley Thompson

Philanthropy Leader

"Cherian Koshy is one of the most profound, ethical, and future-focused voices in fundraising today. *Neurogiving* exemplifies his exceptional ability to blend science, strategy, and heart to deepen our insight into generosity. This book puts into words what so many fundraisers in the field have felt but haven't always been able to articulate. It is a must-read that will transform how you engage with both your work and your donors."

—Julissa Garza

Major Gift Officer

"An essential guide for modern fundraisers, *Neurogiving* blends neuroscience, behavioral insights, and ethical storytelling to transform how we understand, inspire, and sustain generosity in deeply human ways."

—Bernard Ross

Director, =mc consulting, National Arts Fundraising School, & DecisionScience. Edinburgh, Scotland, United Kingdom

"In the fundraising world, many believe that philanthropy is all about how well you can sell. Cherian Koshy's book shouts, 'It's not about you—it's about aligning with the donor!' This is a must-read for CEOs, CFOs, Boards, and fundraisers alike."

—Jim Green

Healthcare Fundraising Leader

cherian koshy

neurogiving

THE SCIENCE OF
DONOR DECISION-MAKING

WILEY

Published by John Wiley & Sons, Inc., Hoboken, New Jersey.
Published simultaneously in Canada.

For general information on our other products and services or for technical support, please contact our Customer Care Department within the United States at (800) 762-2974, outside the United States at (317) 572-3993 or fax (317) 572-4002.

Wiley also publishes its books in a variety of electronic formats. Some content that appears in print may not be available in electronic formats. For more information about Wiley products, visit our web site at www.wiley.com.

Library of Congress Cataloging-in-Publication Data is Available:

ISBN 978-1-394-37045-0 (Cloth)
ISBN 978-1-394-37046-7 (ePub)
ISBN 978-1-394-37048-1 (ePDF)

Cover Design: Wiley
Cover Image: © Usis/Getty Images

Printed and bound by CPI Group (UK) Ltd, Croydon, CR0 4YY

C9781394370450_141025

To the thinkers, teachers, friends, and fundraisers whose wisdom built the very foundations I now walk on—I am not worthy to stand on your shoulders, yet you lifted me anyway.

To those who come after—may this work be not a conclusion, but a foothold. May you go further, think deeper, and build better than I have.

This is for all of you.

Contents

Introduction

Fundraising has long been considered both an art and a science. While the art focuses on creativity and connection, the science is about understanding how people think and feel when making decisions, especially about giving. Neuroscience and behavioral science help us unravel these processes. These fields study how our brain works and how our behavior is influenced by emotions, cognition, and social factors.

Neuroscience focuses on the brain's structure and functions, while behavioral science looks at how those functions influence our actions. When combined, these disciplines offer a clearer picture of how decisions are made, including the decision to give.

In marketing, neuromarketing uses these insights to understand consumer behavior and influence purchasing decisions. While there are similarities, the motivations behind purchasing and giving are quite different. Consumers may ask, "Do I need this?" or "Will I enjoy it?" When it comes to giving, donors are guided by different questions: "Does this reflect my values?" "Do I trust this organization?" and "Will my gift make a difference?" But even deeper, consumer needs are contextual and generosity is inherent, innate.

This distinction matters. Giving is not a transaction. Donors invest in their identity, aligning their actions with their values and beliefs. This is where neurogiving comes in. *Neurogiving* is a new term that merges neuroscience and philanthropy to understand how the brain influences the decision to give. It's the bridge between our intuitive

1

understanding of generosity and the scientific knowledge that helps us connect with donors in ways that feel natural and rewarding.

I chose to describe this as giving versus fundraising because there's nothing—absolutely nothing—that nonprofits or a fundraiser can do to make a person who isn't generous make a gift. If you're a fundraiser and you've sat in that room, you know exactly what I mean. It's why knowing that someone is rich doesn't matter from a generosity perspective. They might make a donation but they aren't a giver. It's not in their soul. You might get one gift but you won't get another one. Trust me, been there, done that.

It's why fundraisers can't simply copy and paste commercial sales tactics into philanthropy. It's why decision architecture—the way choices are framed and presented—must be adapted with an understanding of what makes generosity different from consumer behavior. And it's why the best fundraising isn't about pressure, gimmicks, or persuasion; it's about aligning with how donors naturally think and feel, making it easier and more rewarding for them to give.

Let's put this in context: it's possible for good marketers to convince someone or a lot of someones to want or even need a mobile phone. It's even possible for them to convince a teenager that they absolutely need a specific type of phone like an iPhone instead of an Android and even particular models or features. This may even align with particular values that a teen might have.

It's actually about fundraisers and nonprofits getting out of the way of donors doing the thing they most want to do: be their genuine generous selves. That's neurogiving.

The Promise of Neurogiving

The promise of neurogiving is that when you understand how to connect more deeply, resonate longer, and inspire true loyalty among supporters, it can transform not just your fundraising results but also the entire way your organization builds relationships with donors.

When we understand how the donor brain processes emotions, trust, and decisions, we can design fundraising strategies that work *with* the brain's wiring instead of against it. Knowing *why* stories work justifies prioritizing storytelling. Understanding *how* donors build trust means we can strengthen donor stewardship and retention. Recognizing how generosity naturally arises enables us to craft appeals, design campaigns, and create donor experiences that align with, and don't obstruct, the donor's innate desire to give, making the experience feel meaningful rather than transactional.

Neurogiving isn't just about the ask; it touches every part of the fundraising ecosystem. It shapes how we craft messaging, how we structure giving opportunities, how we steward relationships, how we build long-term loyalty, and even how we evaluate our own success.

This is why neurogiving isn't about fancy technology or Jedi mind tricks. It's about honoring the fact that giving is inherently emotional and social and ensuring that every donor interaction, every message, every event, every thank-you, aligns with that truth.

The Impact: More Than Just Dollars

The promise of neurogiving extends beyond getting more donations. It's about building genuine loyalty. When donors feel deeply connected to a cause, when they feel seen and appreciated, they stick around. They don't just give once. They give again and again. They become advocates. Champions. Even legacy donors.

This is the holy grail of fundraising: not one-time transactions, but lifetime relationships. Neurogiving helps us understand the conditions that nurture and sustain the generosity already present in our supporters. Each chapter ahead reveals new insights, grounded in research and practical application, that help fundraisers create experiences that honor, reinforce, and deepen donor commitment across the entire giving cycle.

Another major promise of neurogiving is that it makes fundraising more effective and efficient—not by manufacturing motivation, but by removing the barriers that stand between a donor's intention and their action. When you understand how giving decisions actually unfold, you can focus your time and budget on what truly resonates. Instead of testing five versions of a message and hoping one sticks, you can confidently send two that are already aligned with how donors think and feel. Instead of debating whether to lead with data or a story, you'll know that stories anchor memory and emotion—and choose accordingly, not by instinct, but by insight.

By aligning strategies with donor psychology, you reduce wasted effort and increase success rates. It's like having a map of the donor's heart and mind, a way to navigate directly to inspiration and generosity, rather than wandering aimlessly.

This doesn't mean everything becomes easy or formulaic. Fundraising will always require creativity, adaptability, and, yes, sometimes trial and error. But it does mean your odds of success go up, your pitfalls become fewer, and your approach becomes more intentional.

How to Use This Book

This book isn't just something to read; it's something to experience, test, and discuss. Whether you're a frontline fundraiser, an executive leader, or someone shaping donor strategy behind the scenes, you'll find ideas here that challenge conventional wisdom and spark new ways of thinking.

I encourage you to read this with your team. Debate these concepts. Test them in your own fundraising efforts. Discuss where you see these principles playing out in real life and where they don't.

Research is powerful and there's lots of it. Trace it back and follow it. But it's even more impactful when applied in your specific context. By engaging in these ideas together, you'll build a shared language for donor behavior and a stronger foundation for how you communicate, engage, and inspire generosity.

The journey ahead will take us through the core drivers of generosity in many different forms, the mechanics of donor decision-making, and the principles behind long-term engagement. You'll discover how small tweaks in messaging, framing, and donor experience can create meaningful changes in your results.

And you'll be equipped to approach fundraising not just as an annual revenue goal but as an ongoing process of building trust, fostering connection, and inviting people into something bigger than themselves. In fact, researchers have shown that neural responses, especially activity in the brain's reward centers, can outperform self-reported preferences in predicting which campaigns will succeed. In a study of actual crowdfunding projects, Genevsky et al. (2017) demonstrated that brain data more accurately forecasted fundraising outcomes than behavioral surveys alone. This opens the door for new, ethically guided ways to test the emotional effectiveness of appeals.

Most important, neurogiving is not about manipulation. You might want to underline that. The goal is authentic, respectful connection, not trickery. Every insight we apply should pass the test: *does this honor the donor and the cause?* If yes, we're likely on solid ground. If not, it's a slippery slope we avoid.

But some people know neuroscience, behavioral science, and decision architecture and can read some of this book to try to "hack" a donor brain. They might try to find a checklist of quick tricks that try to sell an emotion, motivate generosity, or close a gift quickly. I'll be honest. It will work. For some people at some times and for some organizations. But it's not sustainable, and if you think about it, you know that, too.

When done wrong, donors feel like they are being taken advantage of, they start to ignore visit requests, emails, and renewal requests. And donors talk to each other.

When done right, donors will never think, "Oh, they used a neuroscience hack on me." Instead, they'll think, "I love being involved with this cause; it just feels right."

That feeling is what we're after. It's that aligned, almost harmonious state where donor and nonprofit motivations meet and magic happens.

So, as you turn the page to Chapter 1, keep that sense of possibility close. The new wave of fundraising is already forming, and you have the chance to ride it, to create fundraising strategies that not only hit their targets but also inspire and uplift everyone involved. In doing so, you'll be advancing both your organization's mission and the broader practice of fundraising. And perhaps most exciting of all, you'll be helping to forge a future where giving isn't just a transaction, but a deeply fulfilling experience—for donors, for your organization, and for the communities you serve.

That's the promise of neurogiving. Let's begin.

Chapter 1

Foundations of Neurogiving

Fundraising is often seen as the art of touching hearts, but it is also very much about engaging brains. Empathy is a neural strategy. Modern neuroscience has begun to illuminate *why* people give, *how* emotions shape giving decisions, and *what* neural mechanisms underlie empathy and altruism. Understanding these foundations of neurogiving can help nonprofit professionals connect more deeply with donors, not through manipulation or gimmicks, but by aligning fundraising practices with the very wiring of the human brain. While early models such as Sargeant's (1999) focused on rational and relational variables in donor behavior, new findings from neuroscience are revealing an additional layer of understanding. In this chapter, we explore three key areas: the neuroscience of generosity, the intertwined role of emotion in decision-making, and the brain networks of empathy that motivate prosocial behavior. The goal is to understand our donors better, not to "hack" them. Let's begin by looking at how generosity shows up in the brain.

The Neuroscience of Generosity

Charitable giving is more than an act of kindness or a moral choice; it's actually something deeply embedded in our biology. Human brains are literally wired for generosity and this wiring rewards us when we act altruistically. Even 14-month-old babies, when they saw an adult stranger failing to do something, responded by helping without prompting (Warneken & Tomasello, 2007). A growing body of neuroscience research reveals that giving feels good because it engages the brain's reward circuitry in much the same way as enjoyable activities like eating a favorite food or achieving a personal goal. For example, functional magnetic resonance imaging (fMRI) studies show that when people donate to charity, specific reward centers in the brain light up, particularly the mesolimbic reward system (which includes the nucleus accumbens, a key pleasure center). This effect was vividly demonstrated in a landmark fMRI study by Moll et al. (2006), who found that charitable giving activated the same brain areas associated with personal rewards, including the ventral striatum and orbitofrontal cortex. In other words, giving to others neurologically resembles giving to oneself—confirming that altruism is not just moral but also measurably pleasurable. The simple act of making a donation triggers a waterfall of neurotransmitters that produce a positive emotional rush often described as a "helper's high." This neurochemical high confirms something fundraisers have long observed: doing good feels good. Altruism isn't selfless. It's self-rewarding. Your brain was built to buzz when you give.

A growing body of neuroscience research shows that giving engages the brain's reward system, triggering the release of neurochemicals like dopamine, endorphins, and oxytocin. This creates what James Andreoni (1990) termed the "warm glow"—a pleasurable emotional rush linked to altruistic action. Dopamine, the brain's "feel-good" chemical, reinforces the desire to repeat prosocial behaviors, while endorphins produce a mild euphoria and stress relief (Luks, 1991). Research even links helping others with better health and longevity outcomes (Post, 2014). In one study, people who spent money on others reported greater happiness than those who spent on themselves (Dunn et al., 2008).

Meanwhile, oxytocin, sometimes called the "moral molecule," has been shown to increase generosity and trust in experimental settings

(Zak et al., 2007). It's released during emotionally rich experiences, like watching a moving video or hearing a compelling story, and enhances social bonding. Together, these neurochemical responses reinforce a virtuous cycle: giving feels good, which motivates people to keep giving.

For fundraisers, the takeaway is powerful: appeals that trigger emotional warmth and human connection aren't just persuasive—they're biologically rewarding.

Understanding that giving literally triggers pleasure and bonding in the brain has important implications for how we approach fundraising. It enables us to reframe a donation ask not as a cold financial transaction or a loss, but as an opportunity—an opportunity for the donor to experience something positive. In light of this science, inviting someone to give is really inviting them to tap into these biologically rooted joys of generosity. We can confidently say to supporters that giving benefits the giver as well as the cause. Recent research confirms this dual reward. A 2025 systematic review by Chapman and Thai examined over 100 studies and found that incentives appealing to both the donor's self-interest (like personal rewards) and their desire to help others tend to boost giving more effectively than either type alone.

This suggests that giving is most powerful not when it's framed purely as altruism or entirely as self-gain but when it resonates with both the donor's identity and their prosocial instincts. In neurogiving terms, this alignment between self and other is not a contradiction, it's a catalyst.

In practical terms, this means crafting our messaging to highlight the personal fulfillment, purpose, and even fun that donors can derive from making a difference. For example, instead of apologetically asking "please help us," we might emphasize how donating will make the donor feel part of something meaningful or enable them to see a positive change they care about. By aligning our fundraising

9

appeals with this fundamental inherent drive for reward and connection, we help donors subconsciously perceive giving as a win-win scenario: it advances the mission and delivers a dose of happiness and human connection to themselves. In essence, philanthropy can be presented as a healthy, rewarding experience—one that even triggers the brain's pleasure and bonding centers. Recognizing this neurobiological basis of generosity encourages us to create giving opportunities that feel less like obligations and more like rewarding engagements. When speaking with potential supporters, a fundraiser can legitimately say, "By giving, you're not just helping others—you're also doing something wonderful for yourself." This isn't just a feel-good slogan; it's grounded in how our brains work.

The Intertwined Role of Emotion in Decision-Making

If generosity activates our brain's reward circuitry, what does that say about how people decide to give in the first place? One might imagine that donors sit down with a spreadsheet, rationally weighing pros and cons, but neuroscience and psychology tell a different story. Decisions, even high-stakes financial decisions, are profoundly influenced by emotions. We don't think our way to giving, we feel our way there. In fact, Antonio Damasio's groundbreaking research demonstrated that without emotion, we cannot make decisions effectively. Damasio studied patients with damage to emotion-processing areas of the brain; these individuals retained IQ and logic yet became paralyzed in decision-making over even trivial choices. From these observations Damasio (1996) proposed the somatic marker hypothesis, which suggests that our brains attach emotional "marker" signals to past experiences and outcomes, and we rely on those feelings (registered in the body, or "soma") to guide our decisions. In essence, emotions serve as guideposts or shortcuts: based on how an option makes us feel (or how we imagine it will make us feel), our brain leans one way or the other. A purely analytic evaluation, without any emotional weighting, doesn't get us to a decision; it leaves us stuck in endless calculation. Thus, in a very real neurological sense, "purely rational" Spock-like decision-making is a myth—or at least an impossibility for a healthy human brain. Every choice, whether it's buying a car or donating to a charity, involves an emotional component that signals what feels "right" or meaningful.

When it comes to philanthropic decisions, the same principle applies. A donor's decision to give is almost always emotional first and rational second. We might like to think we (and our donors) are entirely rational actors—weighing impact reports, overhead ratios, and so on—but in reality those considerations typically play a supporting role. The spark that actually moves someone to act is emotion: a sense of empathy, or inspiration, or sometimes moral outrage at an injustice. Only after that emotional spark do most donors rationalize or justify the gift with logical reasons ("This charity uses funds efficiently" or "It's tax-deductible," etc.). This sequence has been summarized by one marketer as "emotion first, justification later," and neuroscience would agree. If an appeal doesn't strike an emotional chord, it's unlikely to spur action no matter how logical or fact-filled it is. However, when an appeal does move someone emotionally, the decision to give can be remarkably quick and resolute—with the donor's rational brain essentially saying "Yes, this feels right, let me support it," and then perhaps later articulating the reasons. Damasio puts it succinctly: we don't just think our way to a decision; we feel our way there. For fundraisers, the takeaway is clear: an appeal that engages the heart will drive decisions more effectively than one that only appeals to the head.

Even moral and ethical decisions, which we often assume are the product of high reasoning, are heavily influenced by emotional processing. Consider how people respond to humanitarian crises or ethical dilemmas: often it's the emotional impact of a situation—the tears of a hungry child, or the anger at an injustice—that propels action, rather than a cold calculation of numbers. In fundraising contexts, donors frequently decide to give because something about the cause feels compelling or aligns with their values on a gut level. If a cause "feels right" or a story resonates, the decision can be almost automatic. But if it doesn't evoke any feeling, even the best logical argument may fall flat. The idea of a completely rational philanthropist who only looks at data and ignores emotion isn't just unlikely; it's neurologically implausible. Our brains integrate emotion into every decision, charitable giving included, so effective fundraising needs to honor and speak to those emotions that guide giving.

That said, emotion doesn't work in isolation; it works in tandem with cognition, and sometimes our brains use shortcuts that combine the two. Donors, like all people, rely on mental heuristics, simple mental rules, especially when making decisions under uncertainty or with limited time. Often these heuristics are driven by what information or feelings are most salient. For example, the availability heuristic leads us to judge an issue's importance by how easily examples come to mind. In a giving context, a donor might gauge how urgent or serious a problem is based on a vivid story they recently heard, rather than detailed statistics. If a nonprofit shares a memorable, emotionally charged example such as one family's story of overcoming hardship, that story can loom large in the donor's mind when they decide whether to give, effectively steering their decision by feeling, more than by analytical review. This is not a sign of donor irrationality; it's just human nature. We are all more moved by a concrete story than by abstract numbers, and that affects how we choose to allocate our generosity.

On the flip side, too much information or too many choices can actually hinder decision-making. Psychologists sometimes call this "analysis paralysis," and neurologically it corresponds to the brain's limited capacity to weigh complex options. If a donor is presented with a barrage of data or a menu of a dozen giving options, the cognitive load may dampen the emotional momentum to give. The decision feels complicated, which can lead to hesitation or deferral. Effective fundraisers often intuitively address this by keeping appeals simple and focused: for instance, highlighting one clear call to action rather than many, or suggesting a default donation option. By reducing cognitive overload and not diluting the emotional message, we pave an easier path for the brain to say yes. In practice, this might mean that instead of asking supporters to "choose among our five programs to support," you spotlight one program with a compelling story for this campaign, and ask them to help that specific case. The donor's mind isn't burdened with extra decisions; they can respond more instinctively to the emotional appeal ("This story moved me. I want to help."). In short, emotions drive the desire to give, and a clear, simple context enables the decision.

The interplay of emotion and cognition in donor decision-making also surfaces in how information is framed. The exact same fact can inspire or discourage giving depending on the emotional frame around it. For example, saying "Last year, 50 people just like you joined as $1,000 donors" can evoke a positive feeling of social proof and opportunity, whereas saying "Only 5% of our donors give $1,000 or more" might make a prospect feel isolated or hesitant about giving at that level. The first phrasing invites the donor to proudly join a group; the second inadvertently implies that such a gift is abnormally high (and thus perhaps not "people like you"). Both statements convey a similar statistic, but their emotional resonance differs. The lesson for fundraisers is to always consider what feeling a message will evoke in a potential donor. If the emotion isn't positive or motivating, a reframing may be in order. By honoring the emotional brain in how we present choices, we make it easier for donors to act generously.

At its heart, optimizing donor decision-making is about respecting both the heart and the mind. We need to light the emotional spark and also make the decision process feel natural and straightforward. This means crafting appeals that inspire passion and compassion, while also removing unnecessary roadblocks or confusion. When we do that, we honor the whole person—we appeal to the deeper motivations that move someone to give, and we respect their cognitive need for clarity. In the best cases, a donor might later say, "I didn't have to think twice—it just felt like the right thing to do," and know that the process was easy. That is the ideal intersection of emotion and decision-making in fundraising: the donor's empathy and values are engaged, and the act of giving is as frictionless as possible. As fundraisers, if we can ignite the heart and then guide the decision gently (rather than fighting against the way brains decide), we set the stage for more yes answers that both we and our donors feel good about.

The Brain Networks of Empathy

If emotion is the spark of giving, empathy is often the fuel. Empathy, our capacity to feel and understand what others are experiencing, is the emotional engine that propels so much of human generosity. When we truly empathize with someone's plight, we are motivated to help. But what is happening in the brain when we feel empathy, and why do some stories move us so much more than statistics? Neuroscience research over the past few decades has shown that empathy is not just a poetic concept; it's an observable phenomenon in the brain, involving specific networks of neurons that enable us to "share" in the experiences of others.

One crucial component of empathy is the mirror neuron system. First discovered in the 1990s by Giacomo Rizzolatti and colleagues, mirror neurons are brain cells that fire when we perform an action and when we see someone else perform that action. In other words, parts of our brain mirror the state of others. Subsequent research extended this to emotions: when we observe or imagine someone else's feelings, to a degree our brain activates as if we were feeling the same thing. For example, if a donor hears a vivid story about a child experiencing joy at finally having clean water, the donor's own brain may echo that happiness, simulating the child's relief and joy internally. This neural mirroring is a foundation for empathy. It's as if the brain is saying, "This could be me feeling this." At a very basic level, mirror neurons and related networks let us resonate with others' experiences, creating a shared emotional experience. In a fundraising context, this means a well-crafted narrative doesn't just inform a donor about someone's situation; it can make the donor feel that situation. The story of another person's hardship or triumph can literally echo in the donor's own neural circuits.

Beyond the mirror neuron system, other brain regions are also known to be key players in empathy, especially when it comes to understanding pain and suffering. Brain imaging studies have revealed that when we see someone in pain or distress, it activates many of the same areas that light up when we ourselves experience pain. Notably, regions like the anterior insula and the anterior cingulate cortex, which process the emotional aspects of pain, become active when we witness another's suffering. Tania Singer et al. (2004) famously showed that if your loved one is in pain, your brain's pain matrix is stimulated (though not the sensory pain areas; since you're not physically hurt, the affective/emotional components are). In essence, part of your brain is feeling with the other person. This phenomenon is sometimes described as "shared pain," and it underlies the urgency we feel to relieve others' suffering. It's the reason a parent can hardly bear to watch their child in distress: the parent's own brain is echoing that distress. And it's a big reason why, when we see a tragedy on the news or a heartbreaking story from a nonprofit, we might feel a pang in our chest or a knot in our stomach that compels us to act. Our brains are built to blur the line between self and other in these moments, which is a powerful design for motivating altruism.

Psychologists have long recognized empathy as a key ingredient in altruism. According to the empathy-altruism hypothesis (Batson, 1991), when we feel genuine empathic concern for someone, truly tuning into their suffering or need, we often become motivated to help them even if there's no benefit to ourselves. Empathy creates a selfless urge to improve the other person's condition. In fundraising practice, this means that evoking empathy is essential for inspiring donors to act out of compassion rather than obligation. People are seldom moved to give by statistics alone or by logical arguments about why a cause matters; it is the emotional resonance, seeing oneself in another's shoes, feeling their sorrow or hope, that usually triggers the decision to donate. That's why stories are so potent. As a result, fundraisers find that putting a face and a name to an issue, effectively humanizing the statistics, is critical. It's not that donors don't want to care about the millions in need; it's that our empathy circuitry gets overwhelmed and shuts down when we can't personalize the suffering.

To engage empathy, successful fundraising campaigns focus on stories and imagery that make the cause personal. When donors can see themselves or their loved ones in the story being told, or when they vividly imagine the individuals their gift will help, empathy does the heavy lifting. For instance, showing the before-and-after story of one refugee family rebuilding their life can leave a far deeper imprint on a potential donor than citing a statistic like "there are 1 million refugees in need." By tapping into our natural capacity for empathy, we transform a donation from a transaction into a human connection. The donor is no longer giving to an impersonal cause; they feel they are helping that specific family or that child whom they have come to know through the story. This emotional connection not only increases the chance of an initial gift, but it can also foster loyalty and continued engagement. When someone donates out of true empathy, they've formed a kind of bond with the beneficiary, the donor cares about what happens to Jasmine or Arun (the person in the story), and that means they're more likely to remain interested and involved. In essence, empathy can kick-start a relationship that extends beyond a single donation.

Interestingly, neuroscience is giving us insight into individual differences in empathy and generosity as well. While all healthy humans have the basic neural architecture for empathy, we don't all empathize to the same degree or in the same way. Some people are naturally more attuned to others' emotions—their brains might show stronger activation in those empathy-related regions when they see someone in pain—while others might have a more muted response. Researchers have even linked these differences to generosity. In one study, people who showed stronger brain responses to others' pain and emotion (for example, more activation in the anterior insula when seeing someone in distress) donated significantly more in an economic game, compared to those whose brains showed less of this empathic resonance. By contrast, individuals who had higher activity in brain regions associated with deliberation and impulse control (areas of the prefrontal cortex) tended to give less in the experiment. And in a fascinating twist, when researchers temporarily dampened the activity of the prefrontal "brakes" using transcranial magnetic stimulation, essentially quieting the more analytical, self-regulating part of the brain, participants became about 50% more generous with money tokens in a game. This suggests that our brains may have an inherent altruistic impulse that is sometimes held back by more analytical or self-interested considerations. When the inhibitions are lowered, empathy flows into action more freely. Such findings support a provocative idea: humans might be hard-wired for altruism to a greater extent than we typically realize, and it's often our conscious overthinking or social fear that stops us from acting on those impulses. Of course, this doesn't mean people should give without thinking at all, but it underlines how central empathy is—and that a big part of inspiring generosity is about engaging those deep, automatic empathic responses.

It's also worth noting that empathy, while powerful, has its complexities. Empathy can be biased; we tend to empathize more with those who are similar to us or those who are singular and identifiable, as discussed. There's also a limit to how much distress we can empathize with before we experience empathic distress ourselves or become overwhelmed. This is why effective storytelling in fundraising often balances emotion with hope: we want to engage empathy but not push donors into despair or a feeling of helplessness. Empathy is most motivating when the donor feels connected to the person in need and hopeful that their help will make a difference. That positive frame can prevent the empathy from turning into personal distress or burnout.

For fundraisers, the science of empathy confirms some timeless truths and offers new nuances. It tells us that making a potential donor feel the situation, in an authentic way, is crucial. We do that by telling stories, using images and testimonials, and generally by personalizing the narrative of our cause. Rather than saying, "Millions are hungry," we introduce the one child or one family who represents that crisis. We enable the donor to see the world through that individual's eyes for a moment. We invite the donor into a story. This doesn't mean facts and figures aren't useful—they provide scope and context—but leading with an emotional, human connection is key to ignite the neural circuits of empathy. And once a donor truly empathizes with someone in need, their mindset often shifts from "Why should I help?" to "How could I not?" That shift is the magic of empathy at work in philanthropy.

In practice, engaging empathy ethically means being genuine and respectful with the stories we tell. Neuroscience gives us a kind of "permission" to lean into emotional storytelling, since we know it's how brains connect, but with that comes a responsibility. We should never manipulate or fabricate emotions; instead, we should find the real, human stories in our work that honor the dignity of those we serve and present them in a relatable way. When done right, engaging empathy creates a profound win-win: donors experience the rewarding sense of human connection and purpose, and organizations raise support for those who need help. It's a virtuous circle fueled by our brains' innate capacity for care.

Empathy is the bridge between understanding and action. It is built into our neural wiring through mirror neurons and shared circuits that make us feel a bit of what others feel. It can be nurtured with personal stories and one-to-one connections. And it is a primary driver of altruistic behavior, transforming charitable giving from a mere transaction into a deeply felt human experience. For fundraisers, recognizing the role of empathy means we are not just in the business of conveying information; we are in the business of cultivating human understanding. When a potential donor can look at a situation of need and truly see another human being—to feel their hopes, fears, or relief—that is when the decision to help moves from the head to the heart, and that is when generosity flows most freely.

This idea—that generosity flows most freely when we align with the brain's natural tendencies—contrasts sharply with traditional models of donor engagement. Figure 1.1 compares the conventional "push" model of fundraising with the neurogiving approach that removes barriers and honors intrinsic generosity.

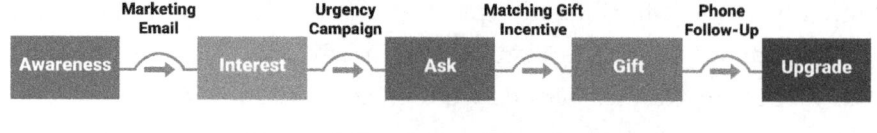

Traditional Push Model
Forcing Donor Progression

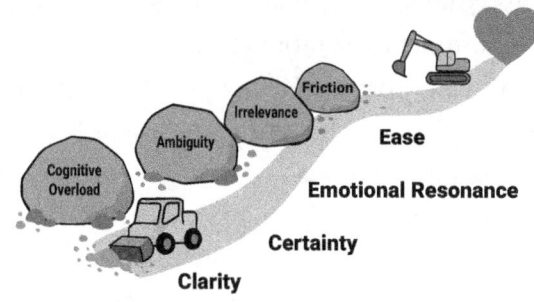

Neurogiving Generosity Flow Map™

Figure 1.1. Traditional Push Path Funnel Versus Neurogiving Generosity Flow Map™

By exploring the neuroscience of generosity, the emotional roots of decision-making, and the brain networks of empathy, modern science affirms something fundamental: giving is an inherently human act, driven by brain systems that reward us for caring about others. As we move forward in this book, we will build on these foundations to see how fundraisers can craft messages and donor experiences that resonate on this neural level, always ethically and authentically. The new wave of fundraising isn't about engineering or tricking the brain; it's about working with the grain of human nature. And human nature, as science shows, is surprisingly generous when we engage it in the right way.

Chapter 2

The Psychology of Donor Decision-Making

Giving decisions might appear spontaneous but behind each act of generosity lies a complex psychological process. Donors rely on mental shortcuts and emotional cues when deciding whether, how, and how much to give. In this chapter, we explore the psychology of donor decision-making in three key areas. First, we examine cognitive biases, which are frames in thinking that can make generosity harder or easier. Next, we look at attention and information processing to see how the brain filters charitable appeals and what captures a donor's focus. Finally, we delve into psychological motivations for giving, from that intrinsic "warm glow" of doing good to extrinsic incentives and social factors. Much of what we know about giving psychology comes from experimental approaches like those compiled by Oppenheimer and Olivola (2011), which lay the groundwork for modern behavioral fundraising. This is the chapter that can easily be taken out of context to try to "hack" a donor brain into giving. Please remember that neurogiving is about straightening a cord that has become tangled. The aim is to provide insights that help nonprofit practitioners design appeals and donor experiences that resonate deeply while staying ethical and respectful.

Cognitive Biases in Giving

Every decision to donate is influenced by more than just facts and logic. Research shows people don't always act as rational calculators; instead, we use heuristics and biases—mental shortcuts—to make decisions. These biases can significantly shape charitable giving. By understanding them, fundraisers can craft appeals that fit how donors naturally think and feel. Here we highlight five common biases in philanthropy: the identifiable victim effect and its neural basis, loss aversion in charitable appeals (prospect theory), anchoring effects in suggested donation amounts, status quo bias and default options in recurring giving, and the availability heuristic in cause selection.

Identifiable Victim Effect and Its Neural Basis

People are far more likely to donate to help one specific person than to support a faceless group. This tendency, known as the identifiable victim effect, has been demonstrated across multiple studies. One named child with a compelling story can elicit more empathy and donations than a paragraph filled with statistics about hundreds of children in need (Small et al., 2013). The emotional connection created by a single narrative engages our brain's empathy systems, while generalized suffering often leads to emotional distancing or overwhelm. Neuroimaging research supports this: Genevsky et al. (2013) found that when people viewed stories about a single, identified individual in need, it activated their nucleus accumbens, the brain's reward center, more strongly than statistics about a group. This neural engagement predicted a higher likelihood of giving, offering a biological explanation for why individual stories outperform abstract appeals.

For fundraisers, the lesson is clear: make the cause personal. Use real, respectful stories that donors can relate to, and highlight one individual whose life can be changed. When we can "see" the person behind the problem, our natural generosity kicks in.

Loss Aversion in Charitable Appeals (Prospect Theory)

Humans are wired to avoid loss more than they are motivated by gain. Behavioral economists Kahneman and Tversky (1979) found that people experience the pain of a loss twice as intensely as the pleasure of a comparable gain. In fundraising, this bias plays out in how appeals are framed. Saying, "Without your help, this program may be eliminated," is more compelling to the average donor than, "Your gift helps us expand this program."

While overly doom-laden messages can feel manipulative, a light touch of loss framing—paired with a hopeful path forward—can effectively trigger urgency and drive action. Highlighting what's at stake if support doesn't come in time gives donors a powerful emotional reason to give. Matching gifts, where another donor will match a gift dollar for dollar, are one of the most effective applications of loss aversion. In a large-scale natural experiment, Karlan and List (2007) found that offering a 1:1 match significantly increased both the likelihood and size of donations. Interestingly, increasing the match ratio beyond that didn't further improve giving—suggesting the psychology of a match matters more than the math.

Anchoring Effects in Suggested Donation Amounts

Anchoring refers to the cognitive bias where people rely on the first number or suggestion they see as a mental reference point. This effect is well documented in both psychology and behavioral economics, including in charitable contexts (Ariely, 2008). For example, a suggested donation of $250 can make a $100 gift feel modest, while that same $100 might seem generous if the top option were only $50.

Fundraisers can apply this bias strategically by setting thoughtful suggested gift amounts. These should reflect the donor's giving history or connect to tangible outcomes. Anchors should stretch generosity without alienating donors, nudging them toward meaningful, attainable contributions.

Status Quo Bias and Default Options in Recurring Giving

Most people tend to stick with the default option, especially when faced with uncertainty. This status quo bias means that preset choices, like opt-in organ donation in some countries, can dramatically shape behavior (Johnson & Goldstein, 2003). In fundraising, making monthly giving the default option, for example, can significantly boost recurring donations.

When donors are offered an easy, no-fuss path, many will take it. Pre-checking a "make this a monthly gift" box (with the option to uncheck), highlighting a recommended giving level, or simplifying donation steps all reduce friction. By designing experiences that align with this bias, nonprofits can turn generosity into a habit.

Designing Better Giving Decisions: Nudges, Friction, and Behavioral Design

Building on the power of defaults, the broader concept of choice architecture offers fundraisers a toolkit for designing giving experiences that align with how people naturally make decisions. Coined by Thaler and Sunstein (2008), choice architecture refers to the way options are presented—and how even small tweaks can dramatically influence outcomes.

For example, simplifying donation forms, presenting a single compelling ask, and providing a suggested amount or deadline can act as gentle nudges. These reduce cognitive effort and subtly guide donors toward generous decisions without pressure. On the flip side, excessive options, unclear language, or multiple competing calls to action introduce friction that makes giving harder, often unintentionally.

Behavioral design isn't about manipulation; it's about minimizing obstacles and clarifying the desired path. Every dropdown menu, checkbox, or narrative structure is a behavioral signal. By reducing friction and creating momentum, you're respecting the donor's limited attention and helping innate generosity happen. If your donation form feels like a tax return, you're doing it wrong. Simple wins. Friction kills generosity.

These behavioral cues are especially important when donors are already operating under cognitive load—too many competing messages, unclear pathways, or emotionally draining content can suppress action. Binder-Hathaway (2018) synthesized findings across dozens of behavioral experiments, confirming that even subtle nudges—like timing, language, or layout—can significantly shift giving behavior. That's why attention, processing, and decision simplicity are so intertwined in effective fundraising.

The Availability Heuristic in Cause Selection

The availability heuristic is a mental shortcut we all use: the easier something comes to mind, the more important it feels. If a cause or crisis is in the news, or if a donor recently heard a moving story about it, it rises to the top of their priorities. This is why natural disasters, viral fundraisers, or personal stories often receive disproportionate attention compared to chronic but less visible problems (Kahneman & Tversky, 1979).

To counter this, fundraisers should keep their cause present and memorable. Vivid storytelling, consistent communication, and connecting to current events can help maintain donor attention. The brain is always filtering for salience; make sure your message gets through because your donor actually wants it to come through.

In addition to cognitive biases, heuristics, and emotional triggers, donors' decisions are influenced by how messages are perceived, and those perceptions can vary significantly among different mindsets, even within the same demographic group.

To better understand this, I've conducted proprietary research using a scientific methodology called mind genomics, developed by Dr. Howard Moskowitz. He's the researcher behind the discovery that the world didn't want one perfect spaghetti sauce, but many, leading to products like chunky spaghetti sauce and Cherry Vanilla Dr. Pepper. Malcolm Gladwell did a whole TED Talk about him!

Unlike traditional focus groups or surveys that ask participants to respond to one message at a time, mind genomics, or preference analysis, uses conjoint analysis and rule-developing experimentation to understand human preference. We start with four key questions, each with four possible answers or statements. These statements are then mixed and matched into short combinations, called vignettes. Each participant sees 24 different vignettes, each a unique blend of one statement from each question, and rates how compelling or relevant it feels. By analyzing patterns across many participants, we can see which specific statements (and combinations) drive the strongest (and weakest) responses across different mindsets.

Working directly with Dr. Moskowitz, I researched how nonprofits could uncover the specific combinations of elements that move a person already inclined to give to action. The methodology is fast, cost-effective, and statistically robust, making it ideal for testing message effectiveness in real-world nonprofit settings. Each study I conducted used this method with donors audiences to understand how message framing influences likelihood to give.

For example, in one study for an organization supporting veterans and their families, we uncovered three distinct donor mindsets: one segment responded best to messages emphasizing direct service delivery and traditional support, such as transition assistance and help for military families. Another segment preferred systemic change, showing high interest in policy reform and advocacy language.

A third group valued a balance, responding best to language about long-term success and dignity for veterans.

Interestingly, these mindsets cut across gender, age, and even veteran status, demonstrating that horizontal segmentation based on how donors think (not who they are) provides deeper insight into donor psychology.

In another study, this time for a global water access nonprofit, we found that two donor personas, let's call them Hugh and Kaitlyn, reacted in near opposite ways to the same messages. For Hugh, data-heavy appeals like "millions of people lack access to water" reduced his likelihood to give, whereas for Kaitlyn, these same facts increased it. Conversely, emotionally framed appeals about impact and dignity motivated Hugh but left Kaitlyn unmoved. Yet within each persona, we also discovered subgroups whose responses aligned more closely with each other than with others in their own category. This revealed a critical insight: donors who look similar on the surface—same age, income, or giving history—can still respond very differently to the same message because of how they think and what they value. In many cases, these internal mindsets explain behavior more accurately than external demographics do.

The implications for fundraisers are profound. Two donors with similar demographics may interpret a message in entirely different ways not because one is more generous, but because the message activates different emotional, cognitive, or moral frameworks. By identifying which elements resonate with which mindsets, organizations can tailor their appeals accordingly, improving response rates and deepening donor engagement.

This approach doesn't just personalize messaging; it reveals *why* personalization works. Donors aren't motivated by generalizations; they're moved by messages that speak to their specific worldview. Generic appeals are like junk mail to the brain. Speak to what your donor already believes and you'll break through. Mind genomics helps uncover those preferences and offers a reliable way to match message to mindset. Nonprofits of all sizes can use these insights to segment appeals by values and message resonance, rather than solely by demographics or giving level.

Attention and Information Processing

Even the most powerful message won't lead to a donation if it never grabs the donor's attention no matter their preexisting generous nature. In today's world, donors are bombarded with information and social media, news, ads, and emails, so charitable appeals are just one part of the din that dampens their generous impulses. The human brain has developed filters to cope with this constant influx. As a result, people will only notice and process a fraction of the messages they encounter. In this section, we examine how attention works in the context of fundraising and how information is processed once a message gets noticed. We look at what kinds of stimuli naturally capture the brain's attention, how cognitive overload can hinder decision-making, and how different thinking styles (intuitive versus analytical) play into giving. By understanding these factors, nonprofits can craft communications that not only reach donors but also resonate and prompt action.

Cognitive Load Theory and Its Impact on Giving Decisions

Once you have a donor's attention, the next challenge is making your appeal easy to understand and act on. If an appeal is too complex or demands a lot of mental effort, some donors will disengage or postpone their generosity decision. Cognitive load refers to the mental processing power required to understand information or make a decision. When cognitive load is high (too much information, too many choices, or confusing instructions), people often experience decision fatigue or "analysis paralysis."

In fundraising, this can happen if we present a potential donor with a cluttered message or a complicated set of options. For example, offering 10 different funds to donate to in one ask might overwhelm someone, whereas highlighting one clear need would be easier to process. Studies in consumer behavior show that when people are faced with too many choices, they are less likely to choose anything at all (Iyengar & Lepper, 2000). The same principle applies to donation options. To avoid this, effective appeals keep things simple: one story, one ask, and a straightforward way to give. If you have multiple things to fund, consider separate, focused appeals for each rather than a single all-encompassing plea. Also, guide the donor on what to do next with clear calls to action. Reducing cognitive load by simplifying your message and donation process will help more people follow through on their initial generous impulse, rather than getting lost in overthinking. The problem isn't that people are unwilling to give, it's that our messaging and engagement strategies often disrupt the natural arc of generosity. Traditional models focus on escalating asks, but they overlook how people actually make giving decisions.

The Generosity Activation Arc shown in Figure 2.1 contrasts the conventional step-based donor journey with a more effective, neuroscience-aligned flow that clears the path to generosity rather than forcing it.

The Power of Feedback Loops

Once a donor completes a gift, the next few seconds and minutes matter more than most organizations realize. In behavioral science, this is the window when a feedback loop can either reinforce generosity or leave the brain with unfinished business.

When donors immediately see the result of their action—a thank-you screen, a short video, a confirmation message that highlights

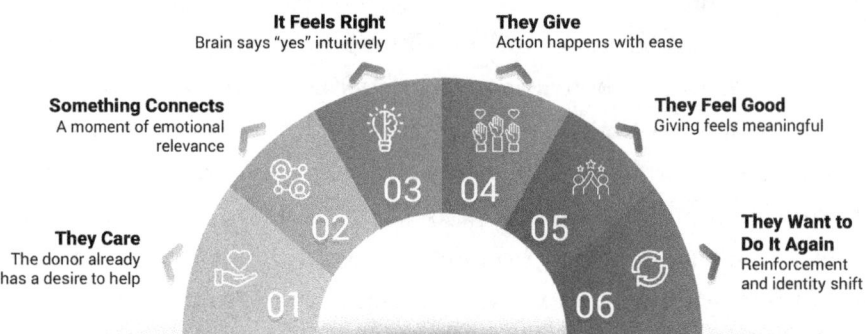

How Generosity Naturally Flows When We Remove Friction

It Feels Right
Brain says "yes" intuitively

They Give
Action happens with ease

Something Connects
A moment of emotional relevance

They Feel Good
Giving feels meaningful

They Care
The donor already has a desire to help

They Want to Do It Again
Reinforcement and identity shift

How We've Traditionally Tried to "Move" Donors

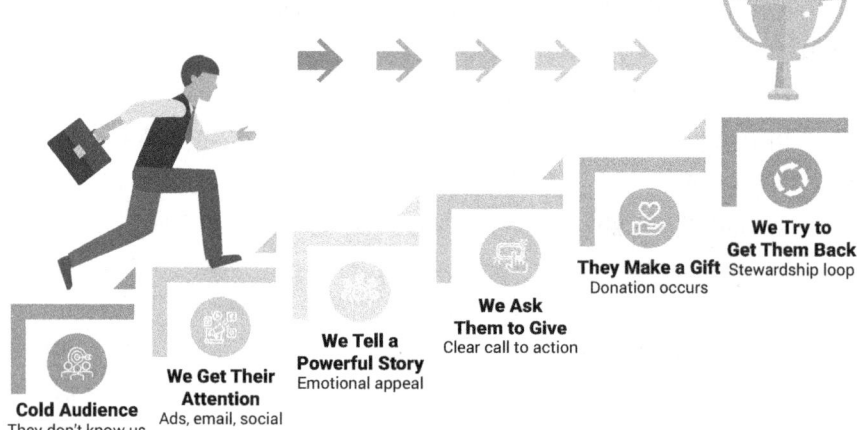

We Try to Get Them Back
Stewardship loop

They Make a Gift
Donation occurs

We Ask Them to Give
Clear call to action

We Tell a Powerful Story
Emotional appeal

We Get Their Attention
Ads, email, social

Cold Audience
They don't know us

Figure 2.1. Generosity Activation Arc: Traditional Versus Neurogiving

the impact—it creates a sense of closure and reward. This release of positive emotion (and often dopamine) is part of what solidifies a memory as good, satisfying, and worth repeating. Without this feedback, the brain doesn't connect the act of giving with a positive emotional outcome, making future generosity less likely.

Even small touches matter. Messages like "You made this possible," or showing a progress bar filling up, help the donor see themselves as a protagonist in the story. This emotional payoff reinforces the behavior neurologically and increases the likelihood of repeated giving. In this way, feedback isn't just about courtesy, it's a behavioral tool that turns action into satisfaction, and satisfaction into habit.

How the Brain Filters Charitable Appeals Among Competing Stimuli

Modern life is an attention battleground. At any given moment, a donor might be skimming through dozens of posts, emails, and ads, and today charitable appeals look like anything else we might see from a for-profit brand. Our brains automatically filter out most of these stimuli, allowing only certain things to capture conscious attention. Given the constant competition for attention, the brain uses filters to decide what to tune in or tune out. For example, if I'm an animal lover, I'll immediately notice a story about a dog rescue in my news feed, whereas I might scroll past a dozen unrelated headlines or cat-related ones! Most generic or routine messages get filtered out. What tends to break through that filter? In most cases, they are charitable appeals that trigger one of a few key attention cues: typically, novelty, emotional resonance, or personal relevance.

If an appeal looks just like every other piece of mail or email, it might never register in a donor's conscious mind. But if it includes something that stands out such as a striking image or subject line or something that immediately feels relevant to the recipient, like their name or a topic they care deeply about, it has a higher chance of making it past the brain's gatekeeper. In essence, fundraisers need to design appeals not just to be compelling in content but also to survive the initial filtering. Leading with an element that is eye-catching or heart-catching can ensure the donor actually notices your message among the many competing stimuli.

Neurological Triggers That Capture Attention (Novelty, Emotion, Personal Relevance)

- **Novelty.** We are wired to notice the new and unexpected. An unusual or surprising element in a fundraising message (an offbeat image, a creative tagline, a story with an unexpected twist) can jolt a donor into paying attention. Neurologically, novel stimuli activate the brain's reward and curiosity centers, making us more alert (Bunzeck & Düzel, 2006). For fundraisers, this means avoiding clichés and sameness. Introduce something fresh in your outreach; even small creative touches can make an appeal stand out from the rest.

- **Emotion.** Emotional content magnetically draws attention. Whether it's joy, sadness, hope, or anger, feelings engage us more than dry facts and pull a reader in. This happens because emotional stimuli engage the limbic system in the brain, signaling that "this matters." In practice, lead with human-centered narratives and imagery that make people feel something. Once a donor is emotionally invested, they are likely to keep reading and ultimately to give. In some additional research I did in partnership with a large technology company, we discovered that emotional subject lines affected open rates. But not just any emotion. In this study, using sentiment analysis, we discovered that positive emotions (relief, gratitude, pride, excitement, and optimism) correlated with higher open rates and negative emotions with lower open rates. The three words that killed open rates? Reminder (−308%), member (−224%), and meeting (−213%). So, if you want to make sure your donors don't open your email, your next subject line should be RE: Reminder member meeting.

- **Personal relevance.** We pay attention to things that relate directly to us or our interests. In a crowd, hearing your own name can instantly cut through the noise. Similarly, a fundraising appeal tailored to a donor's personal context (their community, their past giving interests, or values) will capture more attention than a one-size-fits-all message. Personalization, from simple tactics like using the donor's name and referencing their previous support to segmenting content by donor interest, tells the brain "this is about you." When donors feel spoken to on an individual level, they are more inclined to listen and respond.

Cognitive Processing Styles and Their Effect on Donation Behavior

Humans have two broad modes of thinking, often described as intuitive versus analytical (or "thinking fast versus slow"). Charitable giving is typically driven strongly by the intuitive, emotional mode, a gut-level impulse to help someone in need. However, the analytical side can come into play as well, especially when someone is deciding how much to give or evaluating a charity. Research suggests that too much analytical deliberation can sometimes dampen generosity. For example, when people are encouraged to carefully calculate or reason through a donation decision, they may give less to an emotional appeal than if they follow their first empathetic instinct (Small et al., 2007). For fundraisers, the initial appeal should usually aim at the heart: use narrative and emotion to engage the donor's intuitive desire to help. Once that spark is lit, providing facts or assurances about the charity's effectiveness can help satisfy the rational mind without dousing the emotional spark. But if you lead with an overload of data and logic, you might extinguish the emotional, generous motivation in the first place. Generosity, after all, is rarely ever rational. In practice, "People give with their heart. Then their brain goes looking for a receipt." Design your donor communications accordingly, inspire the donation with emotion, then support it with just enough reason (transparency, impact information) to reassure the donor that their impulse to give is a good decision. That balance will cater to both thinking styles and result in a higher likelihood of a donation.

Psychological Motivations for Giving

Finally, we turn to the underlying motivations that drive someone to make a gift. Understanding these motivations can help fundraisers craft appeals that resonate on a deeper level. People often give for a mix of reasons, some altruistic (focusing on helping others) and some that involve personal benefit or satisfaction. The goal is to appreciate why donors give, so we can remove barriers to generosity in ways that feel rewarding to them and effective for our causes.

Bekkers and Wiepking's Mechanisms That Drive Charitable Giving

After reviewing a large body of philanthropy research, René Bekkers and Pamala Wiepking (2011) identified eight key mechanisms that drive charitable giving: awareness of need, solicitation, costs and benefits, altruism, reputation, psychological benefits, values, and efficacy. This framework reminds us that multiple factors often work together to prompt a donation. For example, a person might give because they become aware of a problem and are asked at the right time, feel empathy, get a good feeling from helping, and trust that their contribution matters. As a practitioner, it's useful to consider these mechanisms in your strategies. Since this framework is addressed in other works and puts more control in the hands of the fundraiser, we will not discuss it in detail here. Effective fundraising appeals often touch on several of these drivers at once. For instance, making sure people know about the need, asking them directly, assuring them that their gift will have impact, and making them feel appreciated. By addressing what motivates donors on multiple levels, you create a more compelling case to give.

Intrinsic Versus Extrinsic Motivation (Self-Determination Theory)

Motivations for giving can be intrinsic (coming from within, driven by the act of giving itself, and aligned with personal values) or extrinsic (driven by external incentives or pressures). Intrinsic motivation is when donating is its own reward—for example, someone gives because it feels good or because it fits their belief that helping others is the right thing to do. Extrinsic motivation might involve things like receiving a gift, a tax benefit, or recognition for donating. Aligned with neurogiving, several psychologists note that people are more likely to sustain a behavior when it is driven by internal interest and values rather than external pressure (Deci & Ryan, 2000). While both play a role, intrinsic motivation tends to lead to more sustained engagement. If people give because they truly care, they're likely to continue giving. Extrinsic rewards can boost generosity in the short term, but they can also undermine it if overused. Studies have shown that offering too many external rewards for a behavior that is already rewarding can reduce the internal motivation to do it (Deci et al., 1999).

In fundraising, this is seen when donors who are bombarded with incentive gifts or gimmicks might start to feel like they only gave to get the reward, rather than for the cause. As a result, they may be less inclined to give again without a similar or greater incentive. The practical insight is to uncover and reinforce intrinsic motives. Fundraisers should emphasize the meaningful impact of the donation and the positive feelings that come from helping while using extrinsic motivators sparingly and thoughtfully. Thank-you gifts or public acknowledgments are fine (people do appreciate them), but they should be positioned as tokens of gratitude, not bribes. When you keep the focus on the cause and the donor's genuine compassion, you nurture a form of motivation that persists and grows, rather than one that disappears if the perks go away.

Altruism Versus Ego Benefits in Giving Behavior

Philanthropy often involves a blend of altruistic and egoistic motivations. On the altruistic side, donors give because they genuinely care about others; they empathize with those in need and want to help purely for the beneficiary's sake. On the egoistic side, donors may also enjoy personal benefits from giving such as feeling good about themselves, gaining social approval, or fulfilling a sense of personal identity (e.g., "I am a generous person."). This doesn't mean donations are selfish; rather, it acknowledges that doing good for others and doing good for oneself can happen simultaneously. In fact, warm glow is an example of an egoistic reward (internal pleasure) that complements altruism. Some economists describe charitable giving as "impure altruism," meaning it's not 100% selfless because the donor also receives something (even if it's just satisfaction) in return (Andreoni, 1990). However, "impure" in this context isn't negative; it reflects a realistic mix of motives. Nobody gives for pure reasons. And that's a feature, not a bug.

For fundraisers, understanding this mix is useful. Appeals can honestly appeal to both: highlight the impact on those in need (altruism) and acknowledge what the donor might gain (pride, community, being part of something important). For example, messages like "Your gift will save lives and you'll join a community of caring neighbors" combine altruistic messaging with an ego boost of belonging and esteem. The key is balance and authenticity. The cause and those benefiting should always remain at the heart of the message (to honor altruistic intent), but it's perfectly fine to also convey to donors that their generosity is valued and that they can take joy and pride in it. By appealing to the whole person—compassion and self-interest—you can motivate giving more effectively than by assuming it's purely one or the other.

The Over-Justification Effect and How Rewards Can Undermine Intrinsic Motivation

The over-justification effect occurs when adding external rewards to an activity that someone already finds rewarding causes their intrinsic interest to decline. In other words, if people start feeling they're doing something for the reward, they may lose some of the pure passion they originally had for the activity (Deci et al., 1999). In fundraising, this is a cautionary tale: if we lean too heavily on incentives, contests, or prizes to drive donations, we risk changing the donor's mindset. They might start to think they donated mainly to get the reward, rather than because they care. For instance, if a nonprofit runs a campaign in which donors are entered into a raffle for a vacation, some people might give primarily to try to win. Those donors could be less likely to give again (when there's no raffle) because the act of giving became tied to an external perk. To avoid over-justification, ensure that any external incentives complement rather than overshadow the real purpose of giving. A matching gift challenge, for example, still keeps the focus on helping the cause (the match just amplifies the impact); this tends to enhance intrinsic motivation ("My gift goes even further.") rather than replace it. Use rewards mainly as a way to celebrate and thank donors for doing what they inherently find meaningful. This way, you preserve the donor's internal motivation, and generosity can remain an expression of their values, not a means to an end.

The Goal-Gradient Hypothesis in Donation Behavior

Have you noticed that fundraising thermometers often seem to fill up fastest at the end of a campaign? This reflects the goal-gradient hypothesis, which suggests that people work harder as they get closer to a goal. In fundraising, donors often become more motivated to give when a campaign is near its target. For example, if a fundraiser is 85% of the way to a $10,000 goal, potential donors seeing that may feel that their contribution could be the one to push it over the finish line, which encourages them to chip in (Cryder et al., 2013). Campaign data frequently shows a spike in donations as the deadline approaches or as the thermometer graphic fills up. This happens partly because donors perceive that their gift will have a more noticeable impact ("I helped complete the goal!") and partly due to a sense of excitement and social momentum. Fundraisers can harness the goal-gradient effect by making progress visible and communicating it. Show donors a progress bar or update ("We're 90% there!") and explicitly invite them to help close the gap. Breaking a large goal into smaller milestones can also maintain momentum ("Only $500 needed to reach our weekend goal of $5,000."). This creates multiple mini–lines that reinvigorate donor enthusiasm. The psychological lift people get from achieving a goal, or helping to achieve it, can be a powerful driver. Just be transparent with your goals and updates; honesty builds trust, and hitting a genuine goal together builds shared pride.

Leveraging these psychological insights can help fundraisers craft more resonant, human-centered appeals that make generosity easier while respecting and empowering donors.

Now that we've explored the psychological principles underlying generosity, let's see how they surface in specific types of donors—across age, wealth, and legacy preferences. These psychological mechanisms show up differently depending on the donor's identity, resources to give, and life stage.

Fundraisers often segment donors by age and generation, hoping to tailor strategies to each group. Research does show *some* differences across life stages. For example, older donors historically contributed more money overall, while younger donors have been more likely to engage through volunteering or issue-specific campaigns (Indiana University Lilly Family School of Philanthropy, 2025). A recent study found that Gen Z and Millennial donors tend to be issue-driven (focusing on causes rather than specific organizations) and heavily tech-enabled in their giving, for instance, using social media and crowdfunding more than their elders. At the same time, younger donors often seek greater transparency and hands-on involvement with causes, whereas older donors may be more trusting of institutions they've supported long-term. These patterns suggest nonprofits can benefit from some understanding of generational preferences. Importantly, generational differences also show up in how donors prefer to receive and respond to communication, a topic we'll explore in more depth later in the book.

However, it's critical not to overgeneralize or rely on stereotypes. Age itself is only one factor, and its predictive power for charitable behavior is waning. A 12-year longitudinal analysis of US giving found that charitable participation has "leveled out" between age groups. Today, younger adults are donating at rates more comparable to older adults than in the past. In fact, income and financial capacity now explain much more about donor generosity than age alone (Collins, 2023). In other words, a wealthy 35-year-old and a wealthy 65-year-old might have more in common with each other in terms of giving patterns than two 65-year-olds of very different means. Life stage matters (younger people have less accumulated wealth and different family obligations), but broad generational labels can be misleading.

Moreover, individuals within a generation are diverse. Not all baby boomers give the same way, and not all millennials share identical motivations. While it's useful to be mindful of trends (for instance, younger donors' comfort with digital engagement), fundraisers should avoid one-size-fits-all assumptions. Yet most fundraising still ignores these insights, favoring segmentation over story, and data slices over donor self-concept. Instead, this chapter focuses on the psychological mechanisms and decision-making processes that influence all donors. These cognitive factors, the heuristics and biases in how humans make giving decisions, often cut across generational lines. By understanding these, nonprofits can better inspire donors of any age. Age-related differences do exist, but effective fundraising taps into the deeper human psychology that drives generosity, rather than relying on simplistic generational generalizations.

Affluent Donors: How Wealth Influences Giving Decisions

Wealth influences more than financial capacity; it shapes how one perceives control, impact, and identity. A donor who can give $50,000 or $1 million or more in one gift understandably requires a slightly different engagement approach than someone giving $50. But beyond the obvious fact that wealthy donors have more financial capacity, what does research tell us about how affluence might change a donor's psychology or decision-making? It turns out that wealth can influence donors' motivations and cognitive patterns in subtle ways—but here, too, evidence cautions against simple stereotypes. Let's explore what studies have found about affluent donor decision-making:

> **Generosity of the wealthy—myth versus reality.** While wealthy individuals give more in absolute terms, they may contribute a smaller percentage of their income compared to others (Piff et al., 2010). However, other studies show

generosity varies widely among high-net-worth individuals, depending on personal values and context (Korndörfer et al., 2015). The point is not that the wealthy are selfish but that their giving is shaped by different dynamics.

Agency, control, and the "self-made" mindset. A key insight into affluent donors comes from psychology: wealth is often associated with an agentic self-concept. People who are wealthier tend to feel a greater sense of control over their lives and outcomes—after all, money provides autonomy and options. In psychological surveys, upper-income individuals report higher levels of self-reliance and a desire to influence their environment (Whillans & Dunn, 2018). By contrast, those with less financial security may place relatively more importance on communal values and interdependence. How does this translate to charitable giving? This 2018 field experiment by Whillans and Dunn demonstrated that they respond better when the ask aligns with their independent, self-efficacious mindset. They like to be seen (and to see themselves) as drivers of change. The practical tip for fundraisers working with high-net-worth donors might be to frame giving opportunities in terms of investment, impact, and personal influence. For instance, instead of "Together we can solve this," one might say, "Your gift can launch a new initiative" or "You have the power to accomplish x with your philanthropy." Empower the donor to feel like a protagonist.

Identity and recognition. Another aspect of affluent donor decision-making is how giving ties into their identity and legacy. For some major donors, philanthropy becomes a part of who they are—an expression of their values, success, and desire to give back. Big gifts often come with opportunities for public recognition (naming rights to buildings, endowments, awards, etc.), which can appeal to donors who take pride in being benefactors. This isn't simply vanity; it's about signaling personal meaning. A qualitative study by Drs. Shang and Sargent noted that making transformative gifts can even shift how wealthy donors view themselves—reinforcing an identity as a "changemaker" or steward of certain ideals (Shang & Sargeant, 2024). However, some affluent donors prefer to give quietly and avoid the spotlight, focusing on the intrinsic reward of doing good. The common thread is that for high-capacity donors, charitable decisions are often woven into long-term personal goals—whether that's family legacy, community impact, or immortality through naming. Fundraisers should recognize these deeper motivations. For example, involving a major donor in the design of a program or soliciting their input can satisfy their desire for agency and partnership. Offering naming opportunities or legacy honors can align with their need to cement their values for posterity. Importantly, genuine gratitude and relationship building are paramount: affluent donors, like any donors, want to trust the organization and feel that their contribution is meaningful. The scale might be larger, but the psychological fundamentals (pride, purpose, trust, connection) remain human and personal.

Altruism with strategy. Wealthy donors may also approach giving with a more strategic or analytical lens. High-net-worth individuals often have advisors, lawyers, or philanthropic consultants guiding their giving, which can introduce more deliberation. These individuals might be interested in data, metrics, or evidence of impact before committing a large sum. This doesn't imply that emotion plays no role; even the most analytical donor is moved by a compelling story, but they may require additional justification to ensure their large gift is used effectively. For instance, major donors might scrutinize a nonprofit's financials (harkening back to overhead aversion concerns) or request detailed proposals. From neuroscience research, we know that counting and deliberation can actually temper emotional impulses to give (Small et al., 2013). So, fundraisers need to strike a balance when engaging affluent donors between heart and mind appeals. Provide the inspiring vision and emotional narrative, but also the facts, plans, and confidence that their significant investment will yield results.

Importantly, affluent donors are not a monolith, but many share psychological characteristics shaped by having ample resources. They often crave agency, appreciate being treated as collaborators, and may think of their philanthropy as part of a broader life mission or legacy. Building trust and demonstrating impact are especially critical with this group. By grounding major-donor strategies in research-backed insights—for example, using empowering language and aligning with the donor's personal values—fundraisers can better connect with wealthy donors in a way that respects their perspective and fulfills their philanthropic aspirations.

Legacy Giving and the Brain: The Neuroscience of Planned Gifts

One of the most fascinating areas where neuroscience and fundraising intersect is in legacy giving: donors leaving gifts in their wills or estate plans (also known as planned giving or bequests). These are unique donations because the decision involves contemplating one's own mortality and the desire to leave a lasting impact beyond one's lifetime. Thanks to the pioneering work of Dr. Russell James, we have a window into what happens in the brain when people consider making a charitable bequest. Understanding these findings can help nonprofits communicate more effectively about legacy giving in a way that resonates with donors' deepest motivations. While we often think of generosity as a choice, neuroscience reveals it's closer to a reflex, when the right emotional and identity-based triggers are present.

Russell James's functional magnetic resonance imaging (fMRI) research revealed that thinking about a charitable bequest activates the brain regions tied to autobiographical memory and self-reflection—particularly the precuneus and lingual gyrus (James & O'Boyle, 2014). In essence, donors visualize the legacy they want to leave, weaving their life story into the decision to give. Legacy gifts are personal narrative decisions, not just financial ones.

Why would a bequest engage the brain's autobiographical regions so strongly? Think about what it means to leave a legacy gift: you're deciding what remains of your resources after you're gone, effectively making a statement about your life's values, the entirety of your generosity story. This naturally triggers thoughts about one's identity, memories, and loved ones. In fact, James's research suggests that encouraging potential legacy donors to reflect on their personal connections and life journey can facilitate the bequest decision. In one experiment, subjects were asked about leaving bequests to family or friends versus to charities. Interestingly, when people thought about bequests to family/friends, brain regions tied to emotion and memory (like the insula and posterior cingulate cortex) were much more active than when they thought about charitable bequests (James, 2013, as summarized by Laskin, 2013). In other words, leaving something to loved ones is automatically emotional; it immediately brings to mind relationships and memories—whereas leaving something to a nonprofit might initially feel more abstract or removed from one's personal story. However, the research also showed that if people consider how a charity connects to their life or the lives of those they care about, the emotional regions can engage for charitable bequests as well (James & O'Boyle, 2014; Laskin, 2013). Sargeant and Shang (2011), using dimensional qualitative research, found that motivations for leaving a bequest include not just altruism but also identity, reciprocity, legacy, and even spite! Critically, they identified with the organization, feeling personally connected, as a central driver. These insights suggest that legacy gifts are less about financial calculus and more about emotional and identity-based alignment. They illustrate how effective giving decisions, especially complex ones like bequests, are deeply tied to self-perception and life narrative.

The implication for fundraisers is powerful: to inspire legacy gifts, we must help donors connect the charity to their sense of self and family. Dr. James advises that gift planners and legacy officers talk with donors about their life story and what matters most to them. For example, asking a donor "What life experiences shaped your passion for our cause?" or "Is there someone you want to honor through a gift?" can invoke that autobiographical reflection. Marketing materials for legacy giving are more effective when they include stories of donors who explain how their personal history led them to include the charity in their will ("We chose to leave a bequest to the hospital where our daughter's life was saved, as a way to extend our family's gratitude to future generations"). By helping donors see a charitable bequest as an extension of their life narrative, almost like adding an important chapter to their autobiography, fundraisers tap into the natural way the brain processes legacy decisions. Legacy decisions aren't anomalies; they're the clearest mirror of what matters most, etched into action by memory and mortality.

Another point from this research is the concept of mortality salience, the awareness of one's own death. Understandably, many people avoid thinking about making a will or estate plan because it's tied to acknowledging mortality. This is a barrier to legacy giving: it's an uncomfortable topic. However, once donors do engage in the idea of a legacy gift, they often find it deeply satisfying to "live on" through a cause they care about. James and O'Boyle's fMRI study (2014) suggests that after the initial hurdle of confronting mortality, the brain's engagement in legacy decision-making can even be positive: people may derive comfort and meaning from imagining the good their bequest will do. The precuneus activation could indicate a kind of peaceful, big-picture reflection on life as donors integrate the charity into their sense of self. As a fundraiser, being sensitive to this emotional journey is key. Early in the conversation, reassurance and empathetic understanding are important ("Take your time … deciding on a legacy is very personal."). As the donor moves toward a decision, focus on the meaning of the gift rather than the mechanics. Highlight how the bequest is a way to leave a legacy aligned with their values, or to memorialize someone dear to them, or to ensure their life's passions continue to make a difference.

Dr. James's contributions to our understanding of planned giving go beyond the scans. He famously concluded that "the story is the answer," both hard science (neuroimaging) and soft science (interviews with donors) converge on the importance of personal story in bequest motivations (James & O'Boyle, 2014). People often decide to make a legacy gift when it "feels like the story of my life leads to this gift." Fundraisers can foster that feeling by listening to donors' stories and linking the organization's mission to them. For example, if a donor used to be a teacher, discussing an education endowment as a way to continue inspiring children could resonate. If a donor lost a loved one to disease, framing a legacy gift to a related charity as "part of your loved one's story living on" can be deeply meaningful. Additionally, providing opportunities for tribute gifts (bequests made in honor of someone) enables donors to combine family and charity, bridging that gap the brain initially perceives between taking care of family and helping a cause. In doing so, the charitable bequest starts to engage the same emotion centers as thinking about family bequests, effectively humanizing the charity in the donor's mind (James, 2013 as summarized by Laskin, 2013).

Ultimately, neuroscience and psychology research have unveiled that legacy giving is not just a financial or transactional choice; it's wrapped up in identity, memory, and meaning. Charitable planners should approach potential bequest donors with this understanding. The goal is to move beyond technical features (tax benefits, etc.) and speak to the heart and mind: who are you? What legacy do you want to leave? How does our cause fit into the story of your life? Fundraising becomes most powerful when it doesn't try to persuade donors to give, but instead helps them remember who they are. By doing so, we honor the profound decision a legacy gift represents and greatly increase the likelihood of facilitating these ultimate acts of generosity.

Crucially, understanding these psychological factors should also remind us to treat donors as people, not ATM machines categorized by age or wealth. Every donor brings their own feelings, biases, and motivations to the table. By appreciating the general principles of how people tend to decide, we can create better experiences for donors of all types. That leads to stronger relationships and, ultimately, more sustainable support for our missions. As you apply the ideas from this chapter, remember to do so with empathy and ethics; the same biases that can boost generosity, if exploited without care, can erode trust. Understanding how donors think isn't just strategic, it's an ethical responsibility to honor, not manipulate, their motivations whether they are digital natives, long-time benefactors, or legacy-minded supporters. Our role is to align with the person's mindset, not to take advantage of it. When done right, fundraising becomes a harmonious process: donors feel understood and joyful in giving, and nonprofits secure the resources to do good, all through approaches grounded in how our brains and hearts actually work.

Chapter 3

The Science of Storytelling and Emotional Engagement

Humans are wired for storytelling. Long before written language, our ancestors shared knowledge, built relationships, and shaped their worldviews through stories. Storytelling is one of the most powerful tools for engaging donors, evoking empathy, and inspiring action. Unlike statistics or facts, narratives activate multiple brain regions, triggering emotional and physiological responses that make information more memorable and persuasive. This chapter explores the science behind storytelling in fundraising. We'll examine how emotional resonance strengthens donor engagement, how developing a storytelling universe fosters long-term connection, and how strategic language choices influence decision-making. By leveraging these insights, nonprofit professionals can craft messages that do more than inform: they can move people to act.

The Neuroscience of Narrative

Storytelling is much more than a buzzword in fundraising; it's rooted in how a donor's brain processes information and connects with a cause. Neural coupling is the scientific name for a remarkable phenomenon that occurs between a storyteller and listener during a compelling narrative. Neuroscientists at Princeton University discovered that when someone listens to a well-told story, the listener's brain activity can mirror the speaker's in key regions associated with understanding and emotion (Hasson et al., 2010). In other words, a compelling narrative literally puts a donor's brain on the same wavelength as the storyteller's. This synchronization doesn't happen with dry facts or statistics; it's a special effect of narrative communication. If you share the story of a child whose life was saved by a donor's gift, the donor isn't just processing the information intellectually; their brain is feeling along with the story. This neural mirroring creates a shared emotional experience, as if the donor is "in the shoes" of the story's characters. Science is confirming what fundraisers know already: a powerful story can align minds and hearts, building empathy and trust at a biological level (Stephens et al., 2010).

Why do stories wield this almost magical influence? Part of the answer lies in how narrative structure activates the brain differently than statistics do. Stories provide context, conflict, and characters, elements that our brains are designed to pay attention to. A list of statistics or factual bullet points might inform, but it rarely transforms. Stories engage the brain's limbic system, our emotional center, whereas raw facts tend to engage more analytical regions. For example, consider the difference between these two approaches: a nonprofit could present a donor with a statistic—"Thousands of families lack clean water"—or it could share a vivid story—"A young mother named Amina walks five miles every day to fetch water for her children … ." The latter paints a picture that engages empathy and curiosity.

Neuroscience helps explain this. A narrative with a classic dramatic arc, one that introduces characters, builds tension or conflict, and then resolves, activates a suite of neurochemicals in the brain, including cortisol and oxytocin. Cortisol is often called the "stress hormone," and it spikes when we pay alert attention to a problem or threat. A good story produces moderate cortisol during moments of tension, which keeps the listener focused. Professor Paul Zak's experiments have shown that character-driven stories can lead to increased oxytocin release in listeners, making them feel more empathy and make generosity easier. As well, Zak found that the combination of cortisol from suspense and oxytocin from empathy was a potent predictor of charitable action, correctly forecasting donation behavior about 80% of the time (Zak, 2015). The takeaway is both powerful and practical: effective stories change our brain chemistry, grabbing attention with a bit of adrenaline and cortisol, and forging human connection through oxytocin, a recipe that can inspire action (Zak, 2015; Zak et al., 2007).

The emotional resolution of a story can activate dopamine pathways in the brain, providing a satisfying reward that enhances recall and motivation to act. From a fundraising perspective, this is pure gold (arguably better than a donation): if a donor's brain associates the act of giving with positive emotional reward, they're more likely to want to repeat that behavior. It's a neurological reinforcement loop.

Another way stories engage the brain is by tapping into our preference for episodic information (experiences, events) over abstract semantic information (facts, figures). Humans are wired to remember through episodes—we learn and recall in narratives ("This happened, then that happened … ."). That's why you might vividly recall the details of a touching program story you heard last year, but you struggle to remember the exact statistics from your annual report. Stories stick because they weave facts into a structure the brain's memory systems prefer. Psychologist Jerome Bruner famously has been misattributed with the concept that a story is 22 times more memorable than a stand-alone fact. While the precise number may be debated the core insight is widely accepted: narratives create multiple memory "hooks." A story has images, emotions, and a logical sequence of events, all of which reinforce learning and recall (Bruner, 1990). By contrast, raw data usually engages only our language and numeric processing, making a much shallower imprint.

For nonprofit practitioners, this means if you want donors to remember your cause and message, embed it in a narrative. We recall personal anecdotes and case studies far better than white papers. One experiment found that even when people are presented with both a statistic and a story, their decisions and recall tend to be driven by the story if it resonated emotionally (Small et al., 2013). Our episodic memory (tied to experiences) simply has a stronger pull than semantic memory (tied to abstract knowledge) when it comes to motivation.

Finally, narrative has a persuasive power through what communication scholars call transportation theory, the idea that when people become absorbed or "transported" into a story, they are more open to its implications and less likely to counterargue (Green & Brock, 2000). Think of the last time you got lost in a novel or a movie; for a while, you emotionally lived in that world. When donors are similarly immersed in a nonprofit's story—picturing the scenes, empathizing with the characters—they experience what Green and Brock (2000) describe as narrative transportation. This immersive state not only makes the experience enjoyable but it also tends to produce attitude and behavior changes consistent with the story's message. In practical terms, if you tell a gripping story about your cause, a donor who is "pulled in" may come out on the other side feeling as though they personally witnessed suffering relieved or a triumph achieved, and that feeling can translate into support. Effective nonprofit narratives often read like a journey—they have a beginning that draws the listener in, a middle that sustains attention through challenges (keeping that cortisol-driven focus), and an ending that provides emotional payoff (triggering oxytocin, dopamine, or a sense of inspiration). When all these elements come together, the audience is not just informed but transformed. This is the science of storytelling at work.

Building Emotional Resonance

If storytelling engages the brain's empathy and reward circuits, how do we ensure our stories actually resonate emotionally with supporters? This comes down to engaging the right brain systems involved in emotional processing when crafting appeals. Central to emotional resonance is the limbic system—particularly the amygdala, a small almond-shaped region that acts as the brain's emotional alarm bell. The amygdala evaluates emotional significance and tags memories with emotional weight. Research has shown that emotionally charged events (whether joyful or traumatic) activate the amygdala and related areas like the hippocampus, which in turn helps encode those events into long-term memory (McGaugh, 2004).

In fundraising terms, this means moments that really hit the heart—a poignant success story, a heartfelt thank-you, a dramatic call for help—are more likely to be remembered by your donors. By creating those emotional peaks, you are literally helping imprint the experience of your cause in the donor's mind (McGaugh, 2004). It's no coincidence that many effective fundraising campaigns have a highly emotional centerpiece (a video, a personal speech, a powerful testimonial). Those peak moments engage the amygdala, which flags the experience as important and "save-worthy." Later on, when that donor thinks about where to give or whether their contribution mattered, those vivid emotional memories come to the surface, reinforcing their connection to your organization.

Emotional resonance also involves neural synchrony through shared experiences—essentially, creating a feeling of being "in it together" with your audience. Earlier we discussed neural coupling between speaker and listener. On a broader scale, when a group of people share an emotional experience, their brains and bodies can literally synchronize. Psychologists have observed, for instance, that audiences at a riveting theater play or a moving piece of music often show aligned physiological responses (heart rate, facial expressions at the same moments). In neural terms, if all eyes in a room are watching the same impactful story, many of the same brain regions will light up in unison across individuals. This creates a kind of social bond; everyone is feeling together. For nonprofits, this is a reason why bringing donors together for events, site visits, or live storytelling sessions can be so powerful. Shared emotional moments build a sense of community and collective empathy. Neuroscientists sometimes call this phenomenon "collective effervescence" in brain terms—a harmony of neurochemical responses among a group (Durkheim, 1912/1995). Practically, it means that by sharing emotional experiences (through stories, videos, or live events) you create group resonance. A donor is not just moved in isolation; they sense that "we"—the community of supporters—are moved and aligned in purpose. That perception of shared emotion can enhance commitment and trust, as people are biologically inclined to bond with those with whom they synchronously experience strong feelings.

Positive and negative emotions engage somewhat different circuitry, and understanding this can guide how we frame our stories. The amygdala and limbic system respond robustly to threats and distress—hence fear-based or urgent crisis appeals instantly grab attention. A story of a child in danger from dirty water might spike a donor's stress response (cortisol, increased amygdala firing), triggering concern and a quick impulse to help. Negative emotions like fear, anger, or sadness activate attention and urgency via the amygdala and insula (regions that process pain and disgust), whereas positive emotions like hope, joy, or pride activate the brain's reward centers (ventral striatum, nucleus accumbens) and social bonding circuits.

Brain imaging studies suggest a clear difference between positive and negative appeals in terms of neural impact. A hopeful story of a community overcoming odds might stimulate the same reward pathway as personal achievement does—releasing dopamine and even endorphins (the "feel-good" opioids that create a mild euphoria). By contrast, a dire warning about a worsening crisis will heighten activity in areas like the amygdala, hypothalamus, and even anterior cingulate cortex (associated with pain detection), which can spur action but also stress. One is not inherently better than the other; it's about how they are used. Negative appeals ("If we don't act, this beautiful forest will be destroyed forever.") are effective at cutting through complacency—they ignite a spark. Positive appeals ("With your help, this forest can thrive for generations.") are effective at sustaining engagement—they light the way. Neuroscience suggests that an oscillation between the two can keep donors emotionally engaged without burnout. For example, effective campaigns often present a problem (engaging attention and concern) but then quickly pivot to a solution or success story (engaging hope and reward), thereby giving the audience emotional resolution instead of leaving them in distress. This mirrors the narrative arc concept: tension (cortisol) followed by resolution (dopamine/oxytocin). From a memory standpoint, ending on a positive emotional note can also be advantageous due to the "peak-end rule"—people remember the peak of an experience and the end of it most (Kahneman & Tversky, 2000). If the end is uplifting, it leaves a warm residue in memory even if parts of the story were upsetting.

Another key element in building emotional resonance is leveraging the brain's mirroring and empathic systems. We touched on mirror neurons previously—those cells that fire both when we do something and when we see someone else do it. They're thought to underlie empathy, enabling us to literally feel a bit of what someone else is feeling. When a donor hears or reads a personal narrative ("As I watched my child struggle with illness, I felt … ."), the donor's brain can mirror the described feelings to a degree. If the story is well crafted, the donor might get a lump in their throat at

55

the same moment the storyteller did, or feel a swell of joy when the protagonist experiences success. This is the neural basis of emotional contagion. Beyond the mirror neuron system, other regions like the anterior insula and anterior cingulate cortex activate when we empathize with another's pain or joy (Decety & Jackson, 2006). So, a story of hardship might literally produce a pang in a donor's neural circuits, and a story of triumph might activate circuits associated with relief and happiness. Harnessing this means making stories as experiential as possible—using first-person perspectives, rich sensory details, and emotional transparency so that the audience can mentally simulate the journey. The more a donor's brain can simulate the experience, the more likely they are to share the emotions. That shared emotion is what drives the urge to help. As fundraisers, if we can get a donor thinking "I feel what they feel," we are much closer to "I want to do something about it."

Emotional resonance also has a lot to do with memory formation, as mentioned. Strong emotions trigger the amygdala-hippocampus tag team to strengthen memory consolidation (McGaugh, 2004). This is why you probably remember exactly where you were during a tragic news event or, on a personal level, why a heartfelt thank-you from someone may stick with you for years. In nonprofit storytelling, details that carry emotional weight (a quote that gave you goosebumps, an image of a beneficiary's genuine smile, a tense moment of uncertainty that resolved positively) serve as anchors in the donor's memory. When donors later recall your campaign, those anchors surface. And importantly, memory and emotion together influence future behavior. A donor who clearly recalls feeling moved by your last story is more likely to open your next email, attend your next event, or make that next gift. In essence, by engaging the brain's emotional systems effectively, you're not only inspiring action in the moment but also laying neural groundwork for ongoing engagement.

Storytelling's power lies not just in its emotional pull but in its precision. When done well, it can speak directly to what a donor values most. This is where reference analysis, using mind genomics training, becomes especially illuminating. While neuroscience tells us *why* stories work—by triggering empathy, reward circuits, and memory—preference analysis helps us understand *which* stories work best for different types of donors.

In one study conducted for a large nonprofit public radio station, we examined how mid-level donors, particularly women over the age of 45, responded to various narrative elements. What we found was not one universal story, but two distinct emotional lenses:

- One group, what we called *cultural stewards*, resonated deeply with legacy-focused messaging: safeguarding beloved programs for future generations, preserving artistic and educational content, and upholding a tradition of excellence.

- The other group, *community anchors*, were moved by stories that emphasized accessibility, inclusivity, and the nonprofit's mission to serve *everyone*, not just elite audiences.

Both mindsets supported the same organization, yet they required different emotional entry points to feel connected. Importantly, messaging that centered purely on financial urgency or institutional need consistently underperformed. What worked instead were narratives that enabled donors to see themselves as active participants in a shared cultural story, whether as protectors of heritage or champions of equity.

In another case, a study for a nonprofit focused on maternal and infant health revealed similarly divergent emotional hooks. Some donors were most compelled by stories of survival and lifesaving impact—clear, emotionally urgent narratives. Others responded better to dignity- and agency-framed messages that honored women and families not as victims but as resilient protagonists.

These findings underscore a critical principle: stories don't move people because they are emotional, they move people when they align with the emotional logic of the stories the donors already tell themselves. Preference analysis enables us to uncover what kind of narrative structure best resonates with different donor mindsets.

The broader takeaway is clear: regardless of your mission—whether it's media, health, education, the arts, or the environment—storytelling is most effective when it's not just emotionally rich, but personally relevant. Using behavioral segmentation to craft stories that match donor preferences is not just smart strategy; it's a form of respect. It honors the diversity of motivations behind generosity and ensures that each donor sees themselves in the story being told.

Developing a Storytelling Universe

Most nonprofits recognize the power of a single good story. But to truly maximize engagement, think beyond one-off anecdotes and toward an ongoing storytelling universe. This means creating a cohesive, interconnected narrative framework for your cause, a series of stories that tie together over time, rather than isolated campaigns that start and stop. Psychologically, people become far more attached to narratives that continue and evolve (with recurring characters or themes) than to stand-alone stories that have no follow-up.

One of the best illustrations is the Marvel Cinematic Universe (MCU): each film on its own is entertaining, but collectively they weave an epic saga that keeps audiences coming back for years. Viewers develop relationships with the characters and anticipation for the next installment. We can apply a similar idea in the nonprofit context. When donors see how each story you share is part of a larger journey or mission, they begin to invest not just in one outcome but in the ongoing saga of your work. They start to care about "what happens next" for your cause, much like a reader cares about the next chapter in a novel.

Building a storytelling universe can significantly strengthen donors' psychological attachment to your organization. Instead of engaging with a single narrative and then drifting away, supporters who perceive a continuing story are more likely to stick around, the way fans stick with a beloved TV series. Each story you tell becomes an episode in an unfolding series. Over time, donors move from being casual listeners to loyal followers who feel almost like participants in your mission's narrative. They aren't just giving to an isolated need; they're investing in the development of a story—a story in which they hope to see progress, setbacks overcome, and successes celebrated. This fosters a deeper level of commitment. In marketing terms, you're improving "customer retention" through storytelling continuity, but in human terms you're building a relationship through narrative. Supporters might start thinking of your cause less as a charity they donate to and more as a journey they are part of. And frankly, even when it's bad, they still stick with you. Who among us hasn't stomached a few bad episodes or season of a show but kept watching anyway through the series finale?

There's a neuroscience angle here as well: ongoing narratives help create neural schemas for your cause. A schema is like a mental framework or story template that our brains use to organize information. When you introduce a new story that connects to previous ones, the brain of your donor can link it to an existing schema ("Ah, this fits into that larger picture I know about."). This means new information is processed more deeply and remembered more easily because it slots into an ongoing context. If over the last year you've shared multiple stories about different children in a literacy program, by the time you introduce the fifth child's story, donors already have a mental model of "kids in the literacy program overcoming challenges." Each new story reinforces and enriches that schema. From a memory

The Science of Storytelling and Emotional Engagement

standpoint, this repetition with variation strengthens recall—donors not only remember the individual stories but also the overarching message that ties them together (Schank & Abelson, 1995). They start seeing patterns and understanding nuances of your work, which educates them in a narrative-driven way. It's much like how each chapter in a book reinforces the overall plot and themes.

So how do we practically create a storytelling universe? It helps to treat your communications like episodes in a connected series rather than one-off appeals. You might begin by identifying your core narrative arc: the big-picture journey of your mission. For instance, the overarching arc might be "community x's journey from crisis to sustainability" or "the fight against disease y from ignorance to cure." This arc becomes the through line that connects individual stories. Every story told then relates back to this larger trajectory. Perhaps Story 1 is about a person at the beginning of that journey (setting the stage), Story 2 is an update showing progress or challenge, Story 3 introduces another facet or character of the mission, and so on. Each piece stands alone but also advances the larger plot. Donors begin to see continuity: the family you featured six months ago is now mentioned in an update, or the problem highlighted last year is referenced as improving this year. Just like episodes in a TV series, each installment resolves some things but also leaves threads that continue.

A powerful technique is to develop recurring characters or themes. In a nonprofit context, "characters" could be real individuals (people served, volunteers, staff) whose stories evolve over time. For example, you might introduce someone in one newsletter and then circle back to their progress later. Or you might have a recurring archetype, like each story features "a dedicated teacher" in different schools, or a "resilient mother" in different communities—a motif that donors recognize. When people see familiar characters or roles reappear, it creates a sense of familiarity and investment

("Oh, I remember her! How is she doing now?"). It's similar to how we get attached to fictional characters; here, donors get attached to real people (or even symbolic characters) related to your cause. The Marvel example fits here: each hero has their stand-alone film, but they also show up in each other's stories, creating a richer tapestry. For a nonprofit, maybe a volunteer featured in a past story later crosses paths with a person served in a new story (e.g., "The nurse who helped Juan in our 2020 story is now running our clinic in 2022."). These linkages signal that all these narratives are part of a common world. It engages the brain's pattern recognition and memory—donors start to build a mental map of your "universe," understanding how people and events are connected.

Another element is the neuroscience of suspense and narrative tension. Just as any good TV season ends on a cliffhanger, you can judiciously use suspense in your storytelling universe to keep supporters eager for updates. Our brains hate unfinished stories. It's called the Zeigarnik effect, a nagging need for closure on incomplete narratives. If you share in a spring update that "we've begun construction on the new well, but the rains are coming early and everything's at risk—we'll know in a few months if the village will have clean water in time," you introduce narrative tension. The donor's mind holds that tension and will feel a strong pull to find out the resolution (did they finish in time?). By designing some of your communications to be part of a to-be-continued arc, you leverage this natural desire for completion. When you later deliver the outcome (hopefully positive), the donor's brain gets the dopamine reward, along with empathy or relief (oxytocin, endorphins) if the resolution is happy. This not only satisfies them but also reinforces their engagement, because it feels good to see progress and to have been emotionally invested in the journey.

An important aspect of a storytelling universe is that it fosters psychological ownership among supporters, especially if you actively invite donors to participate in the story. In other words, donors stop feeling like outsiders looking in, and start feeling like coauthors of the narrative. Some nonprofits do this by giving supporters choices or roles in the unfolding story. For example, you might run a campaign where donors can "vote" on which project to fund next, effectively choosing the next chapter of the story ("Should we expand the school or start a clinic first? You decide!"). When donors cast that vote, they've invested their own agency into the narrative. Or you could invite donors to submit messages or ideas that get incorporated into communications, such as featuring a donor's perspective as part of a story. One organization held a contest for supporters to name a new rescue puppy that would be trained as a service dog, then continued to share that dog's journey under the chosen name. Thousands felt a small sense of ownership because they had been part of the naming and thus part of the story. From a psychological standpoint, these tactics leverage the "Ikea effect"—people place higher value on things they help create (Norton et al., 2012). In neuroscience terms, when we contribute to something, our brain's reward circuit and sense of self get intertwined with the outcome (Sharot et al., 2009). If a donor helps shape the story, even in a minor way, their neural response to the story's highs and lows will be stronger because their identity is now threaded into it.

Let's break down a few practical strategies for developing a storytelling universe (and the brain-friendly rationale behind them):

- **Identify a core narrative arc.** Define the overarching journey that your cause is on, which will unify your stories. Maybe it's "from relief to self-reliance" or "turning the tide on disease." This big arc gives meaning to each chapter. Neuroscience angle: having an overarching narrative provides context (and context is king for memory). Each story becomes easier to process and remember because the brain sees where it fits in the grand scheme (it's like adding folders in a filing system) (Schank & Abelson, 1995).

- **Develop recurring characters/themes.** Introduce characters (real people) who reappear over time or themes that recur. For example, follow a particular family's progress through periodic updates, or repeatedly highlight "hero" volunteers in different stories. Recurring elements create familiarity—the brain likes familiarity because it reduces cognitive load and increases affection (the mere exposure effect). Donors will start to feel like they "know" these people. When a character they recognize shows up, the neural response is similar to seeing an old friend—often triggering warmth and trust (Zak et al., 2007). It also builds continuity: the donor's brain links Story 1 and Story 2 because of the shared element.

- **Plan story arcs over time.** Instead of thinking campaign to campaign, sketch a multipart story. For instance: spring appeal introduces a problem and main characters (Chapter 1), summer newsletter updates on progress/challenges (Chapter 2), year-end report delivers outcome and possibly new questions for the future (Chapter 3). Each piece has its own mini-arc so it's satisfying alone, but together they show development. This trains donors to expect progression. When they know another chapter is coming, they have a reason to stay tuned (just as viewers await the next episode of a series). Anticipation is a powerful engagement tool; it keeps the dopamine trickling in as they look forward to the resolution.

- **Interconnect your stories.** Find ways to weave your stories together. Mention past stories in new ones ("This success echoes what we saw with Maria last year … .") or have storylines cross ("The teacher you met last month is actually mentoring the student in this story."). These callbacks reward attentive

63

donors by making them feel in the know, and even if someone is new, it signals that there is a larger tapestry. Cognitively, it creates a network of associations in memory—each
story reinforces others. One donor might not catch every single reference, but those who follow along will feel like they're
discovering Easter eggs in your narrative universe, which
boosts their engagement and loyalty. Even subtle nods (like
updating on a previous beneficiary's status in a footnote) can
trigger that "aha, I remember them!" moment that strengthens
neural connections.

- **Use multiple channels to tell different parts.** In today's
world, your storytelling universe can be multi-platform. Perhaps your email newsletter carries the main storyline, but your
social media shares side stories or character backstories, and
your annual report ties them all together. This is akin to a trans-
media narrative approach. Neuroscience-wise, engaging donors
on multiple channels can create more touchpoints in the brain
(visual content on Instagram, long-form reading on a blog,
audio in a webinar). The more modalities you involve, the
more encoding paths for memory. Just ensure consistency so it
feels like one universe—the tone and core message should
align (more on continuity in a moment).

- **Invite donors into the narrative.** As mentioned, make
donors *actors* in the story, not just audience. Thank them in
story form ("Because of supporters like you, Chapter 2 was a
triumph instead of a tragedy.") or feature donor stories as part
of your universe. When a donor sees someone like themselves
in the narrative—for example, "Jane donated her birthday to
raise money, and here's the impact she made."—it creates
identification. Social neuroscience shows that seeing a member of one's own group (here, fellow donors) do something

good can trigger vicarious pride and motivation (Molenberghs et al., 2014). It subtly says, *you belong in this story, too.* This increases what psychologists call *psychological ownership* and *identity salience*: donors start to internalize the success of the cause as their own success and the narrative of the cause as part of their personal narrative.

- **Ensure consistency and continuity.** A story universe only works if the world feels coherent. That means maintaining a consistent voice, tone, and style across your stories. If one piece is written in a playful, slangy tone and another is ultra-formal, the donor's brain might not immediately recognize them as the same narrative world. Consistency builds a familiar "story environment" in the brain. Think of it like an author's style—donors should be able to tell it's your organization speaking across different stories. This doesn't mean every piece is identical (variety is good), but underlying values and tone should align. The brain's pattern recognition then lumps these communications together as one entity—*your* story universe—which aids recall and trust (because you seem stable and reliable in your storytelling). From an emotional perspective, a cohesive narrative style prevents what one might call "narrative whiplash." If donors are accustomed to your generally hopeful and empathetic tone, a suddenly cynical or purely clinical story will feel off and can break their immersion.

The benefits of adopting a storytelling universe mindset are significant. Donors begin to anticipate your updates, looking forward to them the way one looks forward to the next episode of a favorite show. This anticipation itself is an engagement win. How many donors eagerly await a nonprofit email? Their understanding of your work deepens as they see multiple facets over time; essentially, you're educating them through narrative without it feeling like a lecture. They also become more adept at telling others about your cause, and because they've internalized the narrative, they can relay the ongoing story to friends, essentially becoming story ambassadors, not just donors. And crucially, their emotional connection grows with each new story if you carry them along a meaningful arc. Just as viewers who binge-watch a series develop strong feelings for the characters, donors who follow a series of connected stories develop a more enduring emotional bond with the people and communities your organization serves. In neuroscience terms, repeated positive exposure builds associative memory and increases the weight of those neural pathways ("Neurons that fire together, wire together."). So, each subsequent story not only has its own impact but also reactivates the emotions of previous stories, compounding the resonance.

One practical consideration: as you craft a storytelling universe, remember to welcome new entrants. Not everyone will have seen "Episode 1." Good storytellers in series formats always provide a bit of context so newcomers aren't lost ("Previously on …"). In non-profit communications, this can be as simple as a one-line recap or ensuring each story can stand on its own and as part of the whole For example, you might reintroduce a recurring character with a brief phrase: "Ever since we first met Maria two years ago when her family fled disaster, she has been working toward rebuilding her life … ." This way a new reader gets the gist, and a long-time reader appreciates the continuity. The goal is a universe that is permeable (anyone can jump in at any time and still be moved) yet richly layered for those who follow along.

Neurolinguistic Programming and Messaging

So far, we've focused on big-picture storytelling and emotional arcs. But equally important is the microlevel of communication: the specific words and phrases we use when speaking to donors. This is where concepts from neurolinguistic programming (NLP) and the psychology of language come into play. The idea behind NLP, originally developed by Richard Bandler and John Grinder (1975), is that language can be engineered to influence thoughts and behavior by appealing to how people represent information in their minds. While some NLP claims are debated, many of its techniques align with known neuroscience and psychology of communication. In fundraising, careful wording can make a significant difference in how a message is perceived by the brain. Phil M. Jones, in his bestselling book *Exactly What to Say* (2018), emphasizes that certain phrases, what he calls "magic words," can reliably engage conversations and reduce resistance in listeners. By understanding why those phrases work on a psychological and neural level, nonprofit professionals can craft messages that not only remove barriers to conversation but also internal barriers to activating the donor's generosity.

One key element is using language patterns that activate specific brain regions, particularly sensory and emotion areas, to make messages more vivid and compelling. For example, sensory-rich language (visual, auditory, tactile words) can stimulate the corresponding sensory cortex in the brain. If you say to a donor, "Imagine the bright smiles of children reading their first book thanks to you," you're using visual and emotional language. The word *imagine* is powerful. Jones (2018) calls it "the 'once upon a time' for adults," because it invites the person to mentally step into a story. When you engage someone's imagination, you're effectively recruiting their visual brain areas (occipital lobe) to paint a picture, and possibly their emotional brain to feel the joy of that scene. Neuroscientific studies have shown that even metaphors can activate sensory brain regions: hearing a phrase like "a sweet victory" can trigger the taste-related cortex and the amygdala more than a literal phrase like "a nice victory" (Citron & Goldberg, 2014). The taste metaphor "sweet" carries a physical connotation that lights up the brain's emotional centers (amygdala) and gustatory areas, giving it extra impact. The upshot: words that evoke senses and concrete imagery aren't just poetic; they literally engage more of the reader's neural hardware. By peppering your appeals with sensory details ("warm meals," "loud laughter," "soft blankets"), you make the donor feel more present in the scene, which heightens empathy and memory for your message.

Jones (2018) gives many examples of subtle phrasing that lowers resistance by framing requests appealingly. One of his famous openers is "I'm not sure if it's for you, but … ." Starting an ask with "I'm not sure if it's for you" paradoxically makes people more receptive; it signals you're not pressuring them, which calms any reflexive defense. The listener's brain hears permission to say no, which ironically makes it easier for them to consider saying yes, since they don't feel trapped. It's a bit of reverse psychology that aligns with what we know about autonomy: people need to feel they have a choice. By acknowledging "this might not be for you," you actually pique curiosity (what is it that might not be for me?) and respect their freedom. Another example: asking "How open-minded would you be about trying …?" instead of "Would you like to try …?" The phrase "how open-minded would you be" cleverly frames the act of considering as a sign of being open-minded, and who doesn't want to view themselves as open-minded? Psychologically, it appeals to the listener's positive self-image and turns a binary yes/no into a scale of open-mindedness (Jones, 2018). The brain's response is to lean toward proving that yes, I am open-minded, thus more likely to give the idea a chance.

NLP also talks about representational systems, basically, people's preferred modes of thinking (visual, auditory, kinesthetic, etc.), and using the right predicates (words) to match those can build rapport. One person might often say "I see what you mean" (a visual thinker), another says "I hear you" (auditory), another "I've grasped the idea" (kinesthetic/tactile). While you won't know each donor's style individually, good fundraising phrasing touches all bases: it uses a mix of seeing, hearing, feeling words so that something resonates with everyone. One sentence might be, "Can you see the impact of your gift? Imagine the faces lighting up as children hear the sound of new books opening, and feel the pride of finishing their first story." In one line, you've hit visual (see, imagine, faces lighting up), auditory (hear the sound), and kinesthetic/emotional (feel the pride). It prompts multiple parts of the brain to engage, as the reader envisions, hears internally, and senses emotion. It also increases the chance that the phrasing will click with the donor's own way of thinking, which creates that "hey, they really speak my language" effect. When a donor feels you just "get" them, trust builds. In neuroscience terms, feeling understood can release oxytocin, yes, that bonding hormone again, because we tend to trust those who we feel are similar to us or validate our perspective (Zak et al., 2007). Matching a donor's representational system in conversation (even in a one-on-one meeting, if you notice they use certain descriptive words, you subtly mirror them) is a known rapport technique in NLP (Bandler & Grinder, 1975). It's essentially training your own communication to meet the listener's brain where it is most comfortable.

Another linguistic tool is using embedded recommendations or suggestions within a sentence. This comes from both advertising research and NLP practice. The idea is to embed the call to action inside a larger statement in a way that the conscious mind might not resist, but the subconscious still picks up the directive. For instance, instead of a blunt "Donate now," you might say, "As you read Maria's story, you might feel inspired to take action now to help and we encourage that." The phrase "You might feel inspired to take action now" is phrased as a possibility, but it contains the embedded suggestion "Take action now." The donor's brain registers that language without the guard up, because it's couched in softer terms. Another

The Science of Storytelling and Emotional Engagement

example: "Many of our supporters decided to give after seeing the impact, it just felt right." This subtly implants the idea that giving is the natural, normal outcome (social proof and embedded command). These techniques must be used ethically and genuinely as the goal is to guide, not deceive. But from a neurogiving perspective, when done transparently ("We encourage that."), it's simply good coaching of the brain toward a decision they already want to make. Politicians and speechwriters do this frequently: they'll bury a slogan or imperative in a story or question. Fundraisers can do similarly by integrating the desired donor action into the narrative flow rather than isolating it as a stark ask. It feels more organic and therefore faces less mental pushback.

Framing and presuppositions also show up in how we ask for specific amounts or commitments. Saying "Would you consider becoming a monthly donor?" is a direct ask. But consider a presuppositional swap: "When you become a monthly donor, you'll join a special group of our most dedicated partners making a difference all year." This sentence assumes the positive action ("When you become … ."), and it immediately paints the reward, not just the impact, but the donor's identity as part of a special group of dedicated partners. In one small swap, it flatters (you could be one of the most dedicated) and frames monthly giving as an elevated status. The brain enjoys status and belonging; neuroscientists have found that social rewards activate similar pathways as monetary rewards (Izuma et al., 2008). So language that confers a little status or belonging can be very motivating.

Last, rapport-building language patterns influence the neuro-chemistry of trust. People are more likely to be persuaded by those they trust and feel connected to. Certain words can foster a sense of closeness. Using the donor's name in communication (in moderation) lights up their brain; we are highly attuned to our own name from an early age (a part of the brain called the medial prefrontal cortex activates when we hear our name, associated with self-related processing). Including words like *together* and *partner* also neurologically incline the listener toward unity. One study found that the word *together* when used in a request increased compliance, likely because it signaled social connection (Jiang et al., 2019). For example, "Together, we can change this" frames the action as a partnership, which triggers that oxytocin-fueled trust and cooperative spirit. It's essentially inviting the donor's brain to shift from viewing you as an external solicitor to viewing you as an ally on the same team. When someone's brain considers you part of their in-group, they react with more generosity and empathy (Brewer, 1979). Simple inclusive language, such as using *we* instead of *you and us*, can make a surprising difference. "We can end hunger in our community" versus "With your help, our organization can end hunger." Both convey collaboration, but the first literally puts donor and organization into one collective we. The donor can mentally place themselves under that umbrella, whereas the second, while appreciative, still separates the parties. Over time, consistently using inclusive language helps cement an identity alignment: supporters start to think of the nonprofit's achievements as their own achievements. And as that identity bond strengthens, so does commitment. People are driven to act in consistency with their identity.

Another aspect of language and trust is tonality and authenticity. The brain is very good at detecting inconsistencies and insincerity, even if not always consciously. Certain messaging patterns can inadvertently create cognitive dissonance. For example, overly formal jargon in what is supposed to be an emotional appeal might make the brain hesitate ("This sounds corporate, not compassionate."). Striking an authentic tone, often conversational and warm, tends to fare better. This aligns with neurochemistry because authenticity cues (like a narrative told in a first-person, vulnerable way) can increase oxytocin release, as we empathize more with a voice that feels human and real

71

(Zak, 2015). Phil M. Jones often stresses the importance of not just what you say but how, for example, delivering a line with empathy and certainty in person, or in writing using punctuation and emphasis to convey a genuine voice. While written appeals don't have tone of voice in an audible way, you can approximate it with choice of words (e.g., "you know," ellipses for pauses, exclamation for excitement). These may seem like small flourishes, but they influence how the reader "hears" your message in their head.

Incorporate some of Jones's practical phrases that have a neuroscientific lens into your fundraising conversations:

- **"Just imagine ..."** As mentioned, this phrase invites visualization. It acts as a direct command to the visual cortex and experiential memory: the donor's mind begins to simulate the scenario, which increases emotional engagement. It's a great setup for painting a sensory scene that the brain can latch onto.

- **"How would you feel if ...?"** This question prompts the listener to project themselves into a scenario emotionally. It's actually an empathy exercise in one sentence. For example, "How would you feel if you couldn't afford the medicine to save your child?" That forces a moment of personal emotional generation—the donor's brain will likely conjure anxiety or sadness as they consider it. This builds empathic concern in a very personal way, which can motivate action.

- **"When would be a good time for...?"** This subtle shift from "Would you do *x*?" to scheduling *when* assumes the person is willing; only timing is in question. It's a classic example of a linguistic presupposition that greases the wheels of decision. The brain, hearing that, skips over *whether* to do it and starts considering *when*, which is a commitment in itself. For instance, a fundraiser asking, "When would be a good time for you to visit our program site?" presupposes the person is open to visiting; they just need to pick a time. Many will go along with that flow, provided they are moderately interested, because it feels natural to answer the question posed.

All of these messaging techniques should be used ethically and with respect for the donor's autonomy. The goal is to communicate in ways that are brain-friendly—that reduce friction and increase clarity and resonance—rather than to coerce. Consistent with neurogiving, our perspective is that the donor is already generous so our goal is to make it as easy as possible to do the thing they most want to do.

Phil M. Jones's "magic words" are essentially about meeting people where they are psychologically. When done right, both fundraiser and donor feel good about the exchange: the donor feels understood, not pressured, and the fundraiser sees better engagement and response. This means crafting language that aligns with how the brain naturally processes words, emotions, and social cues to activate donors' brains more fully. By framing asks in ways that emphasize gains, normalcy, and inclusion, we reduce mental barriers. By matching communication styles and using inclusive, inviting language, we build trust and rapport, encouraging that oxytocin-mediated bond between supporter and organization. It's the fine art of saying things in exactly the right way, not as a manipulation, but as a bridge from the donor's mind to the cause. When combined with the larger storytelling strategies, it creates a powerful synergy: great stories draw people in and open their hearts, and great messaging seals the connection and guides their mind toward compassionate action.

Chapter 4

Identity, Trust, and Long-Term Giving

Building lasting donor relationships goes beyond the initial rush of a successful campaign ask. Currently, donor retention rates across the nonprofit sector hover at distressingly low levels, often about 40% year-over-year, which means organizations are losing the majority of first-time supporters (Sargeant & Woodliffe, 2007). While previous chapters showed how emotional appeals and the brain's reward system might add kindling to the spark of generosity into an initial gift, sustainable philanthropy is rooted in something deeper. Long-term giving relies on a donor's sense of self, their trust in the organization, and the habits that make generosity a regular part of life. In essence, emotion might fan the fire of generosity, but identity, trust, and habit keep it burning for the long haul. In this chapter, we explore how a donor's identity grows around giving, the neuroscience of trust between donor and nonprofit, and how loyalty becomes ingrained through habit formation.

Donor Identity Formation

Why do some donors stick around year after year, turning one-time gifts into a lifelong commitment? A big part of the answer lies in donor identity. Donor identity formation is the process by which a person internalizes the role of "supporter" as part of who they are. In other words, being a donor becomes not just something they do, but something they are. This section explores how giving shapes a donor's self-concept and how nonprofits can nurture an identity that keeps supporters engaged for the long term.

Self-Perception: Giving and Self-Concept

Social psychology offers a powerful insight into how actions shape identity. According to self-perception theory, people infer their attitudes and traits by observing their own behavior (Bem, 1972). In a fundraising context, this means that when someone gives to charity, they start to view themselves as the kind of person who would give. If a donor donates regularly—even small amounts—they gather evidence from their own behavior that "I am a generous person." Each act of giving isn't just a transaction, it's also a piece of self-definition. Over time, a virtuous cycle can emerge: a person gives because they see themselves as generous, and seeing themselves as generous encourages them to keep giving. In essence, the brain takes note of charitable actions and uses them to update the self-concept. Aligning messages with donor identity not only increases donations, it also improves donor satisfaction, as demonstrated by Shang et al. (2008). It's the same principle behind the classic "foot-in-the-door" technique: agreeing to a small request changes one's self-view, making it more likely they'll agree to a larger request later (Freedman & Fraser, 1966). This is why a welcome series for new donors might invite a trivial action like responding to a survey or giving feedback. That additional yes further roots their identity as an engaged supporter.

Consistency, Dissonance, and Identity Maintenance

Once someone embraces a "donor" identity, they naturally want to act consistently with it. Humans have a strong drive for consistency between their self-image and their actions. If a person thinks of themselves as an advocate or helper, failing to support a cause they care about can create internal conflict or dissonance.

For example, a donor who proudly identifies as an environmental advocate will feel a pang of inconsistency if they consider not renewing a gift to an environmental charity. Our brains dislike this kind of self-mismatch. It literally feels uncomfortable. In fact, psychological research shows people are motivated to take actions that affirm important identities (Oyserman, 2009). Continuing to give provides relief from the discomfort of inconsistency and reinforces the valued identity. In neural terms, aligning behavior with self-concept likely engages brain regions that resolve conflict and restore a sense of harmony. By appealing to a donor's cherished identity (e.g., "You have always been someone who stands up for others."), fundraisers can encourage giving as a means for donors to be true to themselves.

Identity Salience in Giving Decisions

Which aspect of a person's identity is most salient (top of mind) at the moment of a donation request can heavily influence their decision. People have multiple identities (parent, professional, volunteer, etc.), and fundraising messages that tap into a relevant identity can make giving feel more personally meaningful. For instance, an appeal that begins "As a teacher, you understand how important education is ... ." immediately triggers the recipient's teacher identity, making the cause resonate on a personal level. When donors see an opportunity to act in line with a salient part of who they are, they are more likely to give. By framing a donation as an expression of values or roles the donor cherishes, nonprofits can boost the likelihood of a positive response. Field experiments by Kessler and Milkman (2016) further demonstrate that priming donor identity such as reminding people of their past giving or invoking a shared community role can significantly increase donation rates, especially among habitual givers. In practice, even simple segmentation and personalization can achieve this. Tailoring messages to align with donor interests or past

77

actions, even general action such as loyalty or generosity, signals to the donor's brain that "this is about me" and invites them to reinforce that self-image through giving.

Social Identity and Group Affiliation

Individual identity is powerful, but so is social identity, the sense of belonging to a larger group. Social identity theory tells us that people derive pride and self-worth from their group memberships (Tajfel & Turner, 1979).

Donating can become not just a personal act but a group identity: "I am part of the community of supporters for this cause." Many successful nonprofits cultivate this by giving their donor base a name or creating a sense of fellowship among supporters. Think of charities that call their repeat donors "partners," "champions," or "family." When donors feel like valued members of a cause, giving is reinforced by a sense of solidarity. There is motivation to uphold the norms and values of the group including the norm of generosity. Public recognition like donor walls or listing supporters in an annual report can amplify this effect, because it visibly links the donor to a community of like-minded givers. Social proof further strengthens group-based motivations: knowing that others "like me" are donating encourages individuals to do the same (Cialdini, 2009). No one wants to be the one member of the "team" who isn't pulling their weight. By fostering an environment where donors see themselves (and others) as part of an impactful collective, nonprofits tap into group identity to drive loyalty and ongoing support. Global donor research reinforces this, showing that charity preferences are often shaped by identity motives: people tend to support organizations that reflect their personal or social identity, such as shared values, causes, or communities (Chapman et al., 2020). My proprietary research reinforces this principle in practice—showing that identity formation and trust are not built by branding alone, but by consistent alignment between messaging and the donor's internal narrative. Across multiple nonprofit subsectors, we've seen that when messaging affirms a donor's worldview, when it "sounds like them" and reflects what they care about, they're more likely to form a durable connection with the organization.

In a study for an arts and cultural nonprofit, we discovered that some donors strongly identified as legacy builders: they wanted to be seen as stewards of the arts and protectors of cultural heritage. For them, trust was reinforced by messages about long-term preservation and intergenerational impact. Meanwhile, another segment was animated by local accessibility and inclusion—seeing themselves not as patrons, but as community advocates ensuring that public resources served all. Messaging that highlighted values and community service created stronger engagement for this group.

Despite supporting the same mission, these donors interpreted the organization's role, and their own, in vastly different ways. What made the difference was not just content, but identity alignment: messaging that reflected the kind of person they believed themselves to be.

This insight holds across issue areas. In another study with an organization addressing maternal and infant health, one donor segment responded to narrative frames focused on agency and dignity, seeing themselves as allies in a movement for equity. Another was more drawn to messaging about measurable impact and saving lives. Over time, each group's trust deepened when follow-up communication reinforced their core motivation, not just the organization's overarching brand.

The broader lesson is this: donors don't just want to believe in the organization, they want to see their values reflected back to them consistently. When that happens, giving becomes part of their identity. And identity is sticky. It motivates future action even when no one is asking, because the donor has internalized the role: "I'm the kind of person who supports this."

Merging Personal and Cause Identities

In truly committed donors, the line between personal identity and cause identity begins to blur. Supporting the cause becomes not just an action they take, but an integral part of who they are. One clear example is seen in membership-based nonprofits. When someone donates and is welcomed as a "member" of an organization, such as a museum, public radio station, or advocacy group, they often start to say things like, "I'm a card-carrying member of XYZ." That phrasing signals pride and identity. However, this identity only flourishes if the organization treats membership as a meaningful affiliation rather than a mere transaction. When framed as a badge of honor ("I belong to this."), membership can dramatically boost loyalty and lifetime giving. Many organizations see this in practice: for instance, a nonprofit that launched with a focus on monthly "membership" donations and community identity reported retention rates above 90%, far higher than typical one-time donor retention.

Donors who strongly identify with a cause often internalize its values. They see the nonprofit's success as a reflection of their own effectiveness or morality. This is why encouraging donors to tell their own story of why they give can be so powerful—as they articulate their motivation, they reinforce the idea that supporting the cause is part of their story and character. In turn, these donors behave almost like ambassadors or owners of the cause. They continue giving not because they are asked, but because it feels like fulfilling a personal mission. At this stage, staying involved is practically a foregone conclusion; it would feel strange not to give. The fundraiser's role shifts from persuading to simply acknowledging and thanking; the donor's identity does the rest. When personal identity and cause identity merge in this way, long-term support becomes second nature. As we previously discussed, self-determination theory suggests that people are more likely to continue behaviors they find inherently rewarding. In fundraising, this means that people are more likely to continue being generous if they feel their giving reflects who they are and that their support genuinely matters.

The Neuroscience of Trust

A donor might give once out of empathy or impulse, but they will only continue to give if they trust the organization to be effective and honest. Trust in philanthropy means a donor believes in the non-profit's integrity and competence—essentially, that the charity will do what it promises with the donor's money. This kind of trust isn't just a vague feeling; it has specific neural correlates and chemical under-pinnings in the brain. In this section, we examine what happens in a donor's brain during trust-based exchanges, how the "trust hormone" oxytocin comes into play, how transparency and authenticity affect the brain's trust calculus, and why consistency over time builds a neurological foundation for loyalty.

Trust in the Brain: Key Regions and Neurochemicals

Trust may seem intangible, but it manifests in the brain in very measurable ways. When we engage in a trust-based exchange—for example, giving a friend money to hold or donating to a charity—certain brain regions light up. Neuroscience studies have shown that decisions to trust activate parts of the prefrontal cortex involved in evaluating social situations and potential rewards, as well as the brain's reward circuitry itself. In trust experiments (like the classic "trust game" where one person entrusts money to another), people who decide to trust often exhibit increased activity in the striatum, a region that processes reward, and reduced activation in fear centers like the amygdala (indicating lowered guardedness). In essence, when trust is established and rewarded, the brain receives positive feedback similar to the pleasure of successful cooperation.

Conversely, breaches of trust can trigger the brain's threat response. Studies have found that when individuals detect untrustworthiness or insincerity, it engages regions that signal caution: for instance, the prefrontal cortex may kick into high gear as the brain scrutinizes the situation (Falk et al., 2010). The takeaway is that trust has a biological signature: it engages the neural pathways of reward and bonding when things go well, and the neural alarms of risk when doubt is raised. Understanding this duality helps explain why building trust is so critical: it encourages donors' brains to associate your organization with positive, rewarding outcomes, rather than wariness.

Transparency and the Brain's Trust Calculus

Trust is built on predictability and evidence. The human brain is constantly assessing: "Is this a good bet?" When a donor gives money to a nonprofit, there is initially some uncertainty, a leap of faith that the organization will deliver results.

This is because the donor's innate generous inclination is mediated by a third party separating them from the outcome of their giving. In most versions of generosity, a donor gives directly to the person and sees that their gift was used for the intended purpose. The existence of a nonprofit organization interrupts that process. It should be no surprise then that we see individual donors move toward other forms of generosity and groups of people engaging in mutual aid where generosity isn't mediated. Generous impulses find a way. That's neurogiving.

If the nonprofit remains a black box (no news after the donation), the donor's brain doesn't get the feedback it requires. That uncertainty can keep the brain's guard up, engaging areas that detect risk or ambiguity.

However, transparency provides the brain with rewarding closure. When donors see exactly how their money was used and what impact it had, it "completes the story" in their mind. For donors, this is satisfying; it resolves the uncertainty and reinforces the neural pathways of trust. Behavioral research backs this up. Donors are far more likely to give again when they believe their gift made a difference and can see the results (Sargeant & Lee, 2004). For instance, some organizations now send donors concrete evidence of impact like photos or GPS coordinates of a project funded by their gift, satisfying the brain's craving for feedback and proof. From a brain perspective, showing outcomes and being open about finances likely activate circuits of reward and relief.

Moreover, transparency builds credibility, which over time conditions the brain to expect positive outcomes from interactions with the nonprofit. That expectation is essentially what trust is—the confident prediction of a good result. In practice, this means nonprofits should report back to donors, share successes and challenges, and be forthright about how contributions are used. Supporting this, a field experiment by Gneezy et al. (2014) found that donor participation significantly increased when donors were told that overhead costs were already covered by another funder, an "overhead-free" framing. This transparency reassured donors that their entire gift would go directly to the cause, boosting both trust and total giving. This is not to suggest that organizations should lean into the overhead myth but rather that the evidence suggest that these frames boost giving.

Authenticity: The Neurology of Sincerity

Donors don't just invest their money, they invest their trust. And the brain is finely tuned to figure out if that trust is warranted. Modern neuroscience suggests that people can subconsciously sense when a message is authentic or not. When a fundraising appeal comes across as exaggerated or "too slick," the brain's vigilance centers perk up, looking for deception. In such cases, instead of eliciting empathy, the appeal might prompt skepticism.

By contrast, authentic communications engage the brain's social empathy network, inviting trust. Real, honest stories that acknowledge both successes and challenges tend to produce a more positive neurological response. In one neuroeconomics study, charity narratives that were perceived as truthful and heartfelt triggered higher oxytocin release (and in turn, greater generosity) than stories that seemed scripted or inauthentic (Zak et al., 2011). On a practical level, this means being truthful is not only ethical but also effective. Admitting uncertainties or limitations, for example, saying, "We can't help everyone, but here's how we are trying," can actually boost credibility. The donor's brain hears honesty and, counterintuitively, trusts you more for it. Authenticity builds a kind of neural handshake: when the nonprofit shows its human side, the donor's brain responds with empathy and trust rather than skepticism.

Consistency Builds Trust in the Brain

Trust isn't built in a day, it's built through consistent experiences over time. Each time a donor has a positive experience that aligns with their expectations, the neural pathways associated with trust get a little bit stronger. The larger the commitment or gift, the larger the trust must be. In order to quickly close a large gift means that traditional forms of trust have to be bypassed by some alternative trust collateral mechanism, typically a personal one. The donor can not trust the organization yet so they rely on trust of the person. But here now we have created a Catch-22: if we establish trust we do so in the person and not in the organization so if the person leaves, that trust departs with them even if the organization has been trustworthy. Building trust in the organization is a critical task that takes time and cannot be taken lightly.

Our brains are pattern recognition machines. If a nonprofit consistently follows through on promises such as delivering aid as advertised, communicating regularly, using donations wisely, the donor's brain gradually shifts into a state of relaxed confidence. Over repeated interactions, the act of trusting becomes less of a conscious decision and more of an automatic response, because the brain has learned "this organization comes through." On the neural level, you can imagine that the "trust circuit" is being myelinated and reinforced with each reliable experience (Fields, 2008). In other words, the brain's trust pathways are strengthening, just like a muscle being exercised. There's even a feedback loop at work: when donors feel heard and appreciated consistently, their brains release rewarding chemicals that make them feel good about the relationship. Those positive feelings then increase the likelihood of trusting and giving again.

By contrast, inconsistency, such as a promised update that never comes or an unfulfilled commitment, is like interrupting a signal. The next time, the donor's brain will be more hesitant, having learned that the pattern was broken. This is why maintaining a steady, positive drumbeat in donor communications and experiences is so crucial. In time, a well-kept promise turns into a baseline expectation of trust. The donor comes to expect integrity and results from your organization, which makes continued giving a natural, low-friction decision supported by their neural "wiring" of loyalty.

Loyalty and Habit Formation

Unlike consumers, in philanthropy, loyalty runs deeper than a rewards card or brand preference; it's also rooted in identity, internalized habits, and emotional commitment. In fact, one of the secrets to donor retention is turning giving into a habit, a regular, valued part of a person's life. When donors give reliably such as every month or every holiday season, it's often because it has become routine. The decision requires less deliberation each time, and in some cases no decision at all (for example, if they've set up an automatic monthly donation). This section delves into how the brain forms and maintains such habits of generosity. We'll explore the neural circuitry of habit formation, how repetition strengthens the "giving pathway" in the brain, the classic cue-routine-reward loop in donor behavior, and how dopamine rewards help lock in patterns of giving. We'll also consider how these habits can break if donors lapse, and what the science says about encouraging lapsed donors to reengage. In short, we're looking at how to go from a one-time spark of giving to a long-term pattern of support that's almost second nature.

Habit Formation in the Brain: Basal Ganglia and Striatum

Why do certain behaviors become automatic? The answer lies largely in a part of the brain called the basal ganglia. The basal ganglia, deep-brain nuclei that include the striatum, serve as the brain's habit center, responsible for converting repeated actions into routine patterns. When we first learn a new behavior, say, a donor makes their very first gift, the decision involves a lot of conscious thought and activity in the higher brain (the cortex). But if that behavior is repeated again and again, the brain starts to "offload" the control to the basal ganglia. Neuroscientists have observed that with enough repetition, a sequence of actions becomes "chunked" into a unit that the basal ganglia can execute almost on autopilot (Graybiel, 1998; Smith & Graybiel, 2016). For example, tying your shoes or driving a familiar route home are actions you likely perform without much conscious awareness, thanks to this chunking.

In the context of giving, if donating to a particular cause becomes part of someone's regular routine, something they do automatically under certain conditions, then retention becomes much easier. The donor doesn't debate each time whether to give; it becomes a default behavior. They have decided that this is how they act on their inherent generosity. Brain scans of habit formation show a distinctive pattern: during early learning, many brain regions are active, but once a habit is formed, neural activity spikes at the beginning and end of the routine, and is quieter in the middle (Graybiel, 2008). This suggests the brain essentially "launches" the habitual sequence at the cue and then lets it run with less conscious control until a conclusion. For fundraisers, our goal is to help them with their generosity commitment and this underscores the value of establishing consistent giving patterns. If you can help a donor "train" their brain to include your cause in their regular life rhythm, the act of giving shifts from a fresh choice each time to a more automatic, ingrained behavior.

Strengthening the Pathways: How Repetition Solidifies Habits

Repetition doesn't just make an action feel easier, it actually changes the brain's wiring. Every time a donor repeats the act of giving, the neural circuit supporting that action becomes a bit more entrenched. Biologically, one way this happens is through myelination. Myelin is a fatty coating that wraps around neural pathways like insulation on a wire, allowing electrical impulses to travel faster. When a behavior is performed over and over, the neurons involved can develop thicker myelin sheaths, essentially upgrading the brain's hardware to make that circuit speedier and more efficient (Fields, 2008). So a habit of giving isn't just a psychological pattern, it's reflected in a stronger, faster signal in the brain. The result? The donor can follow through with their giving habit with less mental effort or resistance.

In parallel, the connections (synapses) between the involved brain cells also strengthen due to repeated use, a phenomenon often summarized as "neurons that fire together, wire together." This is why a habit can be easier to maintain than a series of separate decisions; continuing feels more natural than constantly re-deciding (Wood & Neal, 2007). This means that not only does the physical transmission get smoother but also the likelihood of the whole circuit activating in the future increases. For a donor, this might translate into that feeling of "it just feels right to give—it's part of my responsibility." Their brain has, quite literally, been trained to make generosity a well-trodden neural path.

The Habit Loop: Cue, Routine, Reward

Habits are often described as a loop consisting of three parts: a cue, a routine, and a reward (Duhigg, 2012). This model applies surprisingly well to donor behavior. Consider a simple scenario: a donor receives a reminder email at the end of the month—that's the cue. The donor then goes online and makes their recurring donation— that's the routine. After donating, they feel satisfaction and perhaps see an immediate thank-you message—the reward.

If this loop repeats regularly, the cue will increasingly trigger the urge to perform the routine because the brain has come to anticipate the reward. Neuroscientifically, the brain's reward neurotransmitter, dopamine, starts firing not just when the reward is received, but at the sight of the cue, driving the routine forward (Everitt & Robbins, 2005). In our example, that means over time the donor's brain might get a little hit of good feeling or anticipation as soon as they see that month-end reminder, prompting them to go ahead and donate.

We can harness this loop deliberately: by providing consistent cues (like predictable campaign timelines or reminder nudges) and delivering reliable rewards (the emotional payoff of doing good, reinforced by gratitude or impact updates), we essentially make the donor's habit loop predictable. Eventually, skipping a cycle might even feel odd to the donor just like forgetting one's morning coffee. Their routine of giving becomes ingrained, supported by the brain's own reward expectations. The neuroscience of habit reveals that repeated behaviors are most likely to stick when they're tied to consistent emotional rewards and reinforce a person's identity. This is especially true in giving.

While traditional donor journeys treat giving as a linear funnel—awareness, interest, action, done—the reality is far more cyclical. People don't just give because they're persuaded; they give again because it feels right and affirms who they believe they are.

Figure 4.1 contrasts the conventional donor funnel with the Neurogiving Loyalty Loop™, showing how repeated cues, emotionally rewarding giving experiences, and identity reinforcement build long-term generosity habits.

The Goal-Gradient Effect: Motivation Accelerates Near Milestones

Another tool for deepening engagement is the goal-gradient effect: the behavioral tendency to increase effort and motivation as we get closer to a visible finish line. In fundraising, this means donors are more likely to contribute as a campaign nears its goal.

Psychological studies show that people feel more motivated when they believe their contribution will make a tangible difference—especially when success feels within reach. A donation that gets a campaign from 90% to 100% feels more satisfying than one that only moves the needle from 10% to 11%.

Visual cues like progress bars, countdowns, and campaign milestones trigger this motivation neurologically by creating a sense of urgency and momentum. Donors begin to see themselves as part of a

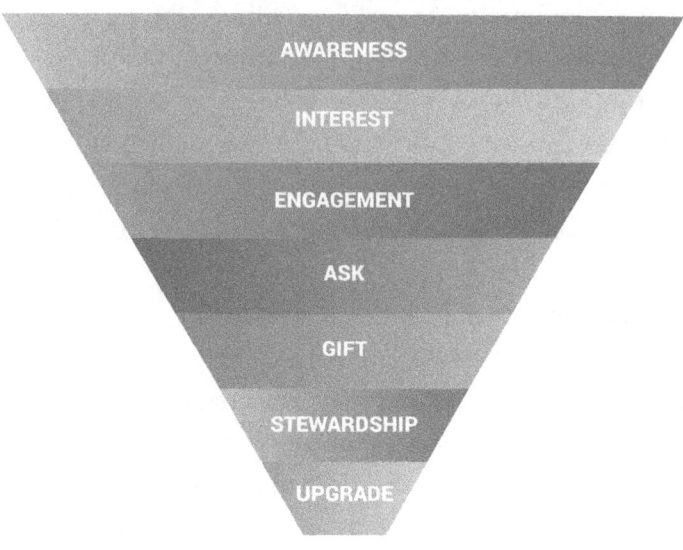

Traditional Donor Funnel

AWARENESS

INTEREST

ENGAGEMENT

ASK

GIFT

STEWARDSHIP

UPGRADE

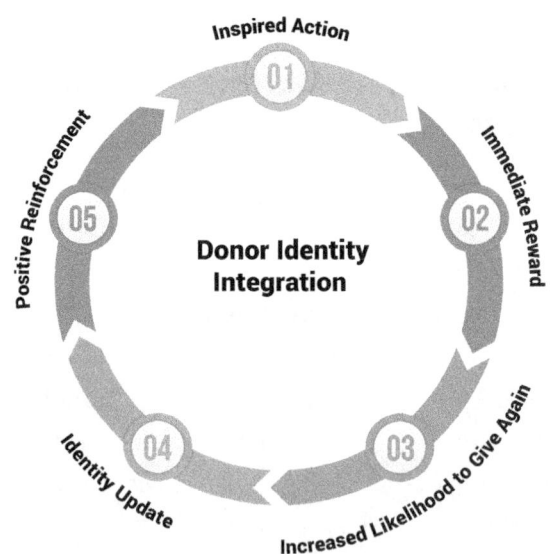

Neurogiving Loyalty Loop™

Inspired Action

01

Immediate Reward

02

Increased Likelihood to Give Again

03

Identity Update

04

Positive Reinforcement

05

Donor Identity Integration

Figure 4.1. Donor Funnel Versus Neurogiving Loyalty Loop™

winning team—and that identity reinforces their commitment. To activate this effect, break large goals into smaller milestones and celebrate progress publicly. You're not just driving donations, you're creating rewarding micro-experiences that build emotional investment over time. Sustaining these emotional wins helps donors associate giving with progress, purpose, and pride, all of which reinforce their long-term loyalty.

Breaking and Rebuilding Donor Habits

Even well-established habits can be broken, and, unfortunately, donor habits are no exception. Life changes, shifts in financial situation, or a lapse in communication from the nonprofit can all disrupt a previously steady giving routine. Neuroscience tells us that the basal ganglia's habit circuit doesn't handle change well. If the cue-routine-reward loop is interrupted when the usual trigger is absent or the reward suddenly diminishes, the brain notices the deviation.

From a neurogiving perspective, it is important for fundraisers to distinguish between habits that are broken because of the donor (life changes, financial situation, etc.) and those that are broken because of the fundraiser (missing impact reports, appeals, friction in giving, etc.). Imagine a donor who always gave during a particular holiday campaign, but the campaign was cancelled one year; without the cue (the event or appeal) the routine might falter. Or consider a monthly donor who suddenly has a bad experience (perhaps one month their credit card was expired, or they felt unacknowledged)—a jolt like that can "break the spell" of the habit, causing the donor to stop and reevaluate ("Maybe I won't continue this … ."). Once a giving habit is broken, the donor's brain returns to a more deliberative state regarding that behavior. The automatic drive is weaker, so renewing the commitment will likely require conscious motivation again.

However, habits leave traces. A lapsed donor often still has the neural wiring of that habit lying in wait, which can be rekindled.

The key to reforming a giving habit is to reintroduce a stable cue and a compelling reward, while addressing whatever broke the cycle in the first place. For example, reaching out to lapsed donors with a personal message ("We missed you and wanted to share the impact you made last time.") might serve as a new cue that sparks the memory of their past positive experience. Pair that with a meaningful reward, perhaps an update that shows exactly what their previous contributions achieved, reigniting the feeling, and you begin rebuilding the loop. It may also help to lower the barrier to reentry: inviting the donor to take a small action (not necessarily a big donation right away) can ease them back into the routine. Success in reforming the habit might come gradually—the donor's trust and identity alignment need to be restored alongside the habit itself. But with patience and consistent positive interactions, even lapsed donors can often return to a regular cadence of giving. Ferguson et al. (2023) found that "cool cooperators"—donors who initially lacked strong emotional engagement—could be reactivated through messaging that affirmed their values and highlighted warm-glow benefits. This suggests that strategic reinforcement of identity and emotional payoff can reignite giving behavior, even among those who previously lapsed.

Identity, trust, and habit don't operate in isolation; they reinforce each other to create lasting donor loyalty. Identity gives the why, trust gives the confidence, and habit gives the rhythm. Together, they create the foundation for donor loyalty. When we align our practices with how people think and behave—not just what they say—we turn giving from a moment into a movement.

Finally, it's worth underscoring that applying these insights should always be done ethically and respectfully. The aim is to genuinely nurture the donor's passion and commitment, not to manipulate. When done right, everyone benefits: the donor finds meaning and joy, and the organization gains enduring support.

Chapter 5

Time Versus Money: The Neuroscience of Different Forms of Giving

When people think about giving, it's often in terms of donating money. But gifts of time, like volunteering in person or virtually, are just as important, and they are experienced differently by generous people. Writing a check, swiping a card, or clicking a button can be meaningful, yet spending an afternoon working for that organization engages us in another way entirely. In fact, for millennia and across the world, generosity doesn't look like the exchange of dollars to a 501c(3) nonprofit organization.

Many donors intuitively sense this distinction: both are generous acts, but they resonate differently in our minds and hearts. Modern neuroscience confirms this intuition has a basis in biology. Donating time and donating money are not neurologically or psychologically identical experiences. In this chapter, we explore these differences. We will look at what brain imaging reveals about each, how volunteering uniquely affects brain chemistry, and how cultural context can shape our altruistic neural responses. Understanding these nuances can help nonprofit professionals appreciate and leverage both forms of giving in complementary ways, engaging supporters in the manner most meaningful to them.

Neural and Behavioral Differences Between Giving Time and Giving Money

Brain imaging insights—volunteering versus financial donations. Cutting-edge brain imaging studies show that while both giving time and giving money activate reward systems, they light up different regions. Time donations more strongly engage areas tied to social connection and emotional processing, such as the ventral striatum and temporal poles. Monetary giving, by contrast, activates the precuneus and areas associated with reflection and cost-benefit thinking (Kwon et al., 2023). This suggests volunteering is processed more like a social experience; financial giving, more like a meaningful transaction.

These neural findings align with how many people describe the two forms of generosity. Volunteering often feels immediately gratifying on an emotional level—a hands-on, experiential kind of reward—whereas donating money, while still rewarding, can feel one step removed or more formal. Importantly, this is not to say that giving money is entirely "cold" or devoid of pleasure. In fact, as we saw in previous chapters, even purely monetary giving can light up the brain's pleasure centers. The act of giving, in any form, engages our brain's reward system. That said, the balance of neural activity differs between time and money. Volunteering appears to tilt more toward social-emotional processing, while monetary giving involves more analytical or value-calculation processing alongside the reward response. It's fascinating that even just asking someone about donating their time, before any mention of money, can increase their likelihood of giving. In a series of experiments, Liu and Aaker (2008) found that prompting people to think about time first activated emotional and identity-related reasoning, which led to significantly higher donations. The emotional lens of time fosters a more generous mindset. In short, giving time tends to be experienced (and encoded in the brain) more like a social interaction or an act of connection, whereas giving money can feel somewhat more like an economic transaction, albeit a generous and rewarding one.

The "experience" of giving time versus money. Why might volunteering ignite stronger reward activity? Think about what volunteering usually entails: immediate, tangible feedback. If you spend a Saturday cleaning up a neighborhood park, by the end of the day you see the park looking trash-free and beautiful. If you tutor a child or serve a meal at a shelter, you directly witness the impact, perhaps a student's newfound confidence or a recipient's gratitude. This real-time feedback likely engages the brain's reward pathways powerfully. It's inherently satisfying to see the effects of your good deed as a kind of instant payoff. Volunteering also often involves face-to-face social interaction, working side by side with others or directly helping someone in need. In essence, volunteering naturally packages together many ingredients that make the brain feel good: human connection, visible impact, physical activity, and a sense of accomplishment. By contrast, when you donate money, the reward can be more delayed or abstract. You might get a thank-you email a week later, or just the internal knowledge that you contributed, which is gratifying, but perhaps less visceral in the moment. Studies in psychology have indeed found that spending money on others increases personal happiness (Dunn et al., 2008), especially when people can vividly see or understand the outcome of their gift. In one experiment, people who spent money to buy a gift for a needy child or donate to charity reported greater joy than those who spent the same amount on themselves (Dunn et al., 2008). Furthermore, making the impact of a donation more tangible can amplify that joy. For example, researchers have noted

95

that when people's donations are connected to a specific beneficiary or project, essentially giving the donor a "story" or image of what their money accomplished, the donors experience a stronger emotional payoff (Aknin et al., 2013). Volunteering inherently provides that tangibility and personal connection. It's "experience-based" giving. This helps explain why many volunteers talk about the activity not as a sacrifice but as something they get as much out of as they give. From the brain's perspective, the experiential nature of volunteering is rewarding in its own right.

Different motivations and mindsets. Alongside these neural differences, there are noteworthy behavioral and motivational distinctions between time-givers and money-givers. Donating money is often motivated by considerations like efficiency, scale of impact, or convenience. Someone might choose to write a check because it's the most practical way they can help, especially if they lack free time or specific skills to offer. Financial donations can achieve things the individual alone cannot (e.g., funding a large project or reaching many people), so donors might feel their money goes further than their personal time could. Moreover, giving money requires relatively little time commitment, which appeals to busy individuals; it enables people with tight schedules to still contribute to causes they care about. In surveys, donors sometimes say they donate funds because they don't have time to volunteer but still want to make a difference. By contrast, donating time is frequently driven by a desire for direct involvement and personal fulfillment. Volunteers often cite reasons like "I wanted to meet the people I'm helping," "I learned so much from the experience," or "It makes me feel more connected and useful." These reasons highlight that volunteering provides experiential and social benefits that writing a check cannot. Research confirms these self-reports: for instance, young adults who continue volunteering tend to do so because of social relationships formed and personal growth experienced through service (Kim & Morgül, 2017).

Volunteering can satisfy deeper psychological needs, the need to belong to a community, to see one's values in action, or to develop skills and purpose. On the flip side, some people prefer giving money specifically because it is less demanding; they might feel they can contribute more effectively through their financial resources than through limited time, or they may simply be uncomfortable or untrained in direct service roles. These differing motivations mean that the very frame of mind people are in when giving time versus money can diverge.

Interestingly, experiments in consumer psychology have shown that prompting people to think about time versus money can shift their attitudes and generosity. In one study, participants first asked about their time ("How many hours do you spend on x?") became more likely to volunteer or donate afterward, whereas those first asked about money became less likely to volunteer (Mogilner, 2010). The theory is that thinking about time puts us in a socially oriented, emotional mindset, focusing on how we connect and what experiences we value, whereas thinking about money triggers a more self-oriented, economic mindset (Mogilner, 2010). Thus, simply the way a charitable appeal is framed ("Give some time to join us in the field." versus "Your $10 can make a difference.") might influence whether people respond with volunteering or with a financial gift. Time framing tends to activate compassion and personal engagement, whereas money framing highlights the utilitarian aspect of giving. This suggests that nonprofits should be mindful of how they invoke these concepts when recruiting support.

Strategic implications—leveraging both forms of giving. Because time and money contributions appeal in different ways, successful organizations often cultivate them somewhat differently. For volunteer recruitment, emphasizing the personal impact and rewarding experience can be very effective, for example, inviting supporters to "come see the difference you can make in one afternoon" or highlighting testimonials like "I got more out of volunteering than I ever expected." Messaging can tap into the social and emotional pay-offs (community, learning, fulfillment) that resonate with the volunteering brain. However, appeals for monetary donations might focus on the scale of impact or the efficiency of converting dollars into outcomes—for instance, "With just $50, we can provide a meal to a family." This speaks to donors who are motivated by making the biggest difference through financial means. That said, there is also a combination of volunteering and donating that nonprofits can use. Often, these two forms of giving reinforce each other rather than remaining separate silos. A person who starts out volunteering for a cause may develop such a strong connection to the mission that they become a financial donor as well. Conversely, someone who donates money and then sees the impact might become curious to get hands on and decide to volunteer. In fact, many individuals do both; they give some time and some money, and they might derive slightly different satisfactions from each. A volunteer who also donates financially could feel doubly invested (emotionally and materially), while a donor who tries volunteering might "get hooked" by the immediate feeling it provides.

Research on donor behavior reflects this crossover: involvement in one mode of giving often predicts increased involvement in the other. Research by Fidelity Charitable (2014) and others finds that people who volunteer tend to donate more to charity than non-volunteers, in part because their engagement and empathy for the cause increase through direct experience. Understanding a supporter's personal preference and circumstances is important—someone early in their career might have more time than money, whereas a mid-career professional might have funds to give but little spare time, and a retiree might circle back to having ample time. By offering pathways for both time and money, and allowing individuals to move between them, nonprofits let people contribute in the ways most meaningful (and neurologically rewarding) for them at each stage of life. The key takeaway is that generosity has multiple channels into the brain: one through the wallet and one through rolled-up sleeves. Both channel into the heart. Neither is inherently "better"; they are two sides of the giving coin. For a holistic fundraising strategy, nurturing both can expand the overall engagement and loyalty of your supporters.

Volunteerism and Brain Chemistry: Why Helping Feels So Good

Why do volunteers so often say they feel great after helping out? In Chapter 1, we introduced the idea of "helper's high," coined by psychologists to describe the euphoria associated with acts of kindness. When it comes to volunteering, that same reward circuitry is certainly activated but volunteering adds extra "ingredients" to the neurochemical mix, particularly through its social interactions. Giving your time tends to engage not only the brain's reward neurotransmitters but also the hormones and neural networks linked to social bonding, empathy, and stress relief, such as oxytocin, serotonin, and endorphins.

The empathy-altruism pathway. While dopamine, oxytocin, and endorphins set the stage for feeling good, another crucial aspect of volunteering's neuroscience is how it engages our brain's empathy circuitry. When you volunteer in person, you're typically confronted with someone else's reality, perhaps someone's struggles, or their gratitude, or just the human presence of those you are benefiting. Our brains are wired to respond to these signals through a mechanism known as the mirror neuron system—brain cells that fire not only when we perform an action (see Chapter 1) but also when we observe someone else performing that action or experiencing an emotion. They enable our brain to mirror or simulate what others are going through, which is thought to be a foundation of empathy. In a volunteering scenario, the effect is even more direct. If you see someone shivering in the cold and you hand them a blanket, your brain's mirror neurons for the sensation of cold and the relief of warmth can fire as if you were experiencing those states. This "self-other resonance" means you literally feel a bit of what others feel (Iacoboni, 2008). Neuroscientists have found that when people witness others in pain or distress, regions like the anterior insula and the anterior cingulate cortex (areas that process our own pain and emotions) activate in response (Decety & Jackson, 2006).

In volunteers, this empathic brain response can be a powerful motivator—feeling even a fraction of someone's hardship can drive us strongly to alleviate it. In fact, remarkable research at UCLA demonstrated that individuals who showed the strongest neural empathic responses (their brain lit up the most in those pain/emotion areas when seeing others suffer) were also the most generous in behavior, giving away the most. Meanwhile, those who showed higher activity in their frontal lobes, associated with deliberation and impulse control, tended to be less generous (Christov-Moore & Iacoboni, 2016). This suggests that our brains may have an automatic altruistic impulse (driven by empathy), which sometimes gets inhibited by more calculated reasoning or self-interest originating in the prefrontal cortex, as tested in further research (Christov-Moore et al., 2017).

The big picture from this research is that empathy is a deep, hard-wired driver in the brain for altruism. Volunteering places us directly in situations that activate this empathy. When you're face to face with someone who needs help, your mirror neurons and emotional networks resonate with their state, creating that compassionate urge to assist. This empathy-altruism pathway is the brain basis for the idea that we help others because we feel their need (Batson, 2011). It is particularly salient in direct service: hearing a person's story, seeing their tears or their smile, can evoke a stronger altruistic response than reading a statistic in a newsletter. Nonprofits intuitively leverage this through activities like site visits or testimonials, but here we see the neuro-scientific reason: those experiences fire up donors' and volunteers' neural empathy, which in turn motivates action.

Leveraging brain chemistry in volunteer programs. For nonprofit practitioners, understanding the neurochemistry behind volunteering offers insight into how to engage and retain volunteers. Essentially, effective volunteer management can be thought of as helping volunteers get those rewarding brain experiences consistently (in ethical ways). Creating opportunities for volunteers to bond, like working in teams, having group orientations or debriefs, or celebrating successes together, will enhance that feeling of connection through the release of oxytocin. Many successful volunteer programs intentionally foster a "team spirit" and community among volunteers (think of volunteer meetups, appreciation events, or even WhatsApp groups for volunteers to chat). This isn't just a nicety; it actually taps into the biology of bonding, making volunteers feel part of something bigger than themselves. Similarly, to engage the empathy-driven reward, it's powerful to help volunteers directly see the impact of their work. If a volunteer tutors a student, periodically show them the student's improvement or let them hear from the student's parents about how the child's confidence has grown. If volunteers pack medical supplies, connect those supplies with a story of a patient who received them. By closing the feedback loop, you trigger the volunteer's emotional circuits, their brain witnesses the beneficiary's joy or relief (even if via a story or photo), and those mirror neurons fire, reinforcing "yes, this mattered, do it again."

In essence, you're aligning the volunteer experience with the neural pathways of empathy and reward. Even thanking volunteers and acknowledging their contribution can feed the cycle; a heart-felt thanks can release dopamine in the volunteer's brain because it signals achievement and social approval. Last, being aware of the stress-reduction aspect of volunteering can inform how we position volunteer opportunities. In today's high-stress world, framing volunteering as a two-way street ("You're helping others, and it might help you feel less stressed and more fulfilled.") can be a compelling message, supported by science. By designing volunteer roles that are meaningful, social, and show progress, we essentially create a positive neurochemical experience for the volunteer, which in turn leads to sustained engagement and word-of-mouth to bring in others. Neuroscience thus affirms an old piece of wisdom: people will keep doing something that makes them feel good. Volunteering, done right, does exactly that, at the level of brain chemistry.

Cross-Cultural Brain Responses: Altruism Across Different Cultures

Generosity is a human universal. Neuroscientists would say that all healthy human brains are equipped with the circuitry for empathy, reward, and social bonding that underlie giving behavior. However, culture plays a profound role in shaping *how* those brain circuits are engaged, whom we feel compelled to help, and what kind of giving is most valued or frequent. In this section, we turn to the question of how cultural context influences the neuroscience of giving time and money. Do people's brains respond differently to acts of generosity in individualistic societies versus collectivistic ones? Are there cultural variations in the oxytocin or dopamine responses associated with helping others? How do cultural norms during one's development influence the neural pathways for altruism? While the fundamental biology of altruism may be consistent across our species, research suggests that cultural values and social norms can modulate the expression of those neural tendencies. It essentially guides the "when, how, and for whom" of generosity. Understanding these differences is especially important for global nonprofits or any organization working with diverse communities of donors and volunteers. An appeal that resonates in one culture might fall flat in another if it doesn't align with local motivations for giving.

Individualist versus collectivist mindsets. One of the broadest cultural distinctions that affects prosocial behavior is whether a culture leans more individualistic or collectivistic. In individualistic cultures (such as the United States, Canada, or Western Europe), personal choice and individual goals are emphasized. Helping others is often framed as a voluntary action that reflects one's personal values or principles. People raised in these cultures might think of giving as a form of self-expression ("I donate to show what I stand for.") or personal fulfillment ("Volunteering helps me grow and learn."). In collectivist cultures (common in many parts of Asia, Africa, the Middle East, and Latin America), the emphasis is on group harmony, family duty, and social responsibility. Helping behaviors are often seen not as extraordinary acts but as expected responsibilities to one's community or family. Research in Japan offers a nuanced view of how trust operates in these contexts. Taniguchi (2013), analyzing data from the Japanese General Social Survey, found that generalized trust was positively associated with irregular volunteering, sporadic or event-based participation, but not with sustained, regular volunteering. This suggests that in some collectivist societies, trust may motivate people to respond to communal needs episodically rather than through ongoing structured service, likely due to cultural norms of in-group cohesion and situational duty rather than continuous personal identity as a volunteer. A person from a collectivist background might feel a strong obligation to volunteer for community events or to donate to help a neighbor in need because that's what a "good member of the group" does. Here, altruism is more tightly interwoven with social identity and obligation. The brain's reward for giving might be linked as much to fulfilling a duty (and avoiding shame) as to intrinsic feelings. Anthropological research has found that in collectivist settings, people often don't even label helping as "charity," it's just part of being family or part of the village.

These cultural differences have been borne out in cross-cultural studies on volunteer motivation. For example, Marcia Finkelstein (2010) found that collectivism was strongly associated with altruistic motivations and a desire to strengthen social ties through volunteering, whereas individualism was more associated with volunteering for personal development or career-related reasons. In a large survey of college students from 13 different countries, students from more individualistic societies were more likely to cite reasons like skill acquisition, personal growth, or "making a difference" as an individual for why they volunteer. By contrast, students from more collectivistic societies more often mentioned duty, reciprocity, or community betterment as key motivations. Notably, the collectivist-oriented volunteers in that study were also more likely to develop a "volunteer role identity"—meaning volunteering became part of who they are, tied to their identity in their community (Grönlund et al., 2011). This makes sense: if volunteering is seen as an integral role to support the group, then being a volunteer is a respected social identity.

In practical terms, a volunteer in the United States might proudly list their volunteer work on a résumé to highlight their initiative and values (personal achievement frame), whereas a volunteer in a collectivist context might engage in the work more quietly as a fulfillment of expected social roles (community contribution frame). The underlying brain experience of reward might differ: the former might get a dopamine boost from personal accomplishment and recognition ("I chose to do something good and I feel great about it."), while the latter might get a stronger oxytocin or social satisfaction boost from solidarity ("I upheld our tradition and feel closely connected with my people."). Both types of reward are valid; they simply reflect different facets of our neurobiology being emphasized.

Cultural influence on oxytocin and dopamine responses. While rigorous neuroscience studies directly comparing brain scans across cultures in giving scenarios are still relatively few, there is intriguing evidence that cultural norms can modulate physiological responses to generosity. One angle comes from cultural neuroscience research on empathy. Studies have found that people tend to have stronger empathic brain responses (e.g., in the insula or mirror neuron system) when observing someone of their own cultural or ethnic group in pain versus someone from an out-group (Avenanti et al., 2010). This suggests that our brains may prioritize empathy for those we consider part of our in-group, which is often culturally defined. In a tightly knit collectivist society, the boundary of the in-group might be very broad (village, tribe, nation), potentially enhancing empathic responses to a wide circle of others as "one of us." In an individualistic society, the in-group might be narrower (close friends, family), with more conditional empathy beyond that.

Culturally reinforced values can either widen or narrow the sphere toward whom empathy (and thus altruistic motivation) is strongly felt. Oxytocin release may follow a similar pattern: oxytocin is known to increase trust and generosity, but predominantly toward those perceived as familiar or part of one's social circle. If your culture emphasizes "all of humanity is one family" (as some religious or philosophical traditions do), then those oxytocin pathways might be engaged even when you help a stranger across the world. Conversely, if cultural norms draw a sharp line between "us" and "them," the brain's oxytocin response might be abundant when helping a neighbor but minimal when considering an outsider. Interestingly, some genetic studies have noted variations in oxytocin receptor genes and dopamine receptor genes across populations, which could influence baseline social sensitivity. For instance, one study on the serotonin transporter gene found that cultures that were historically collectivist had a higher prevalence of a gene variant associated with heightened emotional sensitivity, possibly because cultural practices developed to mitigate the anxiety by providing strong social support (Chiao & Blizinsky, 2010).

By analogy, one might speculate that cultures emphasizing interpersonal harmony could, over generations, "tune" their members through socialization to get bigger neurochemical rewards like oxytocin surges from acts that maintain harmony, whereas a high-adrenaline individualist culture might tune people to get a dopamine rush from standing out or achieving a personal goal, including charitable acts. These are still early hypotheses, but they illustrate the interplay between biology and culture: our universal brain chemicals are the palette, and culture chooses the colors we paint with most.

Norms and neurodevelopment of generosity. Culture doesn't just influence how we give; it actually helps shape our brains from a young age regarding prosocial behavior. Children absorb cultural norms about sharing, helping, and donating through observation and instruction, and these lessons likely influence neural pathways. For example, in some cultures children are routinely involved in communal tasks (caring for younger siblings, helping with harvests, etc.), effectively "training" their reward system to associate helping with positive outcomes like family approval, belonging, and skill mastery.

Neuroimaging work with adolescents gives an interesting window into this process. Developmental neuroscientist Eva Telzer et al. (2010) studied teens from backgrounds that strongly value family obligation (such as many Asian and Latino cultures) and found that when these teens chose to give money to help their family (instead of keeping it for themselves), their ventral striatum lit up with reward activity, more so than when they kept money for personal use. American teens on average showed reward activation for giving as well, but the effect was especially pronounced in youth who had internalized strong collectivist family norms. This kind of evidence suggests that cultural values (like filial piety or communal duty) can heighten the intrinsic reward the brain feels when acting in line with those values. Over time, a culture that reinforces "it feels good to help your group" will create adults for whom that is a neural truth.

Conversely, a culture that emphasizes self-reliance might lead individuals to require a bit more personal resonance or direct benefit to trigger strong reward feelings for helping. Norms also shape what situations elicit empathy. In societies where public displays of emotion are discouraged, people might learn to down-regulate empathic responses in certain contexts, potentially engaging more cognitive control (prefrontal cortex) when confronted with others' suffering. In more expressive cultures, people might more freely empathize, engaging limbic and mirroring systems without as much restraint. These learned patterns become somewhat ingrained in the brain. However, it's crucial to note they are not immutable—cultural exposure can change, and individuals within cultures vary widely.

The neurodevelopment of generosity is a dance between an innate human capacity and the training provided by cultural stories, practices, and expectations.

Examples of cultural variations in giving. To ground this in concrete examples, consider how different cultures frame the act of volunteering (time giving) and how that might engage people's motivations. In the United States, often ranked among the most individualistic cultures, about one-quarter of Americans formally volunteer each year—one of the highest rates globally. Volunteering is framed as a personal choice and even a civic duty; it's common to hear messages like "You can make a difference" or "Be a hero in someone's life," which appeal to personal agency and heroism. School programs require students to do service hours not just to help the community but also to foster personal development and responsibility.

The result is a culture where people volunteer in diverse causes based on personal passion, and being a volunteer is generally seen as a positive aspect of one's identity (something to be proud of). The neural reward here might come from aligning one's actions with personal values and getting validation for it, a mix of dopamine (achievement) and socially triggered oxytocin (community recognition when volunteering is honored publicly). Contrast this with South Korea, which traditionally has a collectivist ethos (rooted in Confucian communal values) but in recent decades has also actively promoted volunteering as part of a modern civic life. South Korean volunteer campaigns often invoke national unity and collective pride. For instance, massive volunteer turnouts for events like disaster responses or international sports events are seen as a point of national honor. High school and college students participate in volunteer clubs in part to contribute to group success and uphold a norm of social contribution (Grönlund et al., 2011). In their case, the motivation might be less "I individually want to do this" and more "we as a generation or group are doing this together." Brain-wise, that might mean a volunteer in Seoul gets a strong feeling of belonging and satisfaction from not letting down the group (activating reward circuits tied to social approval). Meanwhile, in many African contexts like Kenya, helping behavior is deeply embedded in informal networks via principles like *Harambee* (a Swahili term meaning "all pull together").

People regularly volunteer communally in ways that might not be labeled volunteering—for example, helping build each other's homes, or organizing a village fundraiser for someone's hospital bills—because communal interdependence is a way of life. These acts are driven by a mix of altruism, mutual aid, and sometimes expectation that today you for me, tomorrow me for you. The neuroscience of such giving could involve a very direct reciprocity-reward link: one feels good helping now, partly because one knows everyone does this and it secures one's own support system. The cultural norm strongly reinforces that not helping when you could would be socially punishable (leading to feelings of guilt or ostracism), so the brain likely has a low threshold for triggering help.

Seeing a neighbor in need quickly prompts empathy and action because culturally, the mind goes "this could be me or my family next time." Interestingly, in some of these contexts, formal volunteering (through organizations) is less common, and when it does occur, it may be entwined with religious or familial duties. For instance, church groups in Kenya mobilize volunteers for community services, and faith-based motivations (which transcend self versus others by emphasizing duty to God and community) play a big role in driving the neuropsychological reward (perhaps invoking spiritual emotions and meaning networks in the brain as well).

Universal versus culturally specific patterns. Given all these variations, what is universal and what is culture-specific in the neuroscience of giving? The universal elements are the basic building blocks: the joy of helping, the connection we feel, and the internal conflict that can arise when self-interest and altruism collide. Studies have found that prosocial behavior yields positive feelings in countries around the world. One large Gallup survey of 136 countries showed that in over 120 countries, people who donated to charity or helped a stranger reported higher well-being than those who did not, indicating a likely common reward mechanism globally (Aknin et al., 2013). Our brains seem designed to find altruism satisfying at a fundamental level, supporting the idea that "feeling good by doing good" is a human constant.

However, the triggers and expressions of those brain responses are culturally tailored. Think of it like a universal recipe (altruism) that each culture spices differently. In some places, the empathy circuits might be most engaged when hearing about an individual in need (common in Western fundraising: the identifiable individual story), whereas in others, empathy might be more readily engaged by scenarios involving one's own community or kin. The reward circuits might universally activate when giving, but what enhances that activation could be personal recognition in one culture versus communal praise in another. Even the absence of reward, such as feeling nothing or stressed when asked to give, can be culturally shaped. For example, if someone from a culture with low charitable norms is asked to donate to strangers, they might feel more wary or neutral, whereas someone from a highly philanthropic culture might feel automatically compelled or guilty if they don't. Cultural norms also determine whether people feel autonomous or pressured when giving, which can affect the neural experience. In a culture where generosity must be voluntary to feel genuine (individualistic view), a forced donation might not spark the warm glow at all; whereas in a culture where giving is expected, fulfilling that expectation might indeed produce positive feelings and not doing so might produce anxiety.

Despite these differences, it's fascinating that across cultures, humanity has universally developed concepts of charity, volunteerism, and mutual aid. The language and customs differ, but almost every culture has a version of the Golden Rule and encourages helping behavior in some form. This suggests that our brains' altruistic hardware is a shared inheritance, and culture is a powerful software that runs on it, shaping outputs. For nonprofit professionals, this means that when engaging donors and volunteers from different cultural backgrounds, one should pay close attention to cultural cues and values. What motivates a retiree in rural Japan to volunteer might be a sense of civic duty and social belonging, perhaps tied to the concept of *bosai*—community disaster preparedness and mutual help—which became strong after events like the 1995 Kobe earthquake. What motivates a young tech worker in Silicon Valley might be the personal passion for a cause and the unique fulfillment it brings them individually. Neither is more or less legitimate; they are reflections of different cultural stories about why helping matters.

Practical cross-cultural strategies. We've seen that while the desire to help is human, the way it's elicited can be culture-dependent. If you are running fundraising or volunteer campaigns in a multicultural context or in a country not your own, it pays to be culturally neurogiving literate: understanding the local "prosocial brain triggers." For example, in a collectivist setting, emphasizing the community impact ("Together, our village can ensure every child has a meal.") and using group identities ("As members of this community, it's our responsibility … .") may inspire more people, because it taps into the culturally primed sense of duty and belonging. In an individualist context, appealing to personal values or highlighting an individual story ("You can change one person's life.") may connect more with the personal empathy pathway.

Even recognition should be tailored: public praise and awards for volunteering might be very effective in the United States (people strive for that badge of honor), but in cultures that value humility, calling someone out as the top donor or volunteer could embarrass them or discourage others (who might prefer group recognition or no fanfare). One size does not fit all. The lesson is to align with the audience's cultural framework: if religious duty drives giving in one culture, frame your ask in terms of that duty; if personal choice is king in another, emphasize the freedom and personal meaning in choosing to give.

Whether for good or for ill, globalization and communication technologies are also creating some convergence. Concepts of volunteerism and philanthropy are being shared across cultures. For instance, the idea of a corporate volunteer day started in the West has spread to companies in Asia; likewise, the community-driven fundraising circles common in many traditional societies are being adopted by Western communities seeking more collective engagement. Social media campaigns (like Giving Tuesday) have created new "cultures" of giving that transcend national culture to an extent, especially among younger generations who might have more homogeneous "internet culture." Still, even in these global movements, local flavor appears—the hashtags and narratives will often be localized to tap into what moves people there.

Ultimately, understanding cultural differences in the neuroscience of giving underscores a core principle: meet people where they are. The goal, encouraging generosity, is universal, but the avenues to get there must respect cultural context. By doing so, fundraisers can unlock the universal neural rewards of altruism in a way that feels authentic to each culture. Whether it's the rush of pride an individualist feels when hitting a personal fundraising goal, or the deep satisfaction a collectivist feels seeing the community thrive, both are manifestations of the brain's reward for generosity. They simply wear different cultural attire. In embracing these differences, we can inspire more giving across the board, building on the truth that, around the world, helping others is part of what makes us human and our brains are wired to encourage it.

Giving time and giving money fulfill donors in slightly different ways; a strategy that offers people both avenues can maximize donor happiness and commitment.

Chapter 6

Crisis and Emergency Fundraising Neuroscience

In a crisis, decision-making tends to shift into high gear, not just emotionally, but neurologically. Today, crises are unfortunately all too commonplace. Urgent appeals after natural disasters, humanitarian emergencies, or sudden catastrophes can mobilize donors in ways that feel almost reflexive. Their generosity impulse is on overdrive. Understanding what's happening in the brain during these critical moments can help fundraisers craft appeals that resonate without overwhelming. In this chapter, we explore how the generous brain responds under urgency, how disaster psychology shapes giving patterns, what causes compassion fatigue on a neural level, and how to communicate effectively during emergencies. This isn't a theoretical treatise, but a guided tour of the neuroscience that can inform real-life emergency fundraising strategies.

The Neurobiology of Urgency

Urgency triggers a distinctive neurobiological state. When an emergency appeal hits, such as a sudden earthquake or an urgent fundraiser to save a life, donors experience an acute stress response that can alter their giving decisions. At the core of this response is our fight-or-flight system, which floods the body with stress hormones like adrenaline and cortisol. These chemicals heighten arousal and focus attention on the immediate situation. In fundraising terms, this means an urgent appeal can literally put a donor's brain in "alert mode," prioritizing rapid action over careful deliberation. However, cortisol, the primary stress hormone, can have a complex effect on generosity. Recent neuroimaging research found that higher cortisol levels were linked with reduced charitable donations among highly empathic individuals, apparently by impairing parts of the brain that assign value to helping others (Schulreich et al., 2022). In other words, if an appeal induces too much stress, it might backfire for those who deeply resonate with others' pain—stress can dampen their ability to act on their empathy. Striking the right balance is key: some urgency is motivating, but extreme stress risks overwhelming the donor's decision circuits.

The Amygdala and Emergency Appeals

When we talk about urgency and fear, we inevitably talk about the amygdala, the brain's emotional alarm center, constantly scanning for threats and important cues. During a crisis appeal, the amygdala fires rapidly, processing signals of danger or distress in milliseconds. For example, seeing a heartbreaking image of a disaster victim or reading urgent language ("Lives are at risk right now!") will activate the amygdala before the donor even fully realizes it. This swift response is sometimes called an "amygdala hijack," capturing how our emotional brain can momentarily take over in emergencies. From a fundraising perspective, this is a double-edged sword. On one hand, a triggered amygdala means the donor is feeling the crisis—their heart is racing, and they have an emotional impulse to do something. Neuroscience has shown that people who are especially altruistic tend to have amygdalas that are more sensitive to others' distress. In one study, extraordinary altruists, like people who donated a kidney to a stranger, had a larger and more reactive right amygdala in response to fearful faces, suggesting they literally feel others' fear more strongly (Marsh et al., 2014). This heightened amygdala response can translate into a powerful urge to help when encountering an emergency appeal. On the other hand, an overactivated amygdala can also short-circuit rational thought. If people feel too frightened or overwhelmed, they might freeze or avoid the situation to get away from the stress. As we learned in previous chapters, emotion enhances generosity, but in a crisis, the amygdala's surge needs to be coupled with hope and direction to convert fear into positive action.

Temporal Discounting in a Crisis

Human brains are naturally prone to temporal discounting, meaning we prefer immediate rewards over future ones. In calm times, this might make someone more likely to spend $5 on a latte now than save it for a nonprofit next week. But in a crisis, temporal discounting can shift dramatically. An urgent situation essentially makes the future now. The immediate need feels so salient that donors heavily prioritize the present. In effect, the psychological "discount rate" for the future skyrockets. Why donate next month if lives are on the line today? Neurologically, this shift occurs because urgent events heighten emotional arousal and focus attention on the present moment, which is managed by networks in the brain that handle survival and immediate action. In crisis fundraising, this means messaging that highlights immediacy, what's happening right now and the immediate impact of a gift, will naturally engage donors' brains more intensely. The neural reward circuits also come into play: they fire more for rewards that are imminent. So, when donors perceive that their gift will have an instant effect (feeding a family tonight, sending relief today), the brain's reward system engages, reinforcing the impulse to give now rather than later. Urgency, in essence, shrinks the mental distance between the donor's action and the outcome.

Rapid Reaction Neural Circuits

Crises don't give us the luxury of time, and our brains have designed circuits for split-second emotional reactions. When disaster strikes, information often travels along the brain's "low road"—a fast track from sensory input to the limbic system that bypasses slower, deliberate processing. For instance, an alarming news alert or a gut-wrenching photo of a disaster victim can trigger the thalamus and amygdala almost instantly. This rapid route enables us (and our donors) to react emotionally before our conscious reasoning has caught up. The neural circuitry involved includes the amygdala (for fear/alert), the hypothalamus (kicking off the fight-or-flight response via the sympathetic nervous system), and even brainstem areas that increase heart rate and galvanize us to move. These pathways were designed to help us escape threats or respond to urgent needs without overthinking, which, in a fundraising context, can translate to impulsive acts of generosity.

How often have we heard of people spontaneously texting a donation during a disaster telethon or emptying their wallet when confronted with an urgent plea at the grocery checkout? Those spur-of-the-moment gifts are facilitated by these fast emotional circuits. Importantly, while these reactions are quick, they're not mindless. The brain's insula and anterior cingulate cortex (ACC), regions associated with empathy and pain perception, also activate when we witness someone suffering. In an acute crisis, this can be almost instantaneous, a phenomenon sometimes called *visceral empathy*. We quite literally feel a pang of pain on someone else's behalf, as these neural circuits mirror the distress of those affected. That pang can propel a rapid donation as a form of relief, both for the victims and, subconsciously, to relieve our own empathic discomfort. Fundraisers sometimes harness these rapid reaction circuits by creating appeals that grab attention and emotion quickly though they must be careful, as too much shock without guidance can also lead to emotional overload. The bottom line is that the brain is wired to respond first and ask questions later when urgency strikes, which is why those first few seconds of a crisis appeal are so critical.

Visceral Imagery and Immediate Impulses

The phrase *visceral imagery* is almost literal: certain images seem to hit us in the gut. In neuroscience terms, vivid images of suffering or danger activate the brain's visual cortex along with emotion-processing regions to create a powerful, immediate impression. Think of the iconic photograph of a young Syrian boy, Aylan Kurdi, whose image lying lifeless on a beach in 2015 jolted the world's attention to the refugee crisis. Such powerful visuals can stir empathy and action more effectively than any statistic, because they engage our brains' emotion circuits directly (Slovic et al., 2017). When a donor sees a visceral image, their amygdala, insula, and ACC light up with emotional resonance, often before the rational brain has processed what exactly is happening. This can create an immediate giving impulse: a sudden determination to help alleviate the depicted suffering.

Research confirms that negative, emotionally charged images in charitable appeals tend to increase helping behavior more than neutral or positive images (Bak et al., 2024). The beneficiaries' anguished facial expressions, for example, have been shown to elicit empathy and open wallets in a way that happy or abstract images might not. These images essentially serve as a shortcut to the donor's emotional brain, conveying in an instant the gravity of the situation and invoking that core human response: "I have to do something." However, there's a caveat. The same studies note that constant exposure to graphic suffering can lead to desensitization or even aversion. The first time an image shocks us, it has a huge impact; the tenth time, our brain may start to protect itself by numbing out (a phenomenon we'll revisit under compassion fatigue). For fundraisers, the lesson is to use visceral imagery judiciously. A well-chosen photo or video in an emergency appeal can be worth a thousand words; it grabs the brain and heart immediately, but it should be paired with a path to action and hope. That way the donor's immediate impulse (generated by these vivid neural activations) can translate into meaningful help, rather than either being stifled by overwhelm or dulled by repetition.

Disaster Psychology and Giving Patterns

Every disaster seems to spawn two parallel stories in the donor community: one of surging generosity, people often give heroically when tragedy strikes, and another of unevenness, interest that spikes and then fades, some victims helped lavishly while others are overlooked. Psychology and neuroscience together help explain these patterns. In crisis situations, our brains don't respond to need in a linear or purely logical way; they respond based on proximity, perception, emotion, and cognitive appraisals of the event. Let's unpack some key factors: why closeness matters, why one specific victim's story can outweigh a massive statistic, how empathy can be supercharged or short-circuited, how different emotions (fear, hope, solidarity) engage the brain, and how we mentally appraise sudden catastrophes. By understanding these, nonprofit practitioners can better anticipate donor behavior during emergencies and tailor their approaches accordingly.

Psychological Proximity and Neural Response

One powerful driver in disaster giving is psychological proximity—how close (or how connected) donors feel to the crisis. Proximity isn't just physical distance; it can be emotional closeness, cultural or group identification ("It happened to people like me."), or the vividness of imagining oneself in that situation. The closer a disaster feels, the more our brains treat it as our problem. Neurologically, empathy tends to be stronger for those we perceive as close to us. Studies in social neuroscience show that people's empathy circuits (like the anterior insula and premotor mirror neuron areas) are often more active when they see pain or need in someone who is part of their in-group or whom they can easily identify with, compared to a distant stranger.

In disaster terms, donors might feel a bigger jolt of concern for a crisis in their hometown or a country they've visited than for one in a far-off land they struggle to picture. Even without a direct personal link, skillful storytelling can reduce psychological distance. Research on disaster giving found that when donors imagine a disaster happening close to home, it sparks counterfactual thoughts ("It could have been me.") that boost willingness to help (Zagefka & James, 2015).

Essentially, the brain's self-referential and empathetic networks converge: the donor puts themselves in the victims' shoes, and the crisis no longer feels abstract. On the flip side, if something feels very far removed, like an appeal talking about suffering "in 2050" or on the other side of the globe with no relatable details, the brain's emotional response may remain muted. Research generally indicates that simply shifting perspective to a more distant time frame reduced emotional concern and thus donations for a natural disaster. Psychological distance acts almost like a dimmer switch on empathy in the brain. For fundraisers, the implication is clear: wherever possible, decrease the perceived distance. This can be done by emphasizing shared humanity ("a mother caring for her child, just like any of us would"), by highlighting any connections ("This could happen in our community."), or by focusing on relatable details rather than overwhelming statistics. In doing so, you're inviting the donor's brain to treat the crisis as closer and more urgent, lighting up those pathways that say, "This matters to me and I need to help."

Crisis and Emergency Fundraising Neuroscience

The Identifiable Victim Effect in Emergencies

In the aftermath of a disaster, appeals often zoom in on a single poignant story amidst thousands. This is no accident; it leverages a well-documented (but again poorly named) phenomenon known as the *identifiable victim effect*. Simply put, people are far more likely to offer help to a specific, identifiable individual than to an anonymous crowd, even if the crowd's need is objectively greater. The identifiable and urgent case activates emotional and cognitive circuits: we can imagine the person's pain (engaging empathy networks in the insula and ACC) and we often feel a social connection or responsibility (engaging theory-of-mind regions like the medial prefrontal cortex and temporoparietal junction).

By contrast, statistics about large numbers of victims, which are indeed tragic, fail to engage these same circuits, so the tragedy starts to feel like an abstraction. In fact, neuroimaging research indicates that when confronted with unidentified or abstract victims, people's brains may shift into a more analytic mode (e.g., increased activity in the temporoparietal junction as they try to mentalize a vague scenario) (Zhao et al., 2024). It's as if the brain says, "Hmm, I can't feel 10,000 suffering people, I have to think about it," which is a slower, less visceral process and often leads to less generosity. During emergencies, this effect is amplified. The identifiable victim provides a focal point for compassion amidst chaos. Donors may feel overwhelmed by the scale of a disaster ("How can I possibly help everyone affected?") but showing them one person or family to save gives the brain a target for action.

It's motivating ("I can help this child right now.") and it sidesteps the paralysis that can come from statistics. We should note, as compassionate fundraisers, that this effect is a human quirk—it's not entirely rational, but it's real. Acknowledging it isn't manipulative; it's about guiding donors through a natural empathetic entry point.

By highlighting an individual story, we unlock donors' deepest empathetic responses, which can then spill over to benefit many. This is why you'll often see disaster appeals start with one name, one face, one story—it's the spark that lights the fire of giving. And in fact, many donors report that after giving to help "that one story," they felt connected to the larger cause and continued to support broader relief efforts.

Empathic Overarousal and Behavioral Fallout

Disasters dump a huge amount of emotional content on donors. It's not just empathy; it can be empathic overarousal, where people feel too much of others' pain. When we're bombarded with images of devastation and suffering, our capacity to empathize can overshoot, leading to personal distress. Essentially, the empathy switch gets stuck in the "on" position at maximum, and our brain's circuits for feeling others' anguish (again, regions like the anterior insula and ACC) start overloading. This intense empathic arousal can have a few different behavioral consequences. For some people, it propels immediate action. They donate impulsively as a way to alleviate their own distress at seeing others suffer. The act of giving can indeed bring a sense of relief or restore a feeling of control, quelling that empathic angst. This is one reason we often see spikes of giving right as a disaster's most heart-wrenching stories hit the news: people are feeling so much that they urgently need to do something, for the victims' sake and a bit for their own.

However, empathic overarousal can also swing the other way. If the distress feels unmanageable, if the donor's brain perceives that no amount of help they give will make a dent in the suffering, they may shut down emotionally. This is related to what psychologists call the "collapse of compassion," where beyond a certain point of tragedy, our brains start to numb our empathy as a self-protective instinct

(Cameron & Payne, 2011). Neurobiologically, extremely high arousal can trigger the amygdala and stress circuits so much that people go into a freeze or avoidance mode rather than fight-or-flight. It's akin to emotional circuit breakers tripping. A donor might change the channel, scroll past the gut-wrenching post, or avoid thinking about the disaster altogether because it's just too much. Behaviorally, that means no action, no donation, maybe even a defensive shrug of "it's hopeless."

There's also a phenomenon known as empathic distress fatigue that can happen in acute situations: the person feels such acute empathic pain that they turn away to stop the pain, which in a crisis context might mean tuning out the appeals. As fundraisers, being mindful of empathic overarousal is crucial. We want to dial up empathy, but not to 11 with no reprieve. That's why effective disaster appeals often pair the most tragic imagery or stories with glimmers of hope or efficacy ("Your $10 will provide clean water to this family."). By doing so, we help the donor's brain navigate intense compassion without flipping into either panic giving or total shutdown. In essence, we're guiding that powerful wave of empathic arousal toward productive help, rather than letting it crash over the donor unsustainably.

Fear, Hope, and Solidarity: Different Emotional Brain Activations

Crises evoke a complex mix of emotions in donors—fear for those in danger, hope that things can improve, and often a sense of solidarity or togetherness in the face of tragedy. Interestingly, these emotions each tap into different brain regions and pathways, which can influence how donors respond. Fear, as we've touched on, is centered in the amygdala and related limbic structures. When donors feel fear during a disaster (for example, fear that "this could happen to my community" or simply visceral fear from seeing horrifying scenes), their brains heighten alertness and urgency. Fear can be motivating in the short term. It creates a sense that action is needed now but it also carries the risk of paralyzing people if it's not coupled with a solution. In neurological terms, fear can trigger the release of stress hormones and put the brain in a defensive crouch. If an appeal only provokes fear ("The situation is terrifying, everything is awful.") without pointing to a positive action, the donor's brain might stay stuck in threat-processing mode, which is not conducive to making a clear decision to give. That's where hope comes in. Hope is a somewhat understudied emotion in neuroscience, but it's generally associated with the brain's reward and motivation circuits. When we feel hope, say by seeing a survivor pulled from rubble or hearing that donations are making a difference, our brain likely releases dopamine. Regions like the ventral striatum (including the nucleus accumbens) may activate as we envision a better future. Hope essentially tells the brain, "Good outcomes are possible," which shifts a person from a fearful freeze or flight state toward an approach state—they're more likely to move toward the problem to help fix it. In practice, adding even a note of hope ("Thanks to donors, this child was rescued—more need our help.") can biologically encourage donors to engage rather than shy away. Then there's solidarity, that warm sense of "we're all in this together."

Solidarity often comes with feelings of love, empathy, and communal bond. A likely player here is oxytocin, which also has stress-relieving effects and can actually suppress anxiety and reduce stress responses while encouraging caregiving and affiliative behavior. In times of disaster, people often report an incredible coming together: neighbors helping neighbors, strangers feeling like kin. From a brain perspective, oxytocin (and other neuropeptides) may be blunting the fear response (by calming the amygdala) and boosting prosocial feelings. Solidarity also likely engages the medial prefrontal cortex and other "social brain" regions that help us resonate with group identities and norms.

For instance, seeing news of communities volunteering en masse or social media campaigns of people helping can activate a donor's sense of group membership ("Everyone is rallying; I want to join."). That taps into neural reward pathways too—doing good as a collective can be very rewarding, sometimes even more than doing it alone. In practical fundraising terms, successful disaster appeals often balance fear and hope, and evoke solidarity. A message might acknowledge the fearsome reality ("The wildfire has destroyed so much—it's scary.") but swiftly move to hope and solidarity ("But there is hope: communities are coming together, and we can all help rebuild."). By doing so, it engages the full spectrum of the donor's emotional brain: the urgency of fear (act now), the positive motivation of hope (we can make a difference), and the social encouragement of solidarity (join others in doing so). This emotional synergy can be very powerful, leading to both immediate and sustained giving in crisis situations.

Cognitive Appraisals in Catastrophes

While emotions often take center stage in emergencies, there's also a cognitive process unfolding in the background: how donors appraise the catastrophe. Cognitive appraisal refers to our conscious evaluation of what an event means for us and what we can do about it. Even as the emotional brain is surging, the thinking brain, the prefrontal cortex, is trying to make sense of the chaos. This matters because the way a donor mentally frames a disaster will influence their decision to give or not. In the blink of an eye, a potential donor might appraise a sudden catastrophe in terms of challenge ("This is a tough situation, but people can overcome it with help.") or threat ("This is utterly devastating and beyond help."). These appraisals link to different emotional outcomes: a challenge appraisal might come with determination and problem-solving, whereas a pure threat appraisal might come with fear and helplessness.

Neurologically, when the brain appraises an event as something that can be managed or improved, the prefrontal cortex (particularly areas involved in planning and control) stays more engaged and communicates with emotional centers to regulate them. For example, the dorsolateral prefrontal cortex (DLPFC) helps with implementing strategies and controlling impulses. If a donor thinks "I can help by donating; that will make a difference," their DLPFC can focus that intention into action (writing the check, clicking the donate button). Cognitive appraisal also involves the ventromedial prefrontal cortex (vmPFC) when evaluating the personal relevance and value of an action like donating. If the appraisal is, "This is important and donating is the right thing to do," the vmPFC can integrate that value-based decision with emotional input (the vmPFC is a key node in decision-making that connects emotion and value). However, if someone appraises the catastrophe as hopeless, perhaps thinking, "This problem is just too big, nothing I do will matter," we might see a kind of neural deactivation in motivation pathways. Learned helplessness, a concept from psychology, has its neural correlates, too: studies show that if the brain consistently perceives lack of control, it can dampen the normal reward and approach systems (in severe cases contributing to depression-like states). In a moment of crisis, a mini-version of that can occur in a donor's mind: "Why bother? This is unsolvable."

That mindset is poison to fundraising. That's why messaging during disasters tries to shape the cognitive appraisal toward efficacy— showing that help is possible and effective. For example, noting that "just $20 can provide shelter for a family" helps the donor appraise their personal action as meaningful. This engages a sense of control and purpose, activating those frontal brain networks that guide intentional action. Cognitive appraisal also includes attribution: how donors explain the cause of the catastrophe. If they view victims as innocent and the event as unforeseeable, they're more inclined to help; if they (perhaps unfairly) blame human error or think "they

Crisis and Emergency Fundraising Neuroscience

should have been prepared," that can reduce giving. All these inter-pretations are cognitive overlays that can modulate the underlying empathic response.

In summary, even amid the frenzy of a crisis, the donor's brain is performing a quick calculus: what's happening? How bad is it? Can I help? The answers to those questions, shaped by messaging and mindset, will influence neural pathways for either mobilizing action or holding back. As fundraisers, we can't control a donor's internal thoughts, but we can certainly guide appraisals by framing the situation in empowering ways. Reinforce the idea that the crisis, while serious, can be mitigated, and that the donor's action has genuine impact. This way, the cognitive and emotional systems in the brain work hand in hand: the heart feels the need, and the mind affirms that responding is the right and effective choice.

Compassion Fatigue Mechanisms

In the weeks and months after an initial crisis, nonprofits often face a new challenge: specifically, compassion fatigue. This is the phenom-enon where people's capacity to empathize and their willingness to help start to wane after prolonged exposure to suffering. It's as if the emotional well runs dry. But what's actually happening in the brain during compassion fatigue? Understanding the neural mechanisms can shed light on how to prevent burnout—not only in donors, but in staff, volunteers, and anyone continuously exposed to distressing situations. In this section, we'll delve into the pathways of emotional exhaustion, how the brain desensitizes with repetition, and what can be done to keep empathy alive without overwhelming people. We'll also explore the tug-of-war between helplessness and efficacy in ongoing crises—a crucial factor in sustaining engagement—and look at strategies (some even "neural" strategies) for maintaining compas-sion during protracted emergencies.

The Neurology of Emotional Exhaustion

Compassion fatigue isn't just a metaphorical fatigue; it has neurological underpinnings akin to a form of emotional burnout. When someone is repeatedly exposed to traumatic stories or images—for example, humanitarian aid workers hearing countless horror stories, or donors seeing day-after-day appeals about a war—their limbic system (the brain's emotional center) can go into overdrive at first and then hit a wall. One way to think of it is that the continuous activation of empathy-related regions (like the amygdala, insula, and ACC that we've mentioned) eventually leads the brain to down-regulate these responses as a protective measure. It's like the brain saying, "I can't keep feeling this intensely all the time, I need to dial it down." Neurologically, chronic stress plays a big role. If an initial crisis triggered a big spike of cortisol and adrenaline, a prolonged crisis means those stress chemicals may remain elevated or start cycling in waves with each new depressing update.

Over time, high cortisol can actually impair the function of the hippocampus (involved in memory and context) and prefrontal cortex (involved in regulation and decision-making). People might experience this as numbness or difficulty concentrating on yet another sad story. Essentially, the brain's resources for emotion and attention get depleted. There's evidence from caregiver studies that those experiencing compassion fatigue show changes in their brain activity, for instance, reduced activation in empathy-related areas after a while, as if they've become numb, and sometimes heightened activation in areas related to self-protection or shutting down. It's as though the brain flips from "engage with others' pain" to "protect myself from others' pain" mode. In everyday terms, a donor or volunteer might notice they just don't react like they used to: where a heartbreaking image once brought them to tears, now it scarcely raises an eyebrow.

This isn't because they've become cruel or uncaring; it's a kind of neural exhaustion. Another piece of the neurological puzzle is empathic distress versus compassion. Psychologists draw a distinction between empathic distress (essentially taking on the suffering of others, which is draining) and compassion (a warm, caring desire to help, which can actually be nourishing). If a person stays in empathic distress mode too long, they burn out. Their brain might show signs of weariness, constant negative arousal without relief. But if they can cultivate compassion (which has a more positive emotional tone), it engages a slightly different network that includes reward and love-related regions, potentially counteracting fatigue. Emotional exhaustion from compassion fatigue is real, and it's physical. Recognizing it in ourselves and our donors means we shouldn't push the emotional intensity relentlessly without respite. Just as muscles need rest after heavy use, the empathic brain needs recovery to continue functioning well.

Desensitization: When the Brain Numbs Out

One hallmark of compassion fatigue is desensitization, that numbing of emotional response after repeated exposure. The first time we see a particular tragedy, it's shocking; the tenth time, sadly, it can start to feel routine. On a neural level, desensitization is a form of habituation: the brain becomes accustomed to a stimulus and responds less strongly. As discussed previously, if a donor sees graphic images of suffering every day, the amygdala's alarm response to those images might diminish over time. It's not that the images have become any less tragic, but the brain has essentially adjusted its emotional dial. This has been observed in various contexts. Research on media violence shows that people who are repeatedly exposed to violent images show reduced physiological and neural reactivity to them over time (Krahé et al., 2011).

Similarly, with humanitarian imagery, constant exposure can blunt the initial pang of empathy or sorrow that a fresh viewer would experience. You might notice news organizations sometimes vary their approach as a crisis drags on. Early on they show very intense images to convey the horror, but later they might reduce that or people simply stop paying attention. Part of that is audience desensitization. Our brains also engage coping mechanisms. If feeling intensely sad every day is too taxing, the brain might erect a bit of a wall, perhaps increasing activation in cognitive regions to intellectualize the suffering rather than feel it, or triggering more activity in areas that regulate emotion (like the dorsomedial prefrontal cortex) to dampen the emotional impact.

Desensitization isn't absolute. A particularly novel or extreme story can still break through but it raises the threshold for what moves us. For fundraisers, desensitization is a serious concern in protracted crises. It means that the appeals that worked so well initially may lose effectiveness as the audience acclimates. If you send daily emails each with the same type of heartbreaking photo, you might see diminishing returns; donors start glossing over them. Neurologically, once the brain has labeled something as "familiar," it doesn't allocate the same level of attention or emotion to it. There's also a learning component: if a donor gave after the first few appeals and sees things still are bad, they may subconsciously start to feel, "I guess my help didn't change much," leading them to tune out further appeals to avoid feeling ineffective (which ties into helplessness, coming up next).

Combatting desensitization often requires changing up the stimulus. This could mean telling new kinds of stories, using different imagery, or highlighting small wins (to invoke different emotions). It also means not bombarding supporters nonstop; allowing some space can let sensitivity rebound a bit. Think of it like when you step out of a noisy room and then return—the noise hits you again.

131

Likewise, if donors aren't seeing graphic images for a little while, the next exposure may reignite the feeling. The brain's numbness is reversible to an extent; it just needs the right approach. Ultimately, being aware of desensitization reminds us to respect the limits of the human emotional engine. It's not that donors become heartless after a while, it's that their brains naturally protect them by dialing things down. Smart fundraising during long emergencies will adjust tactics to keep reaching hearts that are trying, in self-defense, not to feel quite so much.

Limbic System Regulation: Preventing Empathic Burnout

If the limbic system (emotional brain) is the workhorse of empathy, then regulating the limbic system is key to preventing burnout. What does regulation mean in this context? It's the process of managing emotional responses—not eliminating them (we want donors to care, after all), but keeping them at sustainable levels. In compassionate work, this often involves engaging other parts of the brain to soothe or guide the limbic response. One important player here is the prefrontal cortex, especially the medial and orbitofrontal regions that have connections to the amygdala. These regions act like a wise counselor to the fiery amygdala, telling it, "Okay, calm down a bit" when needed. Previously we mentioned cognitive reappraisal in catastrophes—that's a prime example of prefrontal-driven regulation. If someone thinks, "Yes, this is awful, but there are things we can do," that thought can dial down pure anguish to a determined compassion. Training oneself (or donors) to have these kinds of thoughts can actually show up in the brain: research has found that people who practice reappraising emotional images (finding a more hopeful or distanced perspective) show reduced amygdala activation and increased prefrontal activation.

In a fundraising context, helping donors regulate may sound odd; we often focus on stimulating their emotions. But for long-term engagement, some regulation is necessary. This could mean including messages of reassurance or coping: "We know it's been a lot to take in. Here's how your past support has made a difference … ." Such communication can subconsciously help the donor's brain manage the emotional load by giving it positive material to work with (thus, engaging reward circuits or at least calming circuits). Some nonprofits subtly integrate this by communicating in ways that foster reflection and calm rather than only urgency. An update that shares a hopeful story or expresses gratitude can induce a warm, regulated emotional state in supporters, rather than keeping them in high-pitched anxiety all the time. The limbic system thrives on a balance: enough emotional spark to care, but enough regulation to avoid being consumed by care. Empathic burnout often happens when that balance tips too far toward constant emotional arousal without relief. So in designing campaigns over a prolonged crisis, consider its rhythm, moments of intensity followed by moments of relief. It's akin to how good storytelling has beats of tension and release. This isn't just stylistic; it's neurobiologically sound. It ensures that the donor's limbic system stays responsive but doesn't run away like a train with no brakes. By preventing full-blown empathic burnout, we keep supporters in the game for the long haul, with hearts open but not overwhelmed.

Attention Depletion and Emotional Numbing

Compassion fatigue doesn't only involve emotions, it also involves attention. Paying attention to suffering, day after day, is mentally demanding. Our brains have limited attentional resources, and in a crisis-filled environment or a long crisis, those resources can get depleted. Think of how news fatigue sets in: at first you read every article about a disaster, and later you find yourself skimming headlines or avoiding the news entirely. That is attention fatigue teaming up with emotional fatigue. Neurologically, attention is closely linked with frontal-parietal networks that control what we focus on. When something is novel or urgent, the brain's salience network (including the anterior insula and dorsal ACC) flags it as important, and we direct attention there. But over time, as the crisis becomes "old news," the salience tagging diminishes. It's not that the crisis is resolved, but our brains can't maintain everything as top priority indefinitely. There's a concept called compassion fade or "psychic numbing" where the more people suffer, paradoxically the less attention and compassion each individual seems to receive (as numbers rise, empathy per victim falls). One reason is cognitive: large numbers are abstract and hard to pay attention to. Another reason is simply that our attentional circuits start to tune out repetitive signals.

From a cognitive standpoint, if every email subject looks like "URGENT: Children starving, please help," eventually a frequent donor's brain may categorize that as routine and not bring it to the forefront of consciousness with the same vigor. This is an example of how attention and emotion intertwine. Without attention, even a moving message won't trigger emotion because it gets mentally sidelined. Emotional numbing is often the end result of both the neural desensitization we discussed and this attentional shift. The person isn't actively deciding not to care; their brain is just no longer amplifying those signals. It's a bit like an alarm that's been going off continuously—eventually, you stop hearing it clearly. Attention can also be hijacked by other stimuli. In prolonged crises, eventually some new event or another crisis or just everyday life demands will divert donor attention. Once attentional focus is lost, rekindling the same emotional intensity is hard.

For fundraisers, this underscores the importance of keeping communications fresh and engaging to win that attention back. Using varied formats like videos, personal letters, interactive webinars, or novel angles can re-spark attention. Also, storytelling that evolves gives the brain something new to latch onto. Another tactic is to leverage attention resets: sometimes explicitly acknowledging the fatigue can paradoxically regain attention ("We know you've been hearing about this crisis for months; I want to share why your continued attention is so vital … ."). When donors feel seen and not taken for granted, their attentional guard might lower a bit to listen. In terms of brain chemistry, a fatigued brain might also have imbalances—chronic stress can mess a bit with neurotransmitters that affect concentration (like norepinephrine).

Therefore, occasionally inspiring interest or even curiosity can help, since curiosity engages the systems, which in turn can sharpen attention. Think of how a surprising positive update might cut through the noise: "Guess what? An unexpected outcome from your support … ." Now the donor's brain perks up to learn something new. Our communications should strive to be attention-friendly: clear, succinct when needed (respecting time), and captivating when possible so that donors can mentally stick with a crisis cause even after the initial shock has passed.

Helplessness Versus Efficacy: The Psychology of Ongoing Crises

A critical psychological pivot in prolonged emergencies is the battle between feelings of helplessness and efficacy. Helplessness is that sinking sense of "nothing I do matters," whereas efficacy is the empowered feeling of "I can make a difference." These feelings have profound impacts on a donor's motivation and are reflected in brain activity related to reward and control. In an ongoing crisis (think of a multiyear famine or a protracted conflict), donors might start off feeling efficacious—their first donation feels like it's part of the solution. But if the crisis drags on with no clear improvement, they may slide into helplessness.

From a neurological standpoint, efficacy is rewarding. When we believe our actions have a positive effect, the brain's reward pathway (including the ventral striatum) lights up, reinforcing that behavior. In previous chapters, we talked about the "warm glow" of giving. That glow is tied to these reward circuits releasing dopamine. For the glow to continue in a long crisis, donors need to see or believe in their impact. Otherwise, the dopamine hits diminish. Helplessness, by contrast, can resemble a mild form of depression or defeat in the brain. It might involve less activation of reward circuits and more activation of areas related to pain or disappointment. In extreme cases, people can develop donor fatigue where even the thought of the crisis cues a sort of learned aversion: "Oh, that situation is hopeless, I don't want to engage."

Psychologically, Martin Seligman's classic learned helplessness theory shows that when individuals feel they have no control over outcomes, they often stop trying, even when opportunities to help exist. This is a trap we must avoid in donors' mindsets to avoid squelching their generosity impulse. The good news is that efficacy can be cultivated. Even in dire, long-term crises, highlighting signs of progress or individual success stories can bolster a sense of efficacy. For example, a refugee crisis might not resolve overnight, but sharing the story of one family that rebuilt their life with donor help can give a donor a sense of accomplishment. That, in turn, feeds the brain's reward system—essentially reminding it that giving does work, at least for that one case (which loops back to the identifiable victim effect principle). There's also a social efficacy factor: when donors see many others contributing, they feel part of a collective efficacy ("Together we're moving the needle.").

Brain-wise, knowing one is part of a successful group effort can activate social reward pathways and even oxytocin-fueled feelings of pride and connection. Another aspect is feedback loops. Nonprofits that provide feedback—"Here's what we did with your $50."—are not just being transparent; they're nurturing the donor's efficacy. That positive feedback likely reengages frontal regions that evaluate decision outcomes, showing them, "Yes, that was a good decision; it led to *x*." In ongoing crises, providing these feedback doses is like giving booster shots to the donor's motivation. On the flip side, it's important to be honest about challenges. Sugarcoating can backfire if donors feel misled. But even when being honest ("The situation is still very tough."), pairing reality with actionable hope ("Here's a specific way you can help today.") keeps the door to efficacy open. In essence, managing the helplessness versus efficacy seesaw is crucial. Helplessness is a motivation killer; efficacy is a motivation sustainer. By consistently communicating impact, even small victories, and framing the donor's role as meaningful, we help their brain continue to associate giving with reward, rather than frustration.

Maintaining Empathic Capacity in Prolonged Emergencies

With all the forces that threaten to dull empathy over time, are there ways to actively maintain or even refresh people's empathic capacity during prolonged emergencies? The encouraging answer from both psychology and neuroscience is yes. It requires intentional strategies, much like a fitness regimen for compassion. One approach is variety in perspective. If one aspect of a crisis has become numbingly familiar, introducing a new perspective can reignite empathy. For instance, long after a disaster, donors might tire of hearing from aid agencies, but hearing directly from a survivor in a personal video message could rekindle emotional connection. Neurologically, this new input might activate slightly different social cognition networks. It may engage more of the donor's perspective-taking circuitry in the prefrontal cortex and temporoparietal junction, because now they're imagining this specific person's experience. It's akin to reminding the brain, "Hey, here's a person with fresh emotions to resonate with," breaking the monotony.

On a more tangible level, providing choices or agency in how to help can keep empathy engaged. If donors start feeling like an ATM, empathy can detach. But if you invite them to a hands-on event, or let them choose whether their donation goes to medicine versus education in the crisis, they exercise their own compassion actively. Agency is empowering and can renew emotional investment. The brain likes to feel a sense of control; giving donors a role (even a small one) in the narrative of helping can make their empathic engagement more durable. Last, it's crucial to practice what we might call empathetic pacing. Don't ask someone to shoulder the emotional weight of the whole world at once. During a long crisis, segment the narrative: focus on one aspect at a time. This week, empathize with this community's struggle; next week, highlight another's hope. This pacing prevents overload and enables empathetic response to recover and refocus, rather than being spread thin constantly. Through new perspectives, personal reflection, positive practices, empowerment, and pacing, we can help donors' brains continue to care in a healthy way. This mutual benefit, for beneficiaries and donors alike, is the ideal state of long-term compassionate action.

Effective Crisis Communication

Knowing the brain science is fascinating, but it really pays off when we apply it. Effective crisis communication is about crafting appeals that resonate with the brain's tendencies during emergencies, leveraging the urgency, engaging emotions, but also respecting the cognitive and emotional limits we've discussed.

Framing Messages to Bypass Defensive Brains

In an emergency, donors can experience cognitive defenses: subtle mental barriers that protect them from being overwhelmed or manipulated. These defenses might manifest as skepticism ("Is my donation really going to help?"), avoidance ("I can't handle this news right now."), or rationalization ("I already gave, I can't keep giving."). To effectively communicate, we want to frame messages in ways that lower these defenses. One key is to appeal to System 1 (fast, intuitive thinking) before System 2 (slow, analytical thinking), to borrow psychologist Daniel Kahneman's terms. When a donor's fast, emotional brain is engaged right away, the slower, more skeptical brain often follows along more willingly, or at least doesn't slam on the brakes immediately. This doesn't mean tricking anyone; it means structuring the message so it feels personally relevant and emotionally compelling before throwing in lots of data or requests. For instance, start an appeal with a vivid scenario or a relatable anecdote ("Imagine waking up tomorrow to find your home in rubble ... .") to draw the reader in.

This narrative framing gets the brain's visualization and empathy gears turning. Contrast that with starting with a barrage of statistics— that might cause a donor's analytical brain to scrutinize or even emotionally disengage ("Oh boy, here come the numbers. Do I really want to read this?"). Another framing tip is to avoid triggering guilt or shame as the primary lever. While guilt can motivate giving in the short term, it also often triggers defensive avoidance—people don't like feeling guilty, so they might avoid the source of guilt (your message) in the future. Instead of "How can you stand by while this happens?," frame it as "We know you care and want to help in any way you can." The latter phrasing bypasses the ego's defenses and appeals to the person's identity as caring and capable, which the brain receives as a positive signal rather than an accusation.

Loss framing versus gain framing is another consideration. Emergency appeals often naturally use loss framing ("If we don't act, lives will be lost."), which is powerful for urgency because people generally want to prevent harm. But pure loss framing can also induce that helpless feeling if overdone. A mix—"If we act, we can save lives; if we don't, here's what's at stake."—gives both the jolt and the agency. Research in consumer behavior during crises such as the study by Williams et al. (2014) suggests that making the situation feel immediate and psychologically close heightens emotional response. So framing language to emphasize the present ("right now," "today," "in this very moment") and concrete specifics ("a truck of supplies by Friday") can bypass the brain's tendency to distance itself. The message doesn't get put off to "I'll deal with this later" because it implicitly conveys there is no later to wait for. Additionally, clarity and simplicity in language are crucial. In a crisis, people's cognitive load is often high—they're processing a lot of info and emotions. If our appeals are mired in jargon or complex project details, a donor's brain may raise a defense simply by tuning out ("This is too complicated."). Clear, plain language with a logical flow helps the brain follow along without friction. Think of it as removing speed bumps on the road from the donor's mind to their heart.

One subtle yet powerful framing tool is story resolution. Start with a problem, but end (or at least include) a resolution that the donor can be part of. For example: "X is suffering because of Y. It's devastating. But Z is helping by doing A, B, C. You can join Z to change X's story." This frames the donor not as an outsider being guilted, but as a potential insider, a protagonist who can step in. It aligns with the narrative our brains enjoy—one where problems can be solved through action. By being mindful of psychological defenses and structuring messages to naturally assuage them, we respect donors' mental and emotional comfort while still conveying the urgency of need.

The way we frame our messages, not just what we say, but how we say it, determines whether donors feel emotionally compelled and cognitively equipped to act. These two contrasting frameworks shown in Figure 6.1 illustrate this clearly. The first represents how conventional appeals often fall short by lacking clarity or resonance.

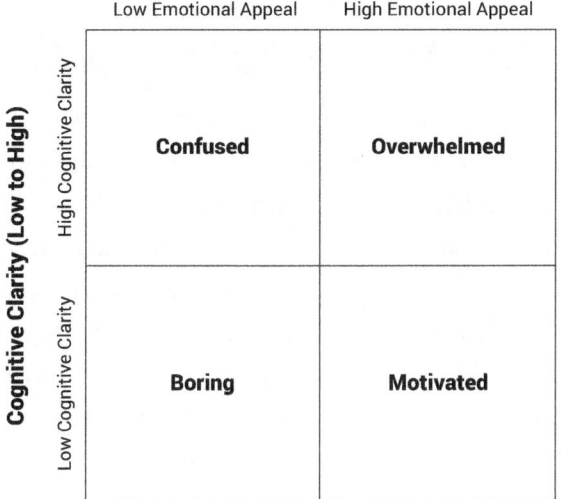

Conventional Donor Message Matrix

Emotional Appeal (Low to High)

	Low Emotional Appeal	High Emotional Appeal
High Cognitive Clarity	Confused	Overwhelmed
Low Cognitive Clarity	Boring	Motivated

Cognitive Clarity (Low to High)

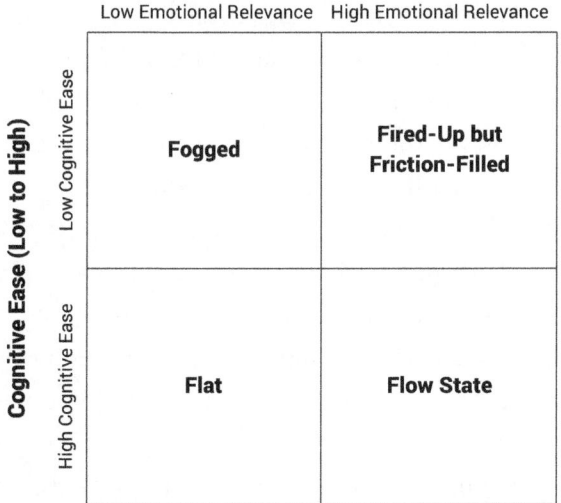

Neurogiving Alignment Map™

Emotional Relevance (Low to High)

	Low Emotional Relevance	High Emotional Relevance
Low Cognitive Ease	Fogged	Fired-Up but Friction-Filled
High Cognitive Ease	Flat	Flow State

Cognitive Ease (Low to High)

Figure 6.1. Conventional Donor Message Matrix and Neurogiving Alignment Map™

Crisis and Emergency Fundraising Neuroscience

The second shows what happens when messages are aligned with how the brain naturally processes decisions.

Fear Versus Hope: A Neurogiving Balancing Act

Fear is a powerful motivator, but as we've discussed, too much of it without relief can paralyze or turn people away. Hope is uplifting and motivating but too much unfounded optimism can make an urgent appeal seem inauthentic or not dire enough. The solution is a balance of fear and hope: essentially, scare people just enough to pay attention and care, then show them there's something they can do to make it better. This sequence maps well onto brain responses. An appeal might start by activating the amygdala with a stark portrayal of the crisis (fear/urgency), and then engage the nucleus accumbens or other reward/motivation areas by introducing a hopeful solution (the potential positive outcome). Consider the two sentences: "A hurricane is bearing down and thousands may lose everything." versus "A hurricane is bearing down but together we can ensure families have shelter and safety." The first is pure fear. The second introduces hope/action. It leads with a vivid statement of the problem (to signal importance to the brain) and quickly follow with a plan or glimmer of success. That brings the emotional trajectory from despair toward optimism. Neurologically, fear heightens attention and urgency via adrenaline, while hope can release dopamine as the brain anticipates a reward (the reward here being a saved life or improved situation). That not only feels good but it also actually counteracts some of the stress response from fear, creating a more approach-oriented state. It's like telling the body, "Don't just freeze or run, you want to move forward and do this."

Solidarity, which we touched on, often rides on the heels of hope: seeing that others are stepping up or that success is possible can produce oxytocin and feelings of connection, further easing fear.

A communicator might explicitly invoke solidarity: "In the darkest times, we see the best in each other." Such a line can reassure the brain's social nature that we're not facing this threat alone. A note of caution: avoid pure doom or pure Pollyanna. Pure doom (all fear, no hope) makes the reader want to shut off the emotion by escaping. Pure overly positive messaging ("Everything will be fine!" in the thick of a tragedy) can ring false, and the brain's skepticism kicks in, possibly even a bit of anger that the seriousness is being underplayed. The mix needs to be authentic: acknowledge the fearsome reality and provide a credible reason to hope through action.

Another idea is to use fear appeals strategically for specific calls to action, and hope messaging in follow-ups. For example, the initial ask might be stark: "Without immediate help, kids will go hungry tonight." But in the thank-you or subsequent updates, emphasize hope and progress: "Thanks to you, kids are eating and recovering." This trains the donor's brain to associate their action with positive feelings, not lingering fear. Some have said "fire in the belly, ice in the head"—meaning a fundraiser should be passionate but also calmly strategic. For donors, maybe it's "fire then light": light a fire of concern, then shine a light of hope and direction. By navigating this balance, we guide the donor through an emotional journey that is compelling but not overwhelming, urgent but ultimately uplifting enough to inspire action.

Temporal Triggers: Now or Never

Crises are all about timing and so are crisis communications. Temporal framing can significantly influence how the brain responds to an appeal. We've already seen how making something feel immediate can increase emotional salience. To activate an immediate neural response, appeals often incorporate what you might call "now or never" cues. These cues tap into our brain's sense of urgency and can even create a slight adrenaline rush, pushing us to act before thinking too long. Phrases like "48 hours left to send help" or "every minute counts" are common for a reason: they instill a deadline in the brain. Deadlines are potent because they engage the brain's executive function (prefrontal cortex) in a goal-oriented way, essentially starting a mental countdown, and also because they can trigger loss aversion (the fear of missing the opportunity to help or prevent harm in time). Neuroeconomics studies have shown that when a reward or opportunity is expiring, the perceived value of taking action can spike. This is related to scarcity effects pushing the "act now" feeling. In an emergency, the reward is saving lives or reducing suffering, which a donor's brain will value more highly if it's presented as happening right now. There's also something to be said about temporal distance and empathy: the farther out in time a consequence is, the less our emotional brain tends to care. That's why climate change appeals, for instance, struggle when talking about year 2100; don't hit our primitive urgency circuits as much. But an earthquake that happened this morning? That's front and center in the emotional timeline. So even for ongoing crises, framing parts of the message in the present tense ("Today, families are facing … .") keeps it temporal and visceral.

Another temporal aspect is speed of feedback. In a rapid crisis, donors often expect or appreciate quick updates, and this can reinforce that their action was timely and mattered. If someone donates to an emergency and hears nothing for a month, their brain might decouple the cause from the action. But a near-immediate update ("Your donation was put to work this week, here's what happened.") keeps the neural link strong between giving and outcome. This also plays into memory: a quick follow-up uses the fresh memory of donating and ties it to a result, which is a learning moment for the brain ("Action led to outcome; do that again next time."). Temporal framing also means being conscious of when you communicate. During a crisis, sending appeals sooner rather than later is generally beneficial because you're catching people while the emotional impact is high. Delaying too long might find people already moving on mentally.

However, within a longer crisis, you might create "micro-urgencies" to reengage people periodically (e.g., "This week, we need to reach x goal to deploy the next phase of aid."). Each micro-urgency resets the clock in the donor's mind and can renew that adrenaline-fueled push to act. Of course, it's important to be honest. Manufacturing urgency where there is none can break trust. But often in real emergencies, there are genuine time-sensitive needs at different stages. Communicating those transparently taps into an authentic sense of "now or never." An interesting neural facet: some folks actually get a little rush from acting under a deadline (procrastinators know this well!). It's that mix of stress and thrill. While we don't want to stress out donors in a bad way, a bit of that countdown pressure can engage a person's competitive or hero instinct—I'm going to beat the clock and help in time! Integrating temporal triggers in crisis fundraising aligns with how our brains allocate urgency. By clearly conveying why now and why not later, we work with the brain's natural focus on the present and near-term future during high-stakes moments. It's another way of saying: this is urgent, because it truly is, and your brain knows how to respond to urgency.

Urgency with Clarity: Guiding Emotional Minds

In the heat of a crisis, communications often lean heavily on emotion—which is critical to spur action. But equally important is maintaining cognitive clarity so that donors know exactly what is being asked of them and how to do it. A highly emotional appeal that leaves someone confused about how to help is a missed opportunity (and can even increase anxiety without resolution). The challenge is that under stress (which our appeals deliberately induce), the brain's higher reasoning can become a bit impaired—the pre-frontal cortex might not process details as efficiently when the amygdala is yelling "Emergency!"

Effective crisis messaging must be crystal clear in instruction and information, almost like giving directions to someone who's a bit flustered (because emotionally, they are). Clarity starts with the ask: what do you want the donor to do? Is it "donate money"? "Volunteer"? "Share this message"? It should be plainly stated. In a state of heightened emotion, people subconsciously seek direction. If our story has moved them to want to help, we should immediately provide the next step, almost like a reflex: "Here's how you can help right now: [link] [phone number] [specific action]." The easier it is to find and comprehend that call to action, the more likely their emotional momentum will carry through to actually doing it. Imagine the brain like a car going 60 miles per hour after reading a gripping story—if the road (to action) is straight and visible, it'll keep going; if it hits a fork with confusing signs, it may brake.

Another aspect of clarity is explaining the use of funds or the impact in simple terms. In crises, donors often worry about where their money will go (partly due to media scrutiny of some disaster scams/inefficiencies in the past). A sentence or two like "Your donation will directly fund emergency shelter and medicine for survivors." gives the logical brain something solid to hold on to. It engages the prefrontal cortex in a reassuring way: "Okay, this makes sense; it's not just throwing money into a void." Also, specific numbers can help—not huge statistics of suffering, but concrete outputs: "$50 provides a food kit for a family of five for a week." This turns an abstract donation into a tangible outcome, which the brain's planning and value networks can process concretely. Clarity also means brevity in many cases. During emergencies, attention spans can be shorter (there's a lot of stimuli flying around). Keeping sentences shorter, using bullet points for key info, and highlighting key phrases in bold can guide a scanner's eye. The brain under stress appreciates when information is chunked and prioritized. Think of how in an actual emergency, instructions are given: short, direct steps ("Exit the building. Meet at the flagpole."). Our emergency fundraising isn't that extreme, but the principle holds—don't bury the lede or the ask in flowery language. Of course, maintain a compassionate tone, but be straightforward in the essentials.

Another component is reducing cognitive barriers: if a donor has to click through three pages to donate, or fill a complex form, that's cognitive overhead that can break the spell. Streamlining the donation process (one-click giving, autofill forms, etc.) is part of communication, too—the user experience side of it. It's like clearing the path so once the donor decides "Yes, I'll help," nothing confusing pops up to deter them. Finally, consider addressing common questions within the appeal if space permits, or in a frequently asked questions link. Questions like "How will my donation be used?" or "Is this organization trustworthy?" may linger in the back of a donor's mind as a form of cognitive defense. Preemptively answering them (briefly) or providing an easy way to find out more (links to financials, etc.) maintains trust and clarity. In short, emotional urgency must be paired with cognitive simplicity. We want the donor's heart racing and their head clear on what to do about it. When emotion says "Go!" and cognition says "I know the way," that's when action happens swiftly and confidently. As fundraisers, being both passionate and plainly instructive in our crisis appeals is not talking down to donors—it's respecting the state we've induced in them and guiding them through it.

Visuals: The Brain's Emergency Fast Lane

We've touched on the power of imagery previously, but it's worth focusing on visual processing as a deliberate tool in crisis communication.

The brain processes visuals faster than text, and a large portion of the human brain is devoted to visual processing. Our history favors quick interpretation of images such as recognizing a threat or a face in an instant. In an emergency fundraising context, a well-chosen image can convey the urgency and emotional tone of the situation before the first word is read.

Visuals aren't decoration—they're decision drivers. A striking photo from the disaster scene can activate the donor's empathic and urgency circuits immediately. For example, an image of a person in distress reaching out for help can galvanize the viewer's mirror neurons and emotional empathy—one practically feels that reach. This primes the donor with emotion that the accompanying text can then build on. Visuals also often stick in memory better than words. Many donors will remember "that picture of the flooded village" or "the video of the hospital running out of supplies" longer than they recall specific statistics. This is crucial for retention and later decision-making—the next time they see an appeal or think about giving, that mental image might come back and nudge them emotionally.

For visual content in crises, ethics, authenticity, and appropriateness are key. Graphic images can evoke strong responses, but there's a fine line between urgency and triggering paralysis or distress. Sometimes a slightly hopeful visual (like a relief worker helping a victim) can be more effective than one of sheer despair, because it pairs need with action, aligning with the fear-hope balance. However, at the immediate onset of a disaster, often the most raw images are what grab attention and convey scale. It's a judgment call—but always consider how an image makes you feel: if it motivates you to help or just makes you want to look away.

The brain's response to visuals is also why videos and live footage have such impact in emergency fundraising (think of telethons showing real-time scenes). Moving images with sound engage multiple senses and can create an immersive empathy experience. One caution: too much visual stimulation (like a very fast, chaotic video) can overload the viewer. A single compelling scene or a testimonial on camera can be more effective than a high-octane montage, because it gives the brain time to emotionally engage rather than just react in shock. Visuals can also be used to show progress and hope—for example, side-by-side images: one of the destruction, one of aid being delivered. This contrast can be powerful, telling a mini-story of "before and after" that underscores the impact of helping. The brain loves stories and visual contrasts; it's a quick way to communicate "problem and solution."

In terms of design, during crisis communications, simplicity tends to win. A clear photo or two, not a cluttered collage, and enough size/quality to feel immediate. Also, captions or text on images can guide interpretation: a short caption like "A mother carries her child through the wreckage in City X" grounds the image in context and often deepens the emotional impact (now you know it's a mother and child, which might trigger parental empathy, etc.). Finally, don't underestimate the psychological influence of colors and layout. Reds and bold colors can signify urgency (our brain associates red with alarms), whereas blues might be used in text for a calming or trust-worthy feel when providing instructions or info. Visual hierarchy (like a bold headline over an impactful image) ensures the brain's attention is grabbed in the right order.

Ultimately, crisis fundraising is about meeting the moment. When the worst happens, bringing out the best in humanity is what we strive for. That means engaging donors in a way that respects their humanity, too—their emotions, their limits, their noblest instincts. The neuroscience insights aren't there to coldly "optimize" dona-tions; they're there to help us align our appeals with human nature at its core. People want to help each other, our brains are wired for it, especially when the need is dire. Our job is to remove the barri-ers and light the path. By understanding the crisis inside the donor's mind, we are so much better equipped to do just that.

Chapter 7

Neuroscience and Behavior in Digital Fundraising

Digital fundraising in the social media age engages our brains in new ways. Online environments, mobile devices, peer networks, and virtual experiences all influence neurogiving. Recent peer-reviewed research in neuroscience and behavioral science sheds light on how social media triggers reward pathways, how mobile interfaces shape communications and decision-making, how peer-to-peer dynamics activate social brain circuits, and how virtual or hybrid events affect attention and empathy. In this chapter, we explore each of these implications on donor behavior.

Social Media and Dopamine Dynamics

Neuroscience of social validation in online giving. Social media feedback mechanisms (likes, shares, comments) tap into the brain's reward circuitry. Functional magnetic resonance imaging studies show that receiving "likes" on one's posts activates the same neural regions as monetary rewards, notably the ventral striatum (Sherman et al., 2016). These regions are key components of the dopamine-driven reward pathway. For example, adolescents viewing their Instagram photos with many likes showed heightened activity in reward-processing areas, alongside brain regions for social cognition and visual attention (Sherman et al., 2016). This suggests that social approval cues provide a neurochemical "hit" of pleasure, reinforcing

151

the behavior. In fact, providing likes to others also engages reward circuits: one study found that when young adults clicked "like" on others' social media posts, their brains showed activation in regions similar to when they receive likes themselves (Sherman et al., 2018). Such social validation can create habitual engagement with social platforms (Meshi et al., 2015). In fundraising, this translates to online donors gaining a rewarding sense of social recognition when their contributions are acknowledged publicly (through donor walls, social media shout-outs, etc.), potentially encouraging repeat giving via these reward pathways.

Dopamine cycles in social sharing and viral fundraising. The cycle of anticipation and reward on social media can become addictive. Every notification or positive comment can produce a burst of dopamine, encouraging users to seek that feeling again (Tamir & Mitchell, 2012). Neuroimaging research by Tamir and Mitchell (2012) revealed that sharing personal information (akin to posting about one's charitable activities) engages the nucleus accumbens and septal area, indicating intrinsic reward. This may explain why campaigns like the Ice Bucket Challenge supporting ALS research spread rapidly: participants not only took prosocial action but also enjoyed the neurochemical rewards of widespread social attention. In an online giving context, donors may experience a "dopamine rush" when their donation post gets likes or when they see fundraising totals climb in real time. However, the dopamine-driven design of social platforms can also lead to compulsive scrolling and attention switching, which poses challenges for keeping potential donors focused on a call to action.

Neural reward pathways of likes, shares, and comments. Converging evidence indicates social rewards such as approval from others share neural substrates with primary rewards. A meta-analysis of 25 studies on vicarious reward (witnessing others' gains) found that activity in the ventromedial prefrontal cortex (vmPFC) was common across studies, whereas striatum activation was more variable (Morelli et al., 2015). This suggests that seeing others benefit (as in charitable outcomes) can engage brain regions tied to valuation and empathy (vmPFC). Meanwhile, direct social feedback such as "likes" tends to activate the striatum in many individuals, much as a tangible reward would (Sherman et al., 2016). Researchers note that the brain does not starkly distinguish between monetary rewards and the social reward of positive feedback—both can trigger dopamine release and feelings of satisfaction (Meshi et al., 2015; Sherman et al., 2018).

For fundraisers leveraging social media, this means that even symbolic rewards (thank-you tweets, badges, shout-outs) can tap into donors' reward circuitry. A recent event-related potential study of online donation pages showed that seeing a large number of peer donors, a form of social endorsement, elicited a stronger P2 brainwave component, indicating early emotional reward processing, compared to seeing few peers (Ye et al., 2022). This early neural response implies that robust social proof on donation platforms immediately triggers a positive emotional reaction in the brain, potentially mediated by dopamine.

Attention fragmentation in digital environments. One downside of the hyper-stimulating social media environment is fragmented attention. Neuroscience research has documented that constant task switching and multitasking online can impair attentional control. Heavy media multitaskers perform worse on tests of sustained attention and cognitive control (Ophir et al., 2009). The brain's prefrontal cortex, responsible for focus and executive function, becomes less efficient when bombarded with simultaneous streams of information, as is common on social feeds. In fundraising terms, a donor browsing Facebook or Instagram is likely experiencing continuous partial attention, quickly skimming and shifting focus, which makes it harder for any single message to stick. Moreover, the allure of novel content releases dopamine in small spurts, reinforcing the urge to scroll rather than stay on one page (De et al., 2025).

This poses a challenge: while social media can bring a charity message to millions, capturing and holding a user's attention long enough to motivate a donation is difficult. Practitioners should be aware that the average attention span online is thought to be just seconds, with some estimates about eight seconds for adult internet users (McSpadden, 2015). To combat attention fragmentation, effective social fundraising content must be highly engaging from the first moments, using emotionally compelling, concise storytelling and visuals to grab attention before the user's focus moves on. Additionally, reducing friction in the donation process (e.g., using autofill forms or in-app giving) can capitalize on brief moments of attention before they dissipate.

Psychology of social comparison in online charitable behavior. Social media naturally promotes social comparison, as users constantly see updates about others' lives and actions. In the context of charitable giving, social comparison can cut both ways. On one hand, seeing peers donate can set a prosocial norm ("everybody's donating") that encourages an individual to do the same. Behavioral experiments have shown that when people are informed that others have given to a cause, they often contribute more themselves, in an effort to match or not lag behind the perceived social standard (Shang & Croson, 2009). On the other hand, seeing extremely high donations by others could trigger an unfavorable comparison or a sense that one's own contribution is too small to matter, potentially discouraging participation. Social media magnifies these comparison effects: donation tallies, leaderboards, or viral charity challenges all make one's philanthropic actions visible relative to others.

Psychologically, people are motivated to maintain a positive self-image and social reputation. Observing friends publicly supporting a cause can spark a mix of altruistic motivation and image motivation, the desire to be seen as charitable (Ariely et al., 2009). Neuroscientific perspectives suggest that upward social comparisons (seeing someone act "better" or more generous) can evoke emotions like admiration or envy, engaging brain regions related to social pain if one feels inadequate or inspiration if one aspires to emulate them (Kedia et al., 2014). For nonprofits, understanding social comparison means designing campaigns that highlight peer involvement at an optimal level. Showing that "people like you are giving" can leverage positive peer influence, while also emphasizing that every gift counts to avoid demotivating those with less to give. Recognition programs such as digital badges for donors can play into beneficial social comparison by allowing donors to showcase their contributions, thereby stimulating others to join without feeling overshadowed.

Practical implications for fundraisers. Social media can powerfully engage the reward systems and social instincts of donors. To leverage this, consider doing the following:

- **Use social proof and recognition.** Highlight the number of people who have donated or positive comments from other donors to trigger neural rewards linked to social validation (Ye et al., 2022). Publicly recognize donors (with permission) to give them a dopamine boost and encourage others through peer influence.

- **Capture attention quickly.** Assume a fragmented attention span. Lead with the most compelling element of your message—a striking image or an emotional story hook—to overcome the brain's tendency to scroll past content amid information overload. Keep content concise and visually engaging to accommodate limited working memory online.

- **Encourage sharing and engagement.** Design campaigns that invite likes, shares, and user-generated stories (e.g., personal reasons for donating). Each act of engagement can reinforce donors' neural reward cycle, making them more likely not only to give again but also to become vocal advocates, further spreading the message (Sherman et al., 2018).

- **Moderate social comparisons.** Frame fundraising goals and examples in a way that inspires but doesn't intimidate. For instance, instead of only showcasing top donors, also share relatable stories of average supporters. This fosters an inclusive social norm that everyone's contribution is valued, mitigating potential negative effects of upward comparison.

Mobile Giving Neuroscience

Cognitive processing differences on small screens. Donor behavior can change when using a smartphone versus a desktop computer due to differences in cognitive processing. Research in consumer psychology indicates that smartphones induce a more emotionally attuned and impulsive mindset. The small screen and intimate nature of phones create what Melumad and Pham (2020) call a "pacifying" effect—users often turn to their phones in moments of stress or idle time for comfort and distraction. This leads to a state of relatively lower self-regulation and more affective decision-making. In one study, participants using smartphones (versus PCs) generated content that was more personal and emotional, presumably because the device makes them feel more at ease and less scrutinized (Melumad & Pham, 2020).

Applied to giving, this suggests that a donor on a mobile device might respond more viscerally to an appeal, relying on gut feeling rather than extensive deliberation. The constraints of small screens (limited text visibility, fewer open tabs) can also reduce analytical comparison of options, pushing users toward heuristic decision processes. People on mobile often prefer quick, clear choices due to the screen size and context, meaning the brain may simplify decisions through heuristics ("This cause feels right.") instead of deep evaluation. Furthermore, mobile interfaces encourage scrolling and swiping, which are fast, stimulus-driven actions; the brain gets used to rapid processing of information chunks on phones. As a result, nonprofits must tailor mobile giving experiences to align with this cognitive style: simple, emotionally resonant messaging and frictionless execution for spur-of-the-moment donations.

Attention span and decision-making in mobile contexts. Smartphones are typically used on the go or amidst multitasking environments, leading to shorter attention spans for any single task. The mobile context often means that potential donors are dividing their attention—for instance, checking a fundraising email while in line at a café or during a quick break. Under these conditions, the brain's capacity for sustained attention and working memory is limited. A donor might only give a few seconds of thought before deciding to donate or move on. Decision-making on mobile tends to favor System 1 thinking (fast, automatic, emotion-driven) over System 2 (slow, deliberate, rational), especially when under time pressure or cognitive load (Kahneman, 2011). Studies using cognitive load manipulations find that when people's mental resources are constrained (as is common on mobile), they rely more on intuitive judgments and emotional cues for choices (Shiv & Fedorikhin, 1999).

In practical terms, a mobile donation ask should accommodate a skimming, hurried mindset: key information (the ask, the impact, the call-to-action button) needs to be immediately evident without requiring extensive scrolling or reading. If the decision to give is not made in that micro-moment, the opportunity may be lost as the user's attention shifts. Additionally, mobile donors tend to complete transactions faster if they decide to give at all—there's often a narrow window between intention and action. This implies that reducing any delay or complexity (extra pages, account creation, etc.) is critical to align with the mobile brain's quick decision loop.

Touch interface neuroscience and donation behavior. Touchscreen interfaces engage the human sensorimotor system differently than mouse-driven interfaces, and this can subtly influence choices. Research by Brasel and Gips demonstrated that using a touchscreen (directly tapping and swiping) versus a traditional mouse interface can alter what information people focus on. In their experiment, touchscreen users considering products placed more weight on vivid, tangible attributes (like images and tactile cues) and slightly less on abstract information (like detailed text descriptions or reviews). This is thought to be because the direct touch interaction creates a sense of physical immediacy or ownership over content—in essence, touching something on screen can make it feel more "real" or self-involving (Brasel & Gips, 2015). A donor using a smartphone touchscreen might respond strongly to vivid imagery or a compelling story that they can swipe through, whereas fine-print details about the charity's financials or long explanations might carry less impact in that mode.

There's also evidence that touch interaction heightens emotional engagement; the very act of tapping "Donate" with one's finger can feel more personal than clicking with a mouse. Neuroscientifically, the somatosensory cortex (processing touch) and even motor-related reward feedback (the satisfaction of completing a tactile action) could reinforce the decision. The implication is that mobile fundraising should leverage rich media and intuitive gestures: for example, swiping through success stories, tapping on impact areas (like an interactive map of projects), or using sliders to select a donation amount. Each of these plays to the strengths of touch interfaces, potentially increasing the donor's sense of connection and immediacy. However, fundraisers should also be mindful of a clumsy interface that leads to mistaps and can introduce friction and frustration, which the brain quickly associates with negative affect, potentially deterring the donation.

The psychology of micro-moment giving decisions. Google's marketing research popularized the term *micro-moments* to describe the brief, intent-driven moments when people turn to their device to act on a need. In a nonprofit context, micro-moment giving might occur when someone feels a sudden surge of emotion—say, after reading a poignant story or witnessing a crisis on the news—and immediately uses their phone to donate. These decisions happen quickly and are often impulsive, guided by whatever information is at hand and the person's emotional state. In the 1950s, Herbert Simon described psychological models of decision-making suggesting that in such hot states, people satisfice—they go with a "good enough" choice that satisfies their intent, rather than exhaustively searching. Thus, if your donation platform or call to action is readily available during that micro-moment, you are more likely to capture the donation.

Conversely, if the user encounters any delay or can't find an easy way to act, the moment passes and the emotional intensity (and dopamine associated with the motivation) may fade. Moreover, micro-moments often have a contextual trigger (time or place). For example, a person may habitually donate small amounts via a charity app while commuting, linking that context to a giving habit. Behavioral neuroscience indicates that such context-dependent routines are stored as procedural memories—cues like location or a particular time can automatically activate the intention to perform the associated behavior (Graybiel, 2008). Nonprofits can encourage micro-moment giving by sending timely prompts (push notifications or texts) that coincide with moments a donor is likely receptive (e.g., during a morning coffee break or when a relevant news story breaks). These prompts should be concise and action-oriented, recognizing that the donor's brain is in a brief decision window.

Temporal and spatial context effects on mobile donation decisions. The mobile donor's mindset can be influenced by where and when they use their device. Unlike a desktop, which is often used in a stationary, work or home setting, mobile use spans many environments—each with distinct cognitive and emotional contexts. Temporal context (time of day, duration of interaction) affects mental energy and focus. Neuroscience research on decision fatigue suggests that later in the day or after many decisions, people have reduced willpower and analytic capacity (Baumeister et al., 1998). If a fundraising appeal reaches a donor late at night on their phone, they might be mentally depleted and either scroll past or, interestingly, could be more prone to a quick impulse donation if the ask is simple (because they won't engage in heavy analysis to counterargue it). Spatial context can also cue different frames of mind—for instance, a person relaxing at home using their phone might be more reflective and open to reading a longer story, whereas the same person on a crowded train may prefer a short, uplifting video.

Mobile neuroscience research has begun examining how our surroundings interact with our phone-based attention. One finding is that merely having a smartphone present, even unused, can occupy some attentional capacity (Ward et al., 2017), implying that mobile users operate with a slightly diminished cognitive bandwidth in general, relative to a fully focused state. Thus, every additional distraction in the environment competes with the donation task. For nonprofits, a key takeaway is to design mobile outreach that is *context aware*. Features like one-click giving (e.g., Apple/Google Pay or saved credit card info) take advantage of mobile donors possibly being in less-than-ideal settings for typing or filling forms. Similarly, using geo-targeted appeals (e.g., "Help families in Des Moines now." sent to a donor when a derecho hits their region) can resonate more because the spatial context is made relevant, grabbing the brain's attentional bias toward local or personally relevant information.

Practical implications for fundraisers. To align fundraising with mobile brain dynamics, consider these strategies:

- **Simplify and streamline.** Given the limited cognitive resources and screen space on mobile, use clear, minimal interfaces. Prominently feature the donation button and use large, legible text. Each additional field or page exponentially increases drop-off on mobile. A/B testing often shows that fewer clicks lead to higher conversion on phones.

- **Leverage emotional appeal.** Mobile donors are often in a laid-back, emotional mindset (Melumad & Pham, 2020). Use compelling visuals and concise stories that quickly evoke empathy. A powerful image or a 30-second video clip can engage the emotional brain far better than a dense paragraph on a phone screen.

- **Utilize touch engagement.** Incorporate interactive elements that encourage the donor to physically engage, like tapping to pick a specific project to support or sliding a marker to choose a gift amount. This not only makes the experience more immersive but also capitalizes on the psychological sense of control and involvement that comes from direct touch (Brasel & Gips, 2015).

- **Timing and context.** Send fundraising communications at times when mobile users are most responsive. Analyze your donor data for when emails or app notifications tend to be opened on mobile (lunchtime, evenings, etc.) and schedule accordingly. Additionally, use urgency wisely. Mobile appeals, phrased as "Donate in the next 10 minutes to achieve x," can motivate immediate action during that micro-moment of attention. But ensure urgency is genuine and not overused to maintain trust.

Peer-to-Peer Fundraising Brain Science

Social contagion mechanisms in networked fundraising. Social contagion refers to how behaviors and emotions can spread through networks almost like a virus. Groundbreaking research using network experiments has shown that generosity is indeed socially contagious. In one experiment, participants in groups played a public goods game where they could donate money for group benefit. When a person gave money, those who observed the act were more likely to give in subsequent rounds, and this effect rippled out to people up to three degrees of separation away (Fowler & Christakis, 2010). The proposed mechanisms for this contagion include generalized reciprocity (paying kindness forward) and peer modeling (seeing giving as the norm). Neuroscientifically, positive social behaviors can elevate neurochemicals like oxytocin, which might make observers more socially generous as well (Zak et al., 2011).

Another study analyzing online donation behaviors found that when users broadcast their pledges on social media, it was associated with more of their friends making pledges, suggesting a network effect (Lacetera et al., 2016). However, in that study, a controlled experiment indicated that the effect was partly due to homophily (like-minded generous people clustering) rather than pure contagion. This nuance is important: true contagion means the act of seeing a peer give causally inspires one to give. While real-life network influence certainly occurs, it may often interact with preexisting similarities and social norms. From a brain science perspective, one person's enthusiastic advocacy for a cause could ignite an emotional resonance in others (through empathy and mirror neurons) and lower psychological barriers by conveying social approval of donating.

The concept of "social proof" (Cialdini, 2009), where we look to others to decide correct behavior, is incredibly powerful in fundraising. If your friends are all participating in a charity run or a crowdfunding campaign, your brain perceives donating as not only acceptable but expected, engaging social conformity circuits. An EEG study by Ye et al. (2022) supports this: they observed a particular brainwave (N2) indicative of cognitive conflict was larger when participants saw fewer peers had donated—implying the brain registered a norm violation or risk ("Why am I being asked to donate if others aren't?"). Conversely, seeing many peers donate reduced that conflict signal and enhanced later reward processing (P3 wave), reflecting greater motivation. In practice, peer-to-peer campaigns harness these contagion dynamics by encouraging supporters to fundraise from their friends, thereby turning private decisions into visible social actions. The more personal and network-driven the appeal (e.g., "I gave and I'm asking you, my friend, to also support this."), the more it leverages the neural inclination to follow suit within one's tribe. Related research has shown that telling donors what others are giving can also influence behavior. Shang and Croson (2009) found that providing social information—such as "Another donor gave $300."— led to significantly higher gift amounts, especially among first-time givers. Social proof, when used ethically, can encourage generosity through subtle benchmarking.

Neural responses to peer pressure versus institutional appeals. Solicitation from a friend or peer can feel very different than a generic ask from an organization. Psychologically, peer requests often carry an element of social pressure or obligation. One reason is that declining a friend's request for charity might threaten the social bond or risk disapproval, which can activate stress responses. Neuroimaging studies on social exclusion and judgment show that being evaluated negatively by peers lights up the dorsal anterior cingulate cortex and anterior insula—regions associated with the pain of social rejection (Eisenberger, 2003). Thus, when someone you know asks you to donate to their fundraiser, your brain may partially treat the decision as a social decision: saying no could subconsciously register as risking pain (disappointment or conflict), whereas saying yes provides social reward (affirmation, belonging). By contrast, an appeal from an impersonal institution (like a mass email from a charity you support) might engage more of a consumer decision framework in the brain—weighing the cause merits, personal values, and budget, possibly involving more activation of the dorsolateral prefrontal cortex for deliberation. That is not to say institutional appeals can't be emotional, but the source matters. A study in the *Journal of Public Economics* found that charitable solicitations were more effective when the asker was someone socially close to the potential donor (Meer, 2011), consistent with the idea that peer influence overrides pure merits of the cause at times.

Neuroscientific research on advice taking similarly shows that information coming from a known, trusted person can reduce activation in skepticism-related regions and increase coupling in reward-related regions (Zak et al., 2011). In peer-to-peer asks, the donor's brain might place a thumb on the scale in favor of giving because it values the relationship with the asker. Additionally, friend-driven appeals often use personalized messaging ("Remember how cancer affected our classmate; I'm raising money in his honor."), which can engage autobiographical memory and emotion networks more strongly than a generic story would. Fundraisers should recognize this dynamic: enabling and training volunteer fundraisers (peers asking peers) can tap into a different motivational pathway than staff-led appeals. However, there is a fine line—too much peer pressure can backfire if people feel coerced. The optimal approach is facilitating genuine peer invitations to give, rather than pressure, preserving the potential donor's sense of autonomy while leveraging the social connection.

The neuroscience of reciprocity in friend-requested donations. Reciprocity is a deeply ingrained social norm and is often visible in peer philanthropy: reciprocating kindness triggers reward-related activity. For instance, when someone is trusted or treated generously in a game and they reciprocate, studies have noted activation in the ventral striatum—as if the brain finds it rewarding to repay goodwill (Rilling et al., 2002). If a friend donated to your charity run last month, you may feel a strong internal pull (a mix of obligation and desire) to donate to their cause this month. Part of this is social accounting—we strive to balance the give-and-take in relationships (Falk & Fischbacher, 2006)—and part is emotional: reciprocating can make us feel good, strengthening social bonds. Oxytocin is released during positive social interactions and has been linked to increased trust and generosity (Zak et al., 2007). It's plausible that when you remember your friend's support for you, that memory (with its positive emotional and neurochemical associations) biases you toward a generous response, facilitated by oxytocin's effect on reducing fear and increasing empathy.

Additionally, reciprocal giving may engage the prefrontal cortex to a lesser degree; it can be a more automatic response because the social norm is well learned ("They helped me, I should help them."). One can see this in donor behavior data—so-called reciprocal donors are those who give in mutual support cycles (e.g., alumni who donate to each other's nonprofits). For nonprofits, the principle of reciprocity suggests that doing favors for donors (like providing value, recognition, or small tokens of appreciation) can neurologically predispose those supporters to give back. Even simple acts like a personalized thank-you note or a shout-out can set up a subconscious urge in the recipient to reciprocate through continued support. In peer fundraising, encouraging participants to donate to one another's pages or to thank their donors publicly reinforces a culture of reciprocity. Importantly, genuine gratitude and generosity, not transactional quid pro quo, should be the tone, since insincere attempts at invoking reciprocity are usually detected and can cause reactance (the brain's defensive response to manipulation, engaging areas like the amygdala).

Identity signaling in public fundraising activities. Many people use charitable activities to express their identities and values. Public acts of giving, whether posting about a donation on social media or participating in a charity challenge, serve as identity signals to one's social group. In economic terms, this is sometimes called "image motivation" (Ariely et al., 2008). Neuroscience hasn't directly measured "identity signaling," but it relates to the brain's reward and social cognition systems. Being seen as altruistic can enhance one's self-concept, activating reward pathways and areas involved in social reward. A neuroimaging study by Harbaugh et al. (2007) showed that donating to charity activated the brain's reward centers even when the donation was mandatory (akin to a tax). When donations are voluntary and public, there is both an internal reward and a potential external reward. The anticipation of positive social evaluation can itself be rewarding; for example, gaining a good reputation stimulates the nucleus accumbens similarly to monetary gains (Izuma et al., 2008). This means that donors may derive additional satisfaction from knowing others will see their generosity.

However, there is a balance to strike, as motivations can be mixed. If signaling becomes too overt (e.g., donors appear to give only for recognition), observers might view it as less authentic, which can reduce the social accolades that make the behavior rewarding. Research in social psychology has found that public recognition can sometimes undermine intrinsic motivation if not handled well (Bénabou & Tirole, 2006). Still, in moderation, identity signaling is powerful. Fundraising campaigns that allow donors to share badges or wear symbols of support (like Livestrong bracelets or charity race T-shirts) essentially recruit donors' desire to broadcast their values. These symbols tap into group identity dynamics: wearing or sharing them aligns the donor with a tribe (e.g., supporters of cancer research), which satisfies the brain's drive for belonging. It also invites conversation and further propagation of the cause within their network. In peer-to-peer fundraising, a participant's identity (say, as a survivor, or as someone running for a cause) is often central to their appeal. They aren't just asking for money; they're inviting others to affirm who they are and what they stand for. Aligning giving with personal identity ("I am the type of person who helps others in need.") reinforces donors' self-concepts and can lead to more sustained engagement, since the behavior is now part of their identity narrative.

Practical implications for fundraisers. Peer-to-peer (P2P) fundraising leverages human social nature. To maximize its impact do the following:

- **Make giving visible and social.** Create opportunities for donors and fundraisers to see each other's contributions. Leaderboards, donor honor rolls, or social media integrations that show when someone donates can activate contagious generosity (Fowler & Christakis, 2010). Seeing peers donate acts as both inspiration and gentle peer pressure for others to join in.

- **Foster community and belonging.** Emphasize the team aspect in P2P campaigns. For example, allow fundraisers to form teams or join virtual communities where they share updates. A sense of "We're in this together" can trigger the brain's group-oriented circuits, leading individuals to cooperate and give more for the group's success.

- **Leverage storytelling by peers.** Encourage your volunteer fundraisers to tell their personal story about why the cause matters to them. These first-person narratives engage empathy far more deeply than institutional appeals. When potential donors read a friend's genuine story, their brain's empathy network engages, and mirror neurons may simulate the friend's emotion, driving a desire to support them.

- **Recognize and reciprocate.** Acknowledge the efforts of fundraisers and the donations of supporters in meaningful ways. Simple acts like publicly thanking a fundraiser or sending a personal note to a donor signal back that the organization values them. This can create a virtuous cycle of reciprocity and loyalty—the supporter who feels appreciated will be neurologically inclined (through positive reinforcement) to continue supporting.

- **Facilitate identity expression.** Give donors shareable content (e.g., "I donated" badges, profile picture frames, or hashtags) so they can announce their support. Most donors won't boast, but many are happy to share to encourage others or mark an accomplishment. Providing a dignified way to do this taps into identity signaling benefits, rewarding donors with social appreciation and reinforcing their philanthropic identity.

Virtual and Hybrid Engagement

Neurological differences between in-person and virtual experiences. As fundraising events and donor interactions have moved online (especially accelerated by the COVID-19 pandemic), researchers have begun to compare how the brain responds in virtual settings versus face-to-face. One clear difference is the richness of sensory input. In person, donors at a gala or meeting experience a full spectrum of nonverbal cues (eye contact, body language, perhaps even touch like handshakes or hugs), which can elevate trust and rapport through subconscious processes. In virtual environments like Zoom calls or livestreamed events, many of these physiological and social cues are reduced or absent. Eye contact is simulated through a webcam but not truly reciprocal, and physical presence is replaced by seeing faces on a screen. Stanford communication researchers have theorized that video calls produce "nonverbal overload"—our brains try to interpret many signals (facial expressions, voice tone, backgrounds) with fewer intuitive anchors, leading to fatigue (Bailenson, 2021).

Indeed, the "Zoom fatigue" phenomenon has been documented, with symptoms like increased exhaustion and difficulty concentrating especially after long video interactions. Neurologically, maintaining focus on a grid of faces requires continuous activation of attentional networks, and the lack of natural movement or orienting (in an in-person meeting our gaze shifts, we take small breaks) can overwork the visual cortex and prefrontal cortex. In-person events also engage the brain's reward systems differently: the energizing effect of being around others can increase dopamine and endorphins (e.g., group singing or applauding can be mildly euphoric). Virtual events struggle to re-create that collective high. However, virtual experiences can still be emotionally powerful if designed well—for example, a compelling virtual reality segment can create a sense of empathy (Herrera et al., 2018)—but generally, the threshold for engaging a donor's emotions might be higher online. Practically, fundraisers should recognize that virtual attendees might feel less naturally "connected" and require more deliberate engagement tactics to keep them emotionally involved (like interactive chats, polls, or periodic breaks to combat fatigue).

Attention and immersion challenges in digital environments. Capturing and holding attention is harder in virtual settings because distractions are just a click away. Cognitive load is a concern: donors participating in a webinar or virtual gala might also be checking email, looking at their phone, or dealing with home environment interruptions. The brain's ability to immerse in the experience is compromised by multitasking. Even if the content is interesting, the medium itself can interfere. For example, in a webinar, a donor's brain is processing the slides on screen, the audio of the speaker, and maybe a live chat simultaneously—this splits attention channels.

If the cognitive load becomes too high (too much information or stimulation at once), the brain may slip into a passive mode where little is retained. Studies on multimedia learning show that people learn and engage better when extraneous cognitive load is minimized and when information is presented in a cohesive, multisensory way that doesn't overwhelm (Mayer, 2009).

For virtual fundraisers, the lesson is to keep things focused: rather than a cluttered screen with many visuals and text, keep the visual field clean and use one primary mode at a time (e.g., show a short video, then stop and have a live speaker, then perhaps a simple slide—avoiding all at once). Additionally, because attention tends to wane quicker online, segments should be shorter and more varied. Research into online attention spans suggests that people start to fatigue in less than 10–15 minutes of continuous screen content unless there's a change of pace (Guo et al., 2014). Immersion, the sense of being deeply engaged, also requires minimizing external distractions. Encourage virtual participants to go full-screen or wear headphones; these simple steps can increase presence by filtering out competing stimuli.

Another challenge is that digital events are often one-way, making it easy for the viewer's mind to drift. Incorporating interactive elements can reengage the brain by requiring active response (even something as simple as "Type your reaction in the chat" or gamified quizzes during a virtual fundraiser can refocus wandering attention by providing a novelty and a task for the prefrontal cortex to handle). In hybrid events (with both in-person and virtual audiences), there's an added complexity of ensuring the virtual audience doesn't feel like observers on the sidelines. Techniques like dedicating an emcee or moderator to interact with the online viewers, or providing exclusive content for them, can maintain their attention and sense of participation.

Multisensory integration in hybrid fundraising events. Hybrid events offer opportunities to blend physical and digital experiences, potentially engaging multiple senses for broader impact. Neuroscience has long established that multisensory integration— presenting information through multiple sensory channels (visual, auditory, tactile, etc.)—can enhance perception and memory. When two or more senses are stimulated in a coordinated way, the brain's superior colliculus and associated cortical areas integrate these inputs, often leading to a stronger combined signal than either alone (Stein & Stanford, 2008). For example, adding audio narration to images is more memorable than either alone, provided they align (Mayer, 2009). In the context of fundraising, an in-person attendee at a hybrid event might see a display, hear a speaker's passionate voice, and feel the vibrations of music or applause, all reinforcing the emotional message.

A virtual attendee typically has just sight and sound; however, creative strategies can introduce other senses or a greater illusion of them. Some organizations have experimented with sending event kits to virtual attendees (including items like snacks or swag) so that during the event they can taste the same dessert as those in person, creating a shared multisensory moment. The psychology here is to create embodied experiences, ones that involve the body and senses, not just the mind. Embodied cognition research sug- gests that engaging the body can influence our emotions and deci- sions (Niedenthal, 2007). Even something as simple as asking virtual attendees to stand up and clap at the end of a speech can increase their physiological arousal and sense of participation, bridging the gap to the in-person experience.

Hybrid events can also use technology like live polls or Q&A to give everyone, regardless of location, a role in the event storyline. The key is coherence: multisensory inputs need to complement the core message rather than distract. When done right, combined sen- sory cues can transport donors into the cause's world—for instance, a virtual reality (VR) or 360-degree video shown at an event can visually and audibly place the donor in a refugee camp, while the room's temperature or a fan blowing could subtly mimic the climate, deepening immersion. While true full-sensory VR for each donor might not be feasible, even partial steps in that direction have been shown to increase presence (the psychological state of "being there") (Gugenishvili & Nyström, 2023). And higher presence is linked to greater empathy and willingness to act (van Loon et al., 2018). Therefore, hybrid events that thoughtfully layer sensory elements stand to engage both the brain and heart of donors more effectively than single-channel approaches.

The psychology of presence and connection in virtual spaces. "Presence" is the feeling of being in a place or experience, even if you physically are not—a crucial goal for virtual fundraising experiences. Presence is a psychological phenomenon supported by neural networks that map our environment and body. In virtual reality research, when presence is high, the brain's responses to the virtual scenario can resemble real-life responses (for instance, feeling vertigo on a virtual ledge, sweating or heart rate increase as if it were real) (Meehan et al., 2002). Outside of VR, even a well-crafted narrative or video can induce a transportive state where someone feels deeply connected to the story.

To cultivate presence and connection in digital donor journeys, storytelling is paramount. A study by Martingano et al. (2021) found that 360° VR videos elicited strong emotional empathy in the moment, but did not necessarily increase long-term cognitive empathy or donations compared to traditional media. This suggests that while presence can heighten immediate emotional responses ("I feel like I was there and it moved me to tears."), other factors like personal relevance and reflection are needed to convert that to sustained action. Therefore, fundraisers should combine immersive tactics with narrative and follow-up. For instance, a virtual tour of a project site gives a sense of place (presence), and pairing it with a live discussion with

172

a beneficiary or field worker can create human connection that the brain treats as a genuine social interaction.

Live video calls have an interesting psychological profile: while not as rich as in-person, seeing a real-time face and voice does engage our social brain (e.g., we mimic expressions, respond to eye gaze). It's been found that the brain can synchronize with others even over video to some extent, reflecting rapport (Kinreich et al., 2017). Thus, ensuring virtual events have live components (not just prerecorded content) can boost the feeling of connection. Also, encouraging attendees to use their own video (for smaller gatherings) or chat comments can switch their role from passive viewer to active participant, which heightens their sense of belonging.

Social identity can be fostered in virtual spaces by using collective language (*we, together*) and rituals (like everyone lighting a candle at the same time at home to signify unity). Our brains respond to such synchrony; doing an action simultaneously with others, even virtually, can increase feelings of unity and affiliation (Valdesolo et al., 2010). Presence and connection in virtual fundraising are about helping the brain to feel "there" and "with others." It won't ever be exactly the same as face-to-face, but through rich media, storytelling, interactivity, and synchronized experiences, virtual engagements can still strongly activate the emotions and social bonds that drive giving. A large-scale analysis of over one million GoFundMe donations by Sisco and Weber (2019) revealed that donor behavior is shaped by subtle identity and social cues. For example, people gave more to recipients with the same last name, and donation amounts increased when donors of the opposite sex were visibly listed. These patterns reflect deep psychological motivations like kinship, signaling, and conformity—even in anonymous digital settings.

Cognitive load reduction strategies for digital donor journeys. When donors navigate digital platforms (whether a website, a donation form, or a virtual event interface), cognitive load—the total mental effort being used—is a crucial consideration. A high cognitive load can lead to confusion, errors, or disengagement as the brain's working memory gets overwhelmed. Cognitive load theory (Sweller, 1988) distinguishes between intrinsic load (inherent complexity of the content), extraneous load (how the information or task is presented), and germane load (mental effort toward learning or the task at hand). Fundraisers obviously can't change the intrinsic complexity of their cause, but they can minimize extraneous load and maximize germane load (i.e., focus the donor's mental energy on the meaningful parts of the decision).

Practical neuroscience-backed tips for this include chunking information: breaking content into bite-sized pieces that are easier for working memory to handle. For example, rather than a long block of text about why to donate, use short paragraphs with clear headings or an infographic. This aligns with the brain's preference for chunking (Miller, 1956, famously noted the 7 ± 2 items in working memory limit). Another strategy is progressive disclosure: only show the donor what's needed at that step of the journey (e.g., first ask for donation amount, then payment info, rather than a single form with dozens of fields). This reduces the perceived task load at each point, preventing the donor's prefrontal cortex from feeling overloaded by too many considerations at once.

Visual clarity is also important: cluttered pages activate more brain regions as the user tries to filter relevant versus irrelevant elements, consuming cognitive resources. In terms of content, using familiar icons and terms helps because the brain can pattern-match quickly without needing to decipher new meanings (for instance, a heart icon for "love"/"fave" or a shopping cart icon for checkout are processed faster due to learned associations). During virtual events, cognitive load can be reduced by guiding attention with verbal cues ("Now focus on this part of the screen … .") or visual cues (highlighting where to look), so the brain isn't struggling to figure out where to direct its limited attentional spotlight. Multitasking should be discouraged gently; for example, an event moderator might explicitly invite the audience to close other tabs and be "fully present," effectively giving permission to focus on one thing. Since we know the brain finds it taxing to context switch, eliminating external pulls can improve the donor's cognitive engagement in the moment.

Last, the use of repetition and summaries can aid memory. People often don't retain everything from a single exposure (the brain might only encode fragments), so repeating key points (not verbatim, but rephrased) or providing a quick recap of the fundraiser's main message or goal can reinforce it in long-term memory. This helps ensure that even if parts of the experience were cognitively demanding, the crucial takeaways (e.g., what the need is and how the donor can help) are not lost. By being mindful of cognitive load throughout the digital donor journey, nonprofits can create experiences that feel "easy" for the brain to navigate—which translates to donors feeling positive and in control, rather than confused or mentally drained.

Practical implications for fundraisers. To make virtual and hybrid engagements neurologically engaging and not exhausting, do the following:

- **Keep it simple and guided.** Whether it's a donation page or a live-stream interface, reduce clutter and guide the donor's eye. Use one primary call to action at a time. In virtual presentations, explicitly tell viewers what to focus on. Reducing extraneous cognitive load will help donors' brains spend their effort on feeling and deciding, not on figuring out how to navigate.

- **Engage multiple senses.** Introduce elements that go beyond just watching a screen. In virtual events, incorporate sound, visuals, and interactive components (polls, Q&A). For hybrid events, consider sending physical kits or using augmented reality or VR components. Engaging more senses can create stronger memories and emotions, as long as each element reinforces your message.

- **Build social connection.** Don't let virtual donors feel like lone observers. Encourage chat discussion, host small breakout conversations, or use social media groups pre/post-event to create communal experiences. Even a simple shared action—like everyone unmuting to cheer at a fundraising milestone—can release endorphins and a sense of togetherness, tapping into our social brain wiring.

- **Test for fatigue points.** Put yourself in the attendee's shoes and do trial runs of events and user tests of online forms. Notice when attention starts to lapse or when the process feels tedious. These are likely points where cognitive load is high or engagement is low. Adjust by trimming content, adding a change of pace, or inserting a moment of surprise or emotion to reengage the brain. For instance, in a virtual gala, break up speeches with a short inspiring video or a live musical performance to reset attention.

- **Follow up to solidify impact.** Recognize that virtual experiences might not imprint as deeply as in-person ones. Plan follow-up communications (email highlights, personal calls, etc.) after an event to reinforce the key emotional moments. The brain consolidates memories and decisions over time, especially during rest, so a well-timed reminder can reactivate the positive feelings from the event and prompt action (like completing a pledge or becoming a recurring donor).

Advances in neuroscience and behavioral research provide valuable insights into how donors think, feel, and act in an increasingly digital fundraising landscape. Social media taps primal reward and social learning systems, mobile giving intersects with our cognitive shortcuts and comfort with handheld devices, peer-to-peer fundraising leverages ancient social brain wiring for reciprocity and peer influence, and virtual engagements challenge us to re-create human connection through screens.

By grounding strategies in this research—using approaches that align with how the brain works—nonprofit practitioners can design campaigns and donor experiences that are not only innovative but also fundamentally resonant with our human psychology and biology. The result is fundraising that feels more natural and compelling to donors, fostering deeper engagement and generosity that can sustain organizations in the digital age.

Ultimately, digital fundraising succeeds when it aligns with fundamental human behaviors and brain responses, just as traditional methods do. This breaks down barriers to exercising generosity in an increasingly online world.

Chapter 8

Ethical Issues in Neurogiving

As neuroscience shapes modern fundraising, ethical considerations become paramount. Unlike consumer neuromarketing, which prioritizes persuasion for sales, fundraising demands higher ethical standards, ensuring donors are inspired, not manipulated, into giving. This chapter explores key ethical concerns, including autonomy, privacy, transparency, and cultural sensitivity. We examine historical ethical violations, lessons from related fields, and ethical frameworks to guide responsible practice. Ultimately, ethical fundraising safeguards trust, donor dignity, and informed choice. By integrating neuroscience with integrity, nonprofits can enhance engagement while upholding the core values of philanthropy.

Consumer Neuromarketing Versus Nonprofit Fundraising Ethics

Fundraising using neuroscience applies neuromarketing insights to charitable giving but nonprofits must tread more carefully than commercial marketers. In consumer neuromarketing, the ethical bar is often set by laws against deception and the market's tolerance for persuasive sales tactics. For example, practices like subliminal advertising were condemned decades ago as deceptive. In 1974, the US Federal Communications Commission warned that broadcasters "should not use subliminal advertising techniques" because they inherently mislead viewers. Commercial advertisers push right up to such legal/ethical lines in pursuit of sales.

Fundraising, however, carries a higher ethical mandate. As described by Rogare, the Fundraising Think Tank, we have a dual duty: a duty to our cause (to raise funds that help beneficiaries) and a duty to our donors (to respect donors' rights and dignity). Fundraising ethicist Ian MacQuillin describe this as a "rights-balancing" approach: fundraising is ethical only when the imperative to ask on behalf of those in need is balanced with the donor's rights to honesty, privacy, and free choice (MacQuillin & Sargeant, 2019). In practice, this means tactics that might be acceptable in consumer marketing such as aggressive emotional marketing or opaque data harvesting are off limits in the nonprofit context. Donors aren't just customers; they are partners in a moral mission, and breaching their trust can undermine not only the relationship with those donors but also the integrity of the cause as well as impact the sector as a whole.

Thus, while a neuromarketer for a retail product might justify a "brain hack" if it boosts sales, a fundraiser must consider a higher standard: will this technique respect the donor, uphold our values, and is it ethical in the fundraising profession? Even if a psychological trigger could increase donations, using it might be unethical if it violates the precepts that nonprofits are expected to maintain. The public and regulators (in some countries) also hold charities to a higher standard of honesty. Nonprofits rely on trust and goodwill, hard to earn and easy to lose, so any neuroscience-informed fundraising must put ethical safeguards first, distinguishing inspiring donors from exploiting them.

Foundational Ethical Theories Applied to Fundraising

We can better understand the ethical lines in fundraising by looking through the lens of classic ethical theories. Each framework—deontological ethics, consequentialism, and virtue ethics, among others—offers guidance on how fundraisers should use (or not use) neuroscience-based approaches.

- **Deontological perspective (duty and rights).** A deontological approach focuses on rules, duties, and the intrinsic rights of individuals. From this perspective, donors must be treated as ends in themselves, never purely as means to an end. Fundraisers have a duty to respect each donor's autonomy and humanity, regardless of the potential monetary gain. In practical terms, this means certain tactics are categorically off-limits if they violate fundamental ethical rules like honesty or consent. For instance, tricking a donor by concealing an influence technique would breach a duty of honesty. A Kantian view would argue that manipulating someone's brain responses without their awareness fails to respect their rational agency.

  In neurogiving, deontology demands transparency and respect: donors should not be deceived or coerced, even if doing so might raise more money. This aligns with professional codes such as the Association of Fundraising Professionals requirement of honesty and donor respect. The "Donor Bill of Rights" in the nonprofit sector similarly asserts donors' rights to be informed and to give voluntarily. Under a deontological ethic, a fundraiser might ask. "Would I consider this tactic acceptable if every donor knew about it?" If the answer is no, then using it treats the donor merely as a means to an end, violating ethical duty.

- **Consequentialist perspective (outcomes and utility).** Consequentialism (including utilitarianism) evaluates ethics by the outcomes of actions. In fundraising, a pure utilitarian might argue that maximizing donations, and thereby helping more beneficiaries, produces the greatest good for the greatest number. From that angle, using neuroscience to boost giving could be justified if it advances the cause. Indeed, many fundraisers feel a duty to ask because their mission's stakes are high. However, a sophisticated consequentialist analysis also weighs potential negative outcomes: undermining donor trust, causing public backlash, or harming the donor community's goodwill. An ends-justify-the-means mentality is dangerous if short-term gains lead to long-term damage. For example, a deceptive neuroscience trick might yield a spike in donations, but if donors later feel manipulated, they may disengage permanently—hurting future fundraising and the nonprofit's reputation. Also, the harm to donor autonomy and privacy are real consequences to consider, not just abstract rights. Ethical theorists note that treating people instrumentally can erode social trust, which is a negative outcome in itself.

In neurogiving, a consequentialist must balance the benefit to beneficiaries against potential harm to donors and the organization. Often, the ethically acceptable path is one of optimal balance: use neuroscience informed techniques to improve fundraising insofar as they don't produce harmful side effects. This mirrors the idea of "harm prevention" in data ethics: nonprofits should prevent not just harm to themselves but also any harm to stakeholders that could result from their approach. For instance, even if brainwave analysis could identify ideal donor targets, the risk of violating privacy or donor trust would outweigh the benefit. The "greater good" in philanthropy is not only measured in dollars raised but also in sustaining a community of willing, respected supporters. Ethical neurogiving, from a consequentialist standpoint, seeks win-win strategies where both mission and donor welfare are advanced together.

- **Virtue ethics (character and integrity).** Virtue ethics asks what a person of good character would do. Instead of focusing on rules or outcomes alone, it emphasizes moral virtues like honesty, compassion, fairness, and prudence. Applied to neurogiving, this approach would encourage organizations to cultivate an ethical culture and for fundraisers to embody virtues in their work. A virtuous fundraiser using neuroscience would demonstrate integrity, for example, exercising honesty about their methods and empathy toward how appeals might affect donors emotionally. Virtue ethics reminds us that fundraising is fundamentally about relationships; traits like trustworthiness and respect are essential to nurture those relationships. If a certain neuromarketing tactic such as a highly manipulative emotional appeal conflicts with the virtue of honesty or care, an ethical fundraiser would avoid it, even if no explicit rule forbids it. Moreover, virtue ethics highlights the importance of intention: are we using neuroscience to genuinely connect with donors and do right by them and the mission, or just to exploit psychological weaknesses? A virtuous approach favors the former, using insights to enhance genuine understanding and connection.

  Over time, acting with virtue builds an organization's moral reputation, which is crucial in the nonprofit sector. Donors tend to remain loyal to charities they perceive as ethically led and mission-focused. In sum, virtue ethics in neurogiving means prioritizing character over any single tactic: even the most cutting-edge brain science must bow to the values of the fundraiser and charity. By cultivating virtues, fundraisers are more likely to intuitively "do the right thing" when faced with ethical gray areas that no rulebook or outcome calculation can fully resolve.

Beyond these, other ethical lenses can also inform neurogiving. For instance, a justice-oriented view might ask if certain communities or individuals could be unfairly targeted or excluded by neuro-driven strategies. An ethic of care would stress maintaining empathy and the donor's well-being in all interactions.

Historical Ethical Pitfalls and Lessons from Related Fields

Neuroscience-based fundraising doesn't exist in a vacuum. It draws from fields with a track record of ethical controversies: marketing, behavioral science, and digital media. Learning from those missteps helps nonprofits anticipate and avoid similar pitfalls. One early warning came from the mid-20th century panic over subliminal advertising. Though the claims were overstated, the backlash revealed how quickly public trust erodes when people suspect psychological manipulation. Today's stealth neuromarketing—using neuroscience to influence behavior without awareness—can provoke the same reaction. Early neuromarketing efforts, such as those at Baylor College of Medicine and Emory University, sparked protest, and in 2011, France amended its bioethics laws to ban the commercial use of functional magnetic resonance imaging (fMRI) in marketing. The message was clear: using brain-scanning tools to influence people without consent crosses a moral and legal line.

While nonprofits aren't scanning donors' brains, similar concerns arise around advanced emotional profiling or artificial intelligence (AI)-driven segmentation. Even well-intentioned use of behavioral insight can feel invasive if not transparently explained. As neuroethicists have warned, the brain is perhaps the most personal space we have. Calls for new rights like "mental privacy" and "cognitive liberty" underscore that the ethical standard is not just what works, but what respects autonomy.

More recent cautionary tales reinforce this. In the Cambridge Analytica scandal, millions of Facebook users were unknowingly profiled and micro-targeted using behavioral science—prompting global outrage and new data regulations. Similarly, Facebook's 2014 "emotional contagion" experiment manipulated users' feeds without informed consent. The result: widespread backlash, not because the science was invalid, but because it was hidden. People don't want to feel like lab rats—especially when they trust your organization.

The fundraising lesson is simple: transparency builds trust. If a donor discovered how you're using neuroscience or behavioral data, would they feel respected—or manipulated? When experimenting with new techniques, err on the side of openness. Just because something works doesn't make it right. And for nonprofits, which operate on public trust, that line matters even more.

The good news: these lessons have spurred progress. The neuromarketing field adopted a code of ethics through the Neuromarketing Science & Business Association, grounded in principles like autonomy, beneficence, and confidentiality. Likewise, fundraising associations such as the Association of Fundraising Professionals, where I'm proud to serve on the global board, and the National Association of Charitable Gift Planners, where I am a member, as well the Chartered Institute of Fundraising in the United Kingdom, the Council for Advancement and Support of Education, the Association of Healthcare Philanthropy, and many other organizations, have updated their codes to address data use, consent, and transparency. These associations are setting and holding the standard for ethical practice in the profession and continuing these discussions.

As neuroscience and behavioral tools become more powerful, scrutiny will increase—and rightly so. The history of related fields shows us: ethical foresight is always better than damage control. It's not enough to ask, "Will this raise more money?" We must also ask, "Does this honor the trust our donors place in us?"

Key Ethical Domains in Neurogiving

Building on these theoretical frameworks and lessons, we can delve into several core ethical issues that neurogiving raises. These include donor autonomy, privacy, transparency, and cultural sensitivity. Each domain is an area where nonprofit practitioners need to uphold higher standards when employing neuroscience in fundraising. However, at its core, remember that neurogiving recognizes that the donor is a generous person, not that the fundraiser is a persuading person. Viewed through this lens, it is the role of the nonprofit to get out of the way of the generosity impulse, to remove the friction, to facilitate the impact and the gift, and to "teach the joy of giving."

Donor Autonomy and Informed Consent

Autonomy. A person's right to self-determination is at the heart of ethical fundraising. Donors should always feel that giving is their choice, prompted but not forced. Neuroscience-based fundraising tactics challenge this if they're used to nudge people against their will at a subconscious level. It's a fine line between influence and manipulation. Ethical theory and nonprofit practice both stress that persuasion must stop short of compromising free will. As Beauchamp and Childress (2001) famously defined it, respecting autonomy means ensuring the individual's informed and voluntary choice. In neurogiving, this translates to methods that guide donors but ultimately leave the final decision to them. For example, using neurogiving research one might craft an appeal that genuinely resonates with a donor's emotions and values engaging their empathy or sense of reward. The donor experiences those feelings and decides to give, which is an authentic decision. Contrast that with a scenario where a fundraiser covertly exploits a donor's psychological vulnerabilities like deliberately triggering anxiety or guilt beyond what the donor would consider fair to push them into an impulsive donation. The latter crosses into manipulation, because it aims to bypass the donor's reflective choice. Academic ethicists warn that if fundraising tactics become so sophisticated that people are "neurologically nudged" without realizing it, true voluntariness is lost.

To preserve autonomy, transparency and consent are key. Donors shouldn't be subjected to psychological strategies that they would not consent to if they knew. Practically, fundraisers can ask themselves, "Am I using knowledge of the brain to help the donor do what they want or to engineer their behavior?" The former is ethical—it respects the donor's agency by giving them compelling information—while the latter treats the donor more like a pawn. Fundraising expert Dr. Adrian Sargeant emphasizes that even in service of the "greater good," we must not strip donors of their agency. Donor trust thrives when they feel their choices are their own. One concrete safeguard is to always give donors an easy way to say no or not right now. Techniques that create a false sense of urgency are particularly suspect. It's one thing to highlight a real deadline or need ("We need 100 donors by midnight to unlock a matching gift.")—it adds urgency if truthfully so. It's entirely another to overstate consequences ("If you don't give now, a life will be lost!" when in fact the situation isn't so dire). The latter is manipulative, as it corners the donor with exaggerated guilt or fear. Respecting autonomy means content and tone of appeals should empower the donor, not overwhelm them. The easiest test of autonomy is asking the donor, "Is this what you really want?"

Many traditional segmentation models are framed around organizational value—how donors perform for us. Neurogiving ethics asks us to consider: how well do our models reflect the donor's mind and motivation? The contrast in Figure 8.1 shows what happens when we shift from extraction to empathy.

Traditional Donor Typology Grid

Engagement Level – Low   Engagement Level – High

Giving Frequency – Frequent

High Frequency + Low Engagement

Passive Givers

They give often but show minimal emotional or personal investment.

High Frequency + High Engagement

Ideal Donors

Highly loyal and emotionally connected. These are your most valuable supporters.

Giving Frequency – Infrequent

Low Frequency + Low Engagement

Lapsed or Low-Value

Infrequent and disconnected donors, often excluded from targeted cultivation.

Low Frequency + High Engagement

Emerging Prospects

Emotionally aligned but not yet consistent. Could be nurtured into stronger supporters.

Generosity Lens Matrix™

Thinking Style – Deliberative   Thinking Style – Intuitive

Motivation Type – Others-Oriented

Deliberative + Others-Oriented

Measured Altruists

They analyze before acting, seeking meaningful impact. Often influenced by data, outcomes, and long-term change.

Intuitive + Others-Oriented

Empathic Givers

Emotionally responsive and guided by instinct, they give quickly when touched by a cause or story.

Motivation Type – Self-Oriented

Deliberative + Self-Oriented

Strategic Supporters

Motivated by alignment with personal goals or identity. Often evaluate benefits or affiliations.

Intuitive + Self-Oriented

Impulsive Contributors

Driven by emotion or immediate reward. Often respond to urgency, convenience, or peer action.

Figure 8.1. Traditional Donor Typology Grid vs. Generosity Lens Matrix™

Privacy and Data Protection

In neurogiving, data is power, and with power comes responsibility. Modern fundraising could involve collecting sensitive data, from online behavior to biometric or neural indicators (like EEG readings, eye-tracking logs, facial emotion analyses, etc.). This raises a host of privacy concerns. Donors have a reasonable expectation that their personal information, especially something as intimate as their neural or emotional responses or as simple as their social media profiles, will be safeguarded and not misused. Privacy is not just a legal checkbox; it's an ethical imperative tied to respect for personhood. Consider that a person's momentary facial expression during an appeal could reveal how they truly felt excitement, anxiety, empathy, or confusion. As of this publication, the technology exists to scrape publicly available information such as social media profiles of a donor and use them to answer a personality test as if they were the donor (such as the big five O.C.E.A.N. test). Using that information, appeals can be created that directly tap into donor preferences that no human could, all without their consent or knowledge. This violates every ethical standard at once. Such information is far more personal than, say, their mailing address. If data is misappropriated, it could be embarrassing at best or even harmful at worst to the donor. Thus, nonprofits venturing into neuro-data must adopt a privacy-by-design mindset.

First, any collection or use of data should be done only with clear consent and for a purpose that benefits the donor and mission. Transparency here doubles as a consent mechanism. Moreover, donors should know what will happen with that data: why is it necessary? Will it be anonymized? Who will see it? How will it be stored? Such openness can actually build trust—donors see that the organization is innovating and respecting their privacy.

Second, data minimization is an ethical principle to follow. Just because a technology can collect dozens of data points per second or score it and apply it doesn't mean the nonprofit should keep all of them or apply them. Collect only what you truly need for the stated purpose. If data isn't yielding actionable insights, don't hoard it "just in case," as that only increases risk. Secure storage is equally critical: sensitive donor data must be protected with the same rigor as one would protect financial or health data. This includes technical measures including encryption, access controls, and policy measures such as limiting which staff or vendors can access raw data. Ethically, that would be a profound betrayal of trust; donors would feel violated at a fundamental level.

By safeguarding donor data, the organization shows that it values the donor as a whole person, not just a source of revenue. On the flip side, abuse of privacy such as secretly tracking facial expressions of website visitors without disclosure would rightly be seen as a breach of ethics and likely law, under regulations like the European Union (EU) General Data Protection Regulation. The bottom line: ethical neurogiving treats data with reverence. Donor privacy is a form of donor respect. When supporters trust that even their subconscious reactions or personal traits are handled with care, they will be more willing to engage with innovative, data-informed fundraising efforts in the future.

Transparency and Honesty in Methods

Transparency is a thread that runs through all ethical principles. It enables autonomy, builds trust, and mitigates potential harms. For nonprofits, being transparent about the practice is important, without necessarily giving away proprietary details. Donors do not need or want a technical lecture about fMRI studies or algorithmic models in every appeal. However, they deserve an honest portrayal that the organization does apply research and testing to make appeals effective and that it does so in line with its values.

What might this look like? It could be as simple as occasional communications where the nonprofit says, "We base our outreach on lessons from behavioral science to better inspire our community." This kind of statement perhaps in a newsletter or on a website FAQ sets the expectation that yes, decision and neuroscience is in play, but it's in service of making the donor experience more engaging and impactful. Importantly, transparency also acts as a moral filter: an organization should avoid any tactic it could not openly explain to its donors. This is a powerful litmus test. If you'd be uncomfortable telling a loyal supporter, "We used a fear-based neuromarketing technique to scare people into donating," then that tactic is likely unethical. By contrast, you should feel fine saying, "We've learned that sharing a heartfelt story at the start of our letter helps readers connect and research shows stories make it easier to understand why generosity matters more than just statistics, so we lead with a personal story." The latter explanation frames a technique that is both effective and ethically sound, and most donors would not be bothered (in fact, many would find it sensible).

Transparency in neurogiving also means sharing learnings and results when appropriate. Some nonprofits have even involved donors in the process, turning experimentation into a collaborative endeavor. For example, after testing two appeal versions, an organization might report back, "Thanks to your feedback, we discovered that including testimonials increased response by 15%, which means we can help more people together!" This level of openness treats donors as partners rather than targets. It can increase buy-in, as supporters feel part of the innovation. Additionally, given the growing public awareness of how data and algorithms are used commercially (people know that big tech and advertisers try to sway them), nonprofits have an opportunity to distinguish themselves. By being transparent, nonprofits can say, "Yes, we also use advanced tools, but ethically—always in support of our mission and respecting your choices." This stance can enhance the organization's credibility. It's much better than behaving like a faceless marketing machine and being lumped in with for-profit actors that some view cynically.

One area where transparency is paramount is when something goes wrong. Suppose a fundraising AI video bot sends out an inappropriate message or a personalization effort misfires, perhaps an algorithm inadvertently references sensitive information about a donor. The ethical response is to communicate with affected donors, apologize, and explain the steps being taken to fix the issue. Hiding or obscuring such incidents would compound the ethical failure. Transparency, in this sense, is tied to accountability. It shows that the nonprofit holds itself answerable to its supporters. Being transparent about neurogiving strategies doesn't mean divulging every detail of your playbook; it means ensuring nothing you do would feel like a secret trick if a donor knew about it. When you maintain that standard, you build lasting trust, the foundation of all philanthropy. Remember, a donor's trust, once broken, is hard to rebuild. Honesty truly is the best policy, especially when employing techniques that could be seen as manipulative if hidden. Research supports this caution: DellaVigna et al. (2012) found that many donors gave under social pressure rather than altruistic desire. When offered a way to opt out before a solicitation, both participation and giving rates dropped dramatically. This highlights how even subtle pressure can drive donations, but potentially erode long-term trust. By keeping things above board, you safeguard your reputation and honor the donor's right to understand how you are engaging them.

Cultural Sensitivity and Global Ethical Variations

While there are some absolute ethical violations in every culture, some ethical standards and perceptions of influence can vary widely across cultures. An approach seen as acceptable and normal in one culture might be viewed as intrusive or unethical in another. Thus, neurogiving in a multicultural or international context requires cultural intelligence and sensitivity. Fundraising is not one-size-fits-all, and neither are ethics. What constitutes respectful persuasion versus manipulation can depend on social norms, values, and even regulatory environments of each region.

For example, consider emotional appeals. In some countries, fundraising advertisements commonly use vivid images of suffering children or animals to evoke empathy and urgency. Donors in those cultures understand this as a usual, if heart-tugging, way charities communicate need. However, in other cultural contexts, such graphic or emotional tactics might be seen as exploitative or in poor taste, perhaps violating norms around dignity or modesty. A full treatise on the ethics of what is unfortunately termed "poverty porn" in the academic literature is beyond the scope of this book. However, it is patently unethical when it violates dignity and consent. That being said, not all emotional images are unethical.

Privacy expectations also differ: European donors, influenced by strict EU data privacy laws and cultural norms valuing privacy, may be far more wary about any collection of personal or psychological data. By contrast, donors in some other regions might be less surprised or offended by data-driven targeting since they are accustomed to it in the commercial sphere. When applying neuromarketing methods like eye-tracking or facial coding internationally, fundraisers should seek local perspective: is this method seen as an innocuous market research technique or as an intrusive test? The answer will guide whether and how to proceed ethically.

There are also differences in how people interpret emotional signals and social cues, which has ethical implications for neurogiving tools. For instance, psychological research has found that facial expressions are not universally interpreted the same way across cultures. A facial coding AI trained on Western expressions might misread an Asian donor's reactions. If a nonprofit relied on such technology without adapting it, they could draw false conclusions, essentially misinterpreting donors, which could lead to inappropriate strategy choices and an ethical lapse of not treating donors as individuals. Culturally aware fundraisers will validate neuroscience-based insights in the local context. For example, the principle of social proof ("Others are donating, so you should, too.") is widely used, but its effectiveness and appropriateness can differ. In some cultures, highlighting that others gave is motivating; in more collectivist societies, it may reassure individuals that they're part of a group effort. In other places, it might clash with values of modesty or independence ("I decide based on my own conviction, not because others did."). Ethically, one should avoid assumptions of universality; just because a tactic is ethical and effective in the United States doesn't automatically make it so in, say, India or Uganda. Engaging local stakeholders or testing approaches with small groups from the target culture can illuminate whether a tactic is seen as respectful.

Additionally, formal ethical codes and regulations for fundraising vary by country. Some nations have strict guidelines against some types of solicitation or specific rules about what donor data can be used for fundraising. For instance, if a country's laws consider psychological profiling of consumers as sensitive, a nonprofit operating there must adjust their neurogiving practices accordingly, even if such profiling is standard elsewhere. The ethical principle of respect implies respecting local norms and laws—doing otherwise could be viewed as a form of ethical insensitivity or even neo-colonialism ("imposing our way of influencing people without regard for their culture"). A culturally sensitive approach might mean forgoing a high-pressure technique in a culture that values polite indirect communication.

Ethical neurogiving requires cultural empathy. It means doing your homework on cultural norms about persuasion and privacy, listening to local colleagues or donors, and being willing to adapt or abandon techniques that clash with those norms. By demonstrating cultural respect, nonprofits not only avoid ethical missteps but also show donors that they are valued as individuals with unique backgrounds. This enhances trust and global reputation. In a diverse world, the most ethical and effective fundraising strategies are those crafted with cultural nuance in mind, proving that empathy, the ability to understand and share the feelings of another, is as crucial when considering your donor's cultural context as it is when telling your beneficiary's story.

Practical Guidelines for Ethical Neurogiving

Understanding these ethical principles is one thing; applying them in daily fundraising practice is another. Nonprofit professionals can follow concrete guidelines to ensure their use of neuroscience in fundraising stays on the right side of the ethical line. Here are some actionable takeaways:

- **Obtain consent and honor autonomy.** If you plan to use any technique, from eye-tracking to AI, get informed consent from participants. Always leave donors room to opt out or say no. Never create a situation where a donor feels their arm was twisted by psychological tactics. Design appeals that invite action, not ones that people later regret under pressure.

- **Prioritize transparency.** Be open about the fact that you test and optimize your fundraising approaches. You don't need to describe every detail of your development strategy, but do communicate an ethos of honesty. For instance, let supporters know, "We use best practices to improve our outreach, and we do it so your donations achieve the most good."

195

Ethical Issues in Neurogiving

- **Protect privacy rigorously.** Treat donor data, especially neuro- or behavior-derived data, with the utmost security and confidentiality. Follow or exceed data protection laws. Use encryption and limit access to sensitive information. Implement policies for data minimization and collect only what you truly need and have permission for. Make sure donors know their data is safe and will never be sold or misused. If you wouldn't want your own data in someone else's hands, don't do it to your donors.

- **Emphasize beneficence and non-maleficence.** These bioethical principles mean "do good" and "do no harm." Ensure your neurogiving techniques are ultimately aimed at mutually beneficial outcomes—more support for the cause and a positive experience for the donor. Avoid anything that might cause psychological distress or harm to donors. Instead, aim for approaches where donors feel uplifted and empowered by giving, which benefits everyone.

- **Apply ethical review and training.** Just as research experiments go through ethics review, consider instituting a review step when implementing new neurogiving strategies. This could be an internal committee or a checkpoint in your campaign planning where you evaluate potential ethical issues. Encourage a culture where anyone on the team can voice concerns about a tactic that feels questionable. Additionally, train your fundraising staff not just in how to use neuroscience insights but also in ethical standards. Equip them with knowledge of these issues so that they can innovate ethically by design, not as an afterthought. An informed team that knows about autonomy, privacy, and so on will naturally incorporate those values.

- **Balance with human touch.** Even as you use AI analytics or psychological approaches that align with ways donors think, keep the human element front and center. Ethical fundraising emphasizes genuine relationship building. Make sure technology augments rather than replaces authentic interactions. For example, use an AI prediction to identify a lapsed donor, but have a real person call to reconnect. This not only respects the donor as a person (not a datapoint) but also serves as a check; humans are more likely to catch when something "doesn't feel right." As a rule, if a tactic would make you feel uncomfortable as a donor, trust that instinct.

- **Stay informed and involve stakeholders.** The ethical landscape is changing. What's acceptable can change as society and technology change. Keep up with the latest discussions on neuroethics and fundraising ethics. Involve diverse stakeholders in discussions, including program staff, donors, and community members to get feedback on whether your approaches align with your mission and values. Sometimes an outside perspective can flag an issue we're blind to internally. By proactively seeking such feedback, you demonstrate accountability.

Following these guidelines helps ensure that neurogiving remains a force for good. When done right, leveraging neuroscience can deepen donor engagement in ways that respect and even delight supporters, for example, by communicating more empathetically, personalizing outreach to donor preferences, or discovering what truly inspires generosity can unlock a donor's truest philanthropic intentions. The key is always to use these powers responsibly. Neurogiving, under strong ethical guardrails, should embrace the spirit of one of the early leaders of the fundraising profession, Hank Rosso, and his definition of fundraising, "the gentle art of teaching people the joy of giving." At its best, neurogiving is scientific insights used gently to enlighten and inspire, never to manipulate or coerce.

An ethically grounded approach to neurogiving is both an obligation and an opportunity. Nonprofit professionals must distinguish their practices from the harder-edged world of consumer neuromarketing by adhering to higher ethical standards, centered on respect for donor autonomy, robust consent and privacy protections, transparency about methods, and sensitivity to cultural context. In a very real sense, how you raise the money is as important as how much money you raise. A donor whose mind and heart are engaged with integrity today will remain a loyal supporter tomorrow. By weaving ethical considerations into the DNA of neurogiving, nonprofits can harness the exciting insights of brain science while staying true to their core values, treating every donor as a free, valued partner in doing good.

Chapter 9

The Future of Neurogiving: Designing for Adaptive Attention, Mediated Trust, and Message Resonance

Future-ready fundraising means designing for adaptive attention, mediated trust, and message resonance, all anchored in ethical experimentation. In other words, the fundraisers of tomorrow will capture donors' scarce attention in a distracting world, cultivate trust even through digital or artificial intelligence (AI)-mediated channels, and craft resonant messages that truly connect with diverse donors' values and identities. Crucially, all of this must be done through a lens of ethical experimentation—trying new approaches, measuring what works, but never at the cost of integrity or genuine human connection. This final chapter explores how we can embrace neuroscience and behavioral science insights to prepare for the future of fundraising while keeping our practices ethical, human-centered, and inclusive.

Adaptive Attention: Capturing Focus in a Distracted World

Modern donors live in an age of distraction. With smartphones buzzing and endless information streams, attention is one of the scarcest resources in fundraising today. Studies show that the average person's focus on a task has shrunk dramatically since the new millennium from a few minutes to well under a minute on average (Mark, 2023)! People multitask and toggle between content in fragmented bursts, which means even the most heartfelt nonprofit message might be glanced at for mere seconds before something else pulls the mind away (Ophir et al., 2009).

This isn't because donors don't care or are less generous; it's because they're overwhelmed. Neuroscience explains why this is happening. Constant exposure to new content (notifications, social media feeds, emails) trains the brain to crave novelty. Each ping or update can release a little hit of dopamine, reinforcing a cycle of scrolling and skimming. Over time, donors' brains get used to quick hits of information and may find it harder to engage deeply with long appeals or dense data. In short, the way people pay attention is changing, and fundraisers need to adapt.

How do we design for "adaptive attention"? First, by acknowledging reality: we must earn attention through clarity, relevance, and emotional appeal. Rather than sending lengthy newsletters or complex annual reports with the expectation of full readership, future-ready fundraisers focus on concise, engaging communication. This might mean using a striking image or story snippet at the top of an email to hook the reader, or breaking content into bite-sized pieces that can be easily absorbed. It also means repeating key points across multiple channels—understanding that a donor might catch part of your message on social media, then see a follow-up email, each reinforcing the other. Consistency and brevity can work hand-in-hand: the same core story or message, distilled to its emotional essence, can be communicated in 90 seconds of video or a single compelling photo with a few lines of text.

Importantly, designing for adaptive attention isn't about dumbing down your content; it's about smart framing. The goal is to respect the donor's limited time and mental bandwidth. For example, leading with an individual beneficiary's story can immediately engage empathy (the "identifiable individual" effect), grabbing attention more effectively than a statistic leading paragraph. Visual cues like bold headings, infographics, or progress bars can guide the scanning eye to what matters most.

We can also leverage timing: if data (or common sense) shows your donors tend to read emails in the evening, or that they respond on weekends when they have more leisure, adapt your send times for when attention is less fragmented. In essence, meet donors where their attention currently lives.

Finally, remember that adaptive attention design is an ongoing process. As attention spans and media habits evolve, fundraisers should treat their communications strategy as a living experiment. Try different formats—short videos, interactive quizzes, minimalist emails—and see which ones hold your audience's focus. Use metrics like open rates, click-throughs, or time on page as feedback. If something isn't capturing interest, be willing to tweak it. This spirit of continuous learning (a theme we'll return to with ethical experimentation) ensures you don't lose donors simply because you failed to adapt to how they consume information. By aligning with donors' brains as they are—busy, curious, and quick to move on—you set the stage for your message to actually land.

Mediated Trust: Building Confidence in a Tech-Mediated World

Trust has always been the bedrock of donor relationships. Donors give to organizations they believe are competent, honest, and aligned with their values. Traditionally, trust was built through personal interactions: coffee meetings, phone calls, seeing programs in action. But today, and even more so in the future, many donor interactions are mediated by technology. From algorithm-curated social media feeds to AI-driven chatbots answering donor questions, there are fewer in-person touchpoints, especially in early donor engagement.

This raises an important question: how do we build and maintain trust when our communication is filtered through screens, algorithms, and automation? The answer lies in being intentionally transparent and human-centered, even within digital channels. Research shows the fundamentals of trust haven't changed: people still look for transparency, reliability, empathy, and competence from nonprofits. Our proprietary study, Donor Perceptions of AI, found that 93% of donors value transparency in how nonprofits use AI (Koshy & Chappell, 2024). Many donors support the use of AI for efficiency but they want to know when it's being used and how. What's changing is the medium through which those qualities must be conveyed.

For instance, if your organization uses AI to personalize emails or handle inquiries, let donors know in a straightforward way. Being upfront—for example, a section on your website that describes how your organization uses (or doesn't use) AI can actually boost credibility. Donors tend to appreciate honesty about AI use; in fact, many support it if it improves efficiency, as long as it's not hidden or pretending to be human (Koshy & Chappell, 2024). The moment a supporter senses they are being deceived (say, a chatbot masquerading as a person), trust erodes.

So, one guide for the future: use high-tech tools, but be higher trust. In practice this means using technology to serve the mission and the relationship, not to pull a fast one on donors. Let them know people still come first. Equally critical is preserving a human touch wherever it counts. Technology should augment, not replace, human connection. For example, an AI chatbot might answer basic questions 24/7—"What's your tax ID?" or "How do I make a stock gift?"—which is convenient for everyone, especially in the middle of the night. But as soon as a conversation gets emotional or complex ("I'm not sure my donation will be enough to honor my late father's memory ...."), the system should hand off to a compassionate human staff member. This kind of hybrid approach ensures that donors feel there is a caring person behind the tech.

Donors still fundamentally trust people and genuine empathy, not machines alone. In fact, our study demonstrated that they care more about human connection than their own privacy (Koshy & Chappell, 2024)! So you might deploy all the latest tech for efficiency, but also schedule personal calls, handwritten notes, or live virtual chats to remind supporters that real humans value their involvement. We should also recognize that trust building may look different for different audiences. A donor who frequently chats with Alexa or Siri might be perfectly comfortable with an AI-driven donation experience and might even find it modern and impressive. By contrast, another donor might find the same experience impersonal or suspicious, preferring a live phone call or a face-to-face meeting.

Future-ready fundraisers will segment their approach to trust: meet donors where they are, not where the technology is. Offer options—for example, allow donors to choose if they want an "instant AI assistant response" or to "hear from a human team member." Empowering donors with such choices signals respect and builds trust through autonomy. Autonomy, as self-determination theory researchers Edward Deci and Richard Ryan (2000) have shown, is key to people feeling respected and satisfied—even in donor relationships, giving supporters some control over how they interact with you can increase their comfort and loyalty.

Beyond transparency and choice, think about how to convey warmth and authenticity over digital channels. Can a piece of software evoke empathy? Surprisingly, with good design, it can come close. An emotionally resonant story told via video or a heartfelt testimonial in an email can trigger the same oxytocin-fueled feelings of connection that an in-person story might. The content still needs to be genuine and human, even if the delivery is digital.

For instance, if you use an algorithm to recommend stories to a donor (perhaps noting that they clicked on climate change content before, so they'll likely enjoy a new climate project update), that personalization can deepen trust if the story itself is real and meaningful. The donor might think, "Wow, they really understand what I care about," rather than "Yikes, they're monitoring my every click"; the difference lies in tone and intent. Always frame personalized outreach as thoughtfulness ("We remembered what you care about.") rather than surveillance. A potential pitfall here is the "personalization paradox"—donors appreciate relevant, tailored content, but if it's too precise or incessant, they may feel their privacy invaded (Aguirre et al., 2015). For example, referencing a donor's exact browsing behavior ("We noticed you spent 5 minutes on our scholarship fund page at 2 a.m. last Sunday ....") will likely creep them out. However, referencing their broadly expressed interests or past support ("You mentioned loving our education initiatives—here's an update on the school you helped build.") feels respectful and appreciative.

The lesson is to personalize with sincerity and restraint. Make the donor feel seen, not scrutinized. Finally, data ethics are paramount in building mediated trust. As nonprofits collect more data and use more tools, they must safeguard donors' information and communicate their practices. A small organization might simply reassure donors, "We will never share or sell your contact info, and we use your data only to improve your experience with us." A larger one might even adopt a public data privacy policy or AI ethics statement. In the coming years, we may see nonprofits touting "ethical tech" badges, similar to privacy seals, to visibly commit to responsible use of technology.

All these efforts boil down to this: trust in a digital world is still earned by character and transparency. Whether interactions happen face-to-face or via app, donors will gravitate to organizations that respect their intelligence, honor their preferences, protect their data, and treat them like partners, not ATM machines. If we can do that, technology becomes an enhancement to trust rather than a barrier. In sum, building mediated trust means proactively infusing every tech touchpoint with honesty, options, and warmth. The medium may be AI, email, or virtual reality headset but the message to the donor is we care about you. The old truth holds: people give to people, and even in the future, our job is to make sure our use of tools never obscures the humanity at the core of philanthropy.

Message Resonance: Crafting Appeals That Truly Connect

In a noisy environment with diverse audiences, relevance is everything. "Message resonance" means your communication deeply connects with a donor's own motivations, values, or identity. The science of neurogiving tells us that when a message resonates, it doesn't just make a donor say "Nice story!"—it can literally activate the brain's reward centers and emotional circuits, giving the donor that warm glow or "this is me" feeling that spurs engagement and activates their inherent generosity.

How do we achieve that resonance? By knowing our donors and tailoring our approach, ethically, to different segments and individuals. One-size-fits-all messaging is becoming a thing of the past. Donors are diverse: culturally, generationally, psychologically. The future of fundraising embraces this diversity through both hyper-personalization and smart segmentation. Imagine it's 2030 and you can customize appeals almost down to the individual—your emails, videos, and web content adjust automatically based on each donor's past interactions and preferences. In fact, that future is already unfolding: nonprofits today have access to tools (often powered by AI) that can send "recommended for you" content much like Netflix suggests shows or Amazon suggests products.

Done well, this level of personalization can make donors feel truly seen and valued. For example, mentioning a donor's specific past contribution ("Your gift of $100 last year provided clean water for 3 families") and tying it to their personal passion ("… and we know safe water is a cause close to your heart.") can be incredibly validating. It tells the donor that their involvement matters and that you remember what they care about. This positive effect of personalization is backed by psychology. People are motivated when their actions align with their identity—a concept in self-perception theory. If your message reinforces a donor's cherished identity ("You are the kind of person who protects the planet." or "You're a generous community builder."), it resonates deeply and encourages continued action. Essentially, personalization can act like a mirror for their values, reflecting back the best version of themselves.

Additionally, neuroscience research suggests that tailoring content format to a person's cognitive style can increase engagement. Some supporters light up at an emotional story, others perk up when they see data and facts, and others respond to visuals. If you know a donor tends to click on infographic links but not long testimonies, you might adjust what you send them. Aligning your communication with each donor's "brain style" increases the chance it feels right to them—that's resonance. However, there's a fine line to walk. Tailoring content also carries risks if misused or overdone. One risk is creating an echo chamber of only what the donor already likes. If we only ever show donors content exactly matching their past behavior, they might never discover other aspects of our work, and their relationship with the organization stays narrow. For instance, a donor who gave to a children's education project might also care about the environment if inspired, but if our algorithm decides "only send education content," we miss the chance to engage them more broadly. So while we tailor for resonance, we should still occasionally invite donors to explore new areas—respectfully and based on genuine overlaps in values ("We know you care about children's health, and clean water is essential to healthy kids … ."). This way, personalization doesn't become a silo.

Use the data donors knowingly give you (their past donations, survey responses, newsletter clicks) more than data scraped without their awareness. And when you do use data, frame it as thoughtfulness: "You mentioned in our survey that you're interested in volunteer opportunities, so we wanted to personally invite you to our community day." This approach is both personalized and permission-based. Crucially, personalization must always be done in service of the donor's experience and the mission, not as a trick to boost short-term revenue. Ethical neurogiving means inspiring, not manipulating. For example, if our data shows a particular donor often gives when a story makes them feel a bit guilty, we should not exploit that by constantly pushing guilt-laden narratives at them. Yes, we want messages to resonate—but not by preying on emotional vulnerabilities. The goal is to uplift and engage donors, helping them feel more connected to the cause, not to trap them in uncomfortable emotions. As a guide, any tailored message should pass an ethics test: would you be comfortable explaining to the donor how and why you tailored it this way? If the answer is yes (because it was to better honor their interests or give them a better experience), you're likely on solid ground. If the answer is no (because you targeted a fear or took advantage of information they didn't know you had), then it's time to rethink.

Cultural background is another critical factor. What resonates in one cultural context might fall flat or even backfire in another. In practice, crafting resonant messages means doing your homework and perhaps dividing your communications strategies: by donor persona, generation, cultural community, or even communication preference. Many organizations already segment their donor lists (by giving level or interests); in the future, segmentation will become even more nuanced, incorporating behavioral and neuro insights. We might have segments like "story-driven empathizers," "analytics-minded impact planners," "community-oriented givers," "recognition seekers," and so on and tailor content for each. The key is that whatever defines a segment should be used to enhance the donor's experience.

If a subset of donors never clicks video links but always reads case studies, give them more rich text stories. If another subset responds to energetic calls to action on social media, focus on engaging them there with shareable content. As you personalize and segment, keep checking in with donors. If a donor indicates "I love the updates about the people I help," that's resonance—keep it up. If another says, "I've been getting a lot of emails that don't interest me," that's a cue to adjust (or to send fewer but more relevant communications). Inviting feedback and listening is part of resonance, too—it shows you care about what they want to hear about.

And of course, always allow donors to opt out or change their preferences; nothing kills resonance like feeling trapped. We'll talk more about feedback loops shortly, but it's worth noting here that resonance is a two-way street: when donors feel a message really speaks to them, they'll often let you know through engagement, and when it doesn't, their disengagement is valuable information so you can realign.

Bringing it all together, "message resonance" in future fundrais-ing means being both smarter and kinder with our communications. Smarter, because we use data and science to align with how differ-ent people think and feel. Kinder, because we use that knowledge to make donors feel good and appreciated, not to manipulate or pressure them. When a campaign is truly resonant, donors often think, "This organization really understands me and what I care about." They feel a personal connection that goes beyond the generic charity-donor transaction. And that feeling—of being understood and valued—is incredibly powerful. It builds loyalty, fosters joy in giving, and ultimately leads to a more fulfilling partnership for both donor and organization.

Anchoring Everything in Ethical Experimentation

We've talked about attention, trust, and resonance as keys to future fundraising success. Underlying all of these is a practice that brings them to life: experimentation. The pace of change in technology and donor behavior means that what worked last year will not work next year. The only way to keep up and truly discover what resonates with your donors is to continually test, learn, and adapt. However, this cannot be a free-for-all—it must be ethical experimentation. That means trying new strategies in a way that respects donors, honors their dignity, and upholds your mission's values.

What does ethical experimentation look like in fundraising? It might help to contrast it with what it is not. It's not randomly testing gimmicks on donors with a "whatever gets more money" mentality. It's not manipulating emotions to see how much guilt or fear you can trigger for a spike in donations. Those approaches may yield short-term gains, but they poison the well of trust and run counter to the spirit of generosity and neurogiving. It may result in gamification and the abandonment of the human aspect of the love of humankind in philanthropy, leaving nothing more than a commodified shell.

Instead, ethical experimentation is rooted in empathy and curiosity. You're testing things to better serve your donors and your cause, not to squeeze donors dry. For example, you might experiment with two versions of an email subject line—one that emphasizes urgency ("Help now to save a life.") and one that emphasizes gratitude ("You can be a hero for someone in need today."). Your goal here isn't to trick anyone; it's to learn which tone aligns with your community more. If urgency works better, you still use it judiciously and truthfully (no false alarms or fake deadlines). If gratitude works better, you incorporate that warmth more often. In both cases, you've learned something about what truly moves your donors. Another example: you could test sending a follow-up thank-you video to half of new donors and just a standard email to the other half, then see which group stays more engaged. If the video group shows higher satisfaction or second gift rates, that's a clue that a more personal touch makes a difference—insight you can use to improve everyone's experience going forward.

The great news is that experimenting has become easier and cheaper with digital tools. What used to require costly studies or consultants can now often be done with simple A/B testing tools in your email platform, or small focus groups via Zoom and so on. Even small nonprofits can adopt a learning mindset. Institutional constraints like budget or size shouldn't deter you from trying things on a smaller scale. If you don't have fancy software, you can still do something as basic as sending two different letters in alternating batches to your mailing list and comparing the responses. Or you can survey your donors with free online tools to ask for their preferences and feedback. If you lack internal resources, encourage staff to read up on the latest research (many useful insights are available in articles, webinars, and, yes, books like this one!).

The point is to bake experimentation into your culture: regularly ask "What if we tried this differently?" and then see what happens, always with an eye on donor satisfaction as well as dollars. Ethical experimentation also means accepting "failure" as learning, without sacrificing donor trust. Not every new idea will work, and maybe that new event format flops or the AI-driven newsletter you tried gets lukewarm feedback. The key is to be transparent and responsive.

If something doesn't land well with donors, acknowledge it, adjust, and thank them for helping you learn. Donors are generally quite understanding when you involve them in the process. In fact, many appreciate being part of an organization that is forward-thinking and honest. For instance, you might tell your supporters, "We're experimenting with a new way of sharing updates via text messages. Let us know what you think!" This kind of openness turns experimentation into a collaboration with your community, rather than a top-secret lab project.

Finally, anchor your experiments in your ethics by having some red lines and guidelines upfront. As a team, decide what you will never do, even if some guru claims it raises more money. Will you send emotionally manipulative images of suffering without context? No—because dignity of those you serve and respect for your donors trump shock value. Will you trick donors with "urgent" asks that aren't truly urgent? No—because honesty is non-negotiable for trust. By clearly defining such boundaries, you ensure your testing never devolves into "ends justify the means." Instead, you focus on positive innovation: how can we make giving more joyful? How can we communicate impact more clearly? How can we involve donors more in the mission?

These are great questions to experiment with, and they all respect the donor's agency and goodwill. The future belongs to organizations that pair science with conscience. You need the science (behavioral insights, data analysis, A/B tests) to navigate a changing landscape effectively. But you need the conscience (ethical grounding, empathy) to ensure that navigation never loses sight of why you're on this journey: to do good with people, not to do things to people. When ethical experimentation is your norm, you continuously refine your approach in alignment with your donors' hearts and minds.

That leads to fundraising that not only raises more money but also does so in a way that donors feel great about, which in turn fuels sustained support. In a sense, you create a virtuous cycle: test and improve how you engage donors, which makes donors happier and more loyal, which improves results, which gives you more freedom to further experiment and personalize, and so on. Before wrapping up, let's consolidate some of these ideas into a handy toolkit you can apply in your own work.

Neurogiving Toolkit: Strategies for Future-Ready Fundraising

To help bridge theory into practice, here's a quick reference toolkit of actionable strategies derived from neurogiving principles. Think of this as a checklist or a set of tips you can use right away to design fundraising approaches that align with attention, trust, and resonance insights:

Capture attention with purpose. Design your communications for easy, friction-free engagement. Use clear, bold headlines and compelling visuals or stories to pique the reader's generosity impulse in seconds. For example, start an email or post with a single striking image or an emotional one-liner that creates curiosity. Keep content concise and scannable—assume your donor will give you just a few seconds to decide whether to keep reading. Make those seconds count with meaningful, relatable content upfront.

Design for cognitive ease. In any donor interaction (web page, email, event), reduce unnecessary complexity. Fewer fields on a donation form, a single clear call to action in an email, and bite-sized informative content all help an overwhelmed, generous brain say yes instead of "I'll do this later."

Streamlining the experience (especially for first-time engagements) respects donors' limited attention and makes it easy for them to follow through on generosity.

Personalize, but keep it human. Use the information you have to personalize the donor experience in thoughtful ways—greet donors by name, acknowledge their past support or interests ("We know you care about the environment, so we thought you'd love this update on our tree-planting project."). Small touches like birthday notes or reference to their locale ("Friends in your city have been volunteering this month.") can delight donors. However, always review personalized content with a human eye to ensure it feels genuine, warm, and not overly intrusive. The goal is a personal connection, not a creepy accuracy.

Segment and tailor messages. Recognize that different donors respond to different approaches. Don't send the exact same appeal to a long-time donor and a new donor. Segment your audience and tailor messaging accordingly. Perhaps create two versions of a campaign letter—one emphasizing tradition and legacy for some, another emphasizing innovation and immediate impact for others. Test which segments respond to which style and refine over time. This way each donor feels the message "speaks to me."

Augment trust with transparency. Proactively communicate your trustworthiness, especially when using new technology or data. If you employ AI or new digital tools in outreach, let donors know how and why. For example, include a note: "You're receiving this recommendation because you told us in a survey you love our arts programs." Remind donors their privacy is respected ("We never share your data. This is simply to serve you better."). Also, keep showing the real humans behind the work—share staff stories, behind-the-scenes glimpses, or sign emails with a real name and photo. These signals reassure donors that there are caring people at the helm, even as you innovate.

Close the loop on impact. One of the strongest ways to encourage future giving is to show donors the impact of their last gift. Build this into your routine: if someone donates, set a practice (or an automated workflow) to send a follow-up within a few weeks that vividly illustrates what their gift made possible. It could be a testimonial, a short success story, or even a simple stat ("Thanks to you, this family has clean water now."). This feedback fulfills the donor's psychological need to feel effective and appreciated. It reinforces that good feeling they had when giving, effectively rewarding the brain and increasing the likelihood they'll give again.

Invite involvement and feedback. Treat donors as partners. Ask for their input occasionally—whether through a quick survey ("What updates would you like to see more of?") or in a more engaging way ("Reply to this email with one word for how our last event made you feel!"). When donors do give feedback or suggestions, acknowledge it and, whenever possible, act on it. For instance, if several donors say the newsletter is too long, shorten it—then mention, "You spoke, we listened" in the next edition. This loop shows donors you value their voice, building loyalty and trust.

Embrace continuous learning. Make experimentation a habit, not a one-off. A/B test subject lines, call-to-action buttons, or images to see what resonates best. Try small pilots of new ideas (maybe a text message campaign to a small group, or a new event format for select invitees) and measure the response. Keep a spirit of curiosity—after each campaign or donor interaction, ask "What worked well? What could we do differently?" Consider keeping a shared "learning log" in your team where you note insights (e.g., "Donors responded strongly to stories about individuals; we should include more in our fall appeal."). Over time, these small lessons add up to big improvements in how you connect with supporters.

Each of these strategies is grounded in respecting how donors think and feel. The toolkit isn't about tricks or complex analytics (though data can help); mostly, it's about thoughtfulness and intentional design. Even a small nonprofit with no budget for new software can implement many of these ideas—it costs nothing to write a warmer thank-you, or to segment an email list by interest, or to simplify a donation form. Being "future-ready" doesn't require every bell and whistle; it requires understanding the principles of attention, trust, and resonance and making creative use of whatever resources you have to act on them. Start with one or two strategies and build from there. Every step closer to a neurogiving approach is a win—for your donors and your mission.

Ethical Reminder: How Not to Use This Book

As we conclude, let's reaffirm a core tenet that's been woven throughout this chapter (and indeed, the whole book): neurogiving is not a license to manipulate; it's a toolkit to enlighten and enhance genuine connections. In the excitement of new science and strategies, it might be tempting for some to view these insights as hacks to make donors do what you want. That is not the spirit in which this knowledge should be applied.

So, a brief reminder of how not to use this book: do not use neurogiving principles as a mind control manual. They are not that, and trying to coerce or deceive donors will ultimately backfire.

For instance, knowing that urgency and loss aversion can spur action does not mean you should constantly frighten donors with doomsday messages or trick them with false scarcity. Doing so would erode the very trust and goodwill that you're trying to build. Similarly, understanding that certain stories tug heartstrings doesn't give license to exploit emotions or fabricate narratives. Authenticity is paramount.

Donors' generosity comes from a place of wanting to do good, and our job is to nurture that impulse, not twist it. Remember that philanthropy is about people, not transactions. Every donor is a human being with their own dreams, values, and reasons for giving. Neurogiving insights are there to help us align with those human elements: to speak to a donor's values, to honor their attention and intelligence, to make giving joyful and meaningful for them. If anyone were to use these techniques to cleverly upsell donors on things they don't care about, or to guilt-trip them into giving beyond their comfort, they would be betraying the trust at the heart of fundraising.

As the legendary fundraiser Hank Rosso said, "fundraising is the servant of philanthropy." The science and tactics in this book are in service to that idea: to better serve the donor's noble intentions, not to serve the fundraiser's short-term agenda. Also, be mindful of institutional integrity. Just because we can segment donors finely or automate personalized messages doesn't mean we treat donors like lab rats or data points. Ensure everyone on your team approaches neurogiving strategies with empathy. For example, if a data analysis shows a certain donor segment is less responsive, the answer is not to write them off or hit them harder with asks; it's to understand them more deeply or give them the space they need.

Ethical fundraising respects a donor's right to say no or "not now." High-pressure tactics have no place in a neurogiving-informed future—not only are they unethical but they're also increasingly ineffective as people grow savvy to them. Trust and respect are the currencies of lasting donor relationships, and no neuroscience insight is worth sacrificing those.

In short, how not to use this book can be summarized as this: don't treat it as a cheat sheet for tricking people. Instead, use it as a guide for aligning your work with human nature in the most positive way. The difference often comes down to intent. If your intent is to care for your donors, to inspire them and fulfill their aspirations to make a difference, then employing psychology and neuroscience will feel natural and ethical. If your intent slips into get the gift at any cost, then even neutral techniques can become manipulative. Always check your intentions and remember the ethical responsibility you hold as a steward of donors' trust and generosity.

As we look to the future of fundraising, the exciting tools and research will keep emerging—AI, brain scans, big data, you name it—but our moral compass must remain steady. Use these advancements to enhance the human connection, not replace it. Use them to listen better to your donors, not to drown out their voice. Use them to create more meaning in giving, not to make giving feel like a tech-driven transaction. If you ever find yourself plotting a strategy that makes you uneasy if the donor knew about it, that's a red flag. Step back and recalibrate.

To conclude, the heart of neurogiving is empathy. We delve into brain science and behavioral economics not to strip the heart out of fundraising, but to inform it—to make our relationship with donors more attuned to their needs and experiences. When applied ethically, these insights can indeed lead to more effective fundraising, but importantly, everyone wins: donors feel more fulfilled and understood, and nonprofits raise support in a way that strengthens relationships rather than straining them. That's the future we should strive for.

Neurogiving is about honoring the indwelled generous human spirit, not exploiting it. Keep that principle front and center, and you

217

The Future of Neurogiving

will not only raise more money but you also will do so with integrity, ensuring that generosity remains a joyful, voluntary expression of the best in us. That is how this book is meant to be used, and not used.

Now, equipped with both inspiration and caution, go forth and design the future of fundraising—one that is adaptive, trustworthy, resonant, and, above all, deeply human. Let science be your ally and ethics be your anchor, and you'll navigate the coming changes with wisdom and heart.

The next chapter of philanthropic history is yours to write, and with the right approach, it promises to be a bright and bountiful one for all involved.

Neurogiving

References

Aguirre, E., Mahr, D., Grewal, D., de Ruyter, K., & Wetzels, M. (2015). Unraveling the personalization paradox: The effect of information collection and trust-building strategies on online advertisement effectiveness. *Journal of Retailing, 91*(1), 34–49. https://doi.org/10.1016/j.jretai.2014.09.005

Aknin, L. B., Barrington-Leigh, C. P., Dunn, E. W., Helliwell, J. F., Burns, J., Biswas-Diener, R., Kemeza, I., Nyende, P., Ashton-James, C. E., & Norton, M. I. (2013). Prosocial spending and well-being: Cross-cultural evidence for a psychological universal. *Journal of Personality and Social Psychology, 104*(4), 635–652. https://doi.org/10.1037/a0031578

Andreoni, J. (1990). Impure altruism and donations to public goods: A theory of warm-glow giving. *The Economic Journal, 100*(401), 464–477. https://doi.org/10.2307/2234133

Ariely, D. (2008). *Predictably irrational: The hidden forces that shape our decisions.* HarperCollins.

Ariely, D., Bracha, A., & Meier, S. (2009). Doing good or doing well? Image motivation and monetary incentives in behaving prosocially. *American Economic Review, 99*(1), 544–555.

Avenanti, A., Sirigu, A., & Aglioti, S. M. (2010). Racial bias reduces empathic sensorimotor resonance with other-race pain. *Current Biology, 20*(11), 1018–1022. https://doi.org/10.1016/j.cub.2010.03.071

Bailenson, J. N. (2021). Nonverbal overload: A theoretical argument for the causes of Zoom fatigue. *Technology, Mind, and Behavior, 2*(1). https://doi.org/10.1037/tmb0000030

Bak, S., Yeu, M., Min, D., Lee, J., & Jeong, J. (2024). Charitable crowdfunding donation-intention estimation depending on emotional project images using fNIRS-based functional connectivity. *PLoS One, 19*(5), e0303144. https://doi.org/10.1371/journal.pone.030314

Bandler, R., & Grinder, J. (1975). *The structure of magic* (Vol. 1). Science and Behavior Books.

Batson, C. D. (1991). *The altruism question: Toward a social-psychological answer.* Psychology Press.

Batson, C. D. (2011). *Altruism in humans.* Oxford Academic.

Baumeister, R.E., Bratslavsky, E., Muraven, M., & Tice, D. M. (1998). Ego depletion: Is the active self a limited resource? *Journal of Personality and Social Psychology, 74*(5), 1252–1265.

Beauchamp, T. L., & Childress, J. F. (2001). *Principles of biomedical ethics* (5th ed.). Oxford University Press.

Bekkers, R., & Wiepking, P. (2011). A literature review of empirical studies of philanthropy: Eight mechanisms that drive charitable giving. *Nonprofit and Voluntary Sector Quarterly, 40*(5), 924–973.

Bem, D. J. (1972). Self-perception theory. *Advances in Experimental Social Psychology* (Vol. 6, pp. 1–62). Academic Press.

Bénabou, R., & Tirole, J. (2006). Incentives and prosocial behavior. *American Economic Review, 96*(5), 1652–1678.

Binder-Hathaway, R. (2018). The effects of behavioral interventions on charitable giving: A meta-analysis. *Global Giving* https://doi.org/10.2139/ssrn.3336244

Brasel, S. A., & Gips, J. (2015). Interface psychology: Touchscreens change attribute importance, decision criteria, and behavior in online choice. *Cyberpsychology, Behavior, and Social Networking, 18*(9), 534–538. https://doi.org/10.1089/cyber.2014.0546

Bratslavsky, E., Muraven, M., & Tice, D. M. (1998). Ego depletion: Is the active self a limited resource? *Journal of Personality and Social Psychology, 74*(5), 1252–1265.

Brewer, M. B. (1979). In-group bias in the minimal intergroup situation: A cognitive-motivational analysis. *Psychological Bulletin, 86*(2), 307–324. https://doi.org/10.1037/0033-2909.86.2.307

References

Bruner, J. (1990). *Acts of meaning*. Harvard University Press.

Bunzeck, N., & Düzel, E. (2006). Absolute coding of stimulus novelty in the human substantia nigra/VTA. *Neuron, 51*(3), 369–379.

Cameron, C. D., & Payne, B. K. (2011). Escaping affect: How motivated emotion regulation creates insensitivity to mass suffering. *Jurnal of Personality and Social Psychology, 100*(1), 1.

Chapman, C. M., Masser, B. M., & Louis, W. R. (2020). Identity motives in charitable giving: Explanations for charity preferences from a global donor survey. *Psychology & Marketing, 37*(9), 1277–1291. https://doi.org/10.1002/mar.21362

Chapman, C. M., & Thai, H. A. (2025). Incentivizing charitable giving: A systematic review of self- and other-benefiting incentives for donating money. *Nonprofit and Voluntary Sector Quarterly*. Advance online publication. https://doi.org/10.1177/08997640251348411

Chiao, J. Y., & Blizinsky, K. D. (2010). Culture–gene coevolution of individualism–collectivism and the serotonin transporter gene. *Proceedings of the Royal Society B: Biological Sciences, 277*(1681), 529–537.

Christov-Moore, L., & Iacoboni, M. (2016). Self-other resonance, its control and prosocial inclinations: Brain–behavior relationships. *Human Brain Mapping, 37*(4), 1544–1558.

Christov-Moore, L., Sugiyama, T., Grigaityte, K., & Iacoboni, M. (2017). Increasing generosity by disrupting prefrontal cortex. *Social Neuroscience, 12*(2), 174–181.

Cialdini, R. B. (2009). *Influence: Science and practice* (Vol. 4, pp. 51–96). Pearson Education.

Citron, F. M., & Goldberg, A. E. (2014). Metaphorical sentences are more emotionally engaging than their literal counterparts. *Journal of Cognitive Neuroscience, 26*(11), 2585–2595.

Collins, L. 2023. Giving trends: The role of age and income in charitable giving. Giving USA. Retrieved from https://givingusa.org/giving-trends-the-role-of-age-and-income-in-charitable-giving/.

Cryder, C. E., Loewenstein, G., & Seltman, H. (2013). Goal gradient in helping behavior. *Journal of Experimental Social Psychology, 49*(6), 1078–1083.

Damasio, A. R. (1994) Descartes' error: Emotion, reason, and the human brain. PhilPapers. https://philpapers.org/rec/DAMDEE

Damasio, A. R. (1996). The somatic marker hypothesis and the possible functions of the prefrontal cortex. *Philosophical Transactions of the Royal Society of London. Series B: Biological Sciences, 351*(1346), 1413–1420.

De, D., El Jamal, M., Aydemir, E., & Khera, A. (2025). Social media algorithms and teen addiction: Neurophysiological impact and ethical considerations. *Cureus, 17*(1), e77145. https://doi.org/10.7759/cureus.77145

Decety, J., & Jackson, P. L. (2006). A social–neuroscience perspective on empathy. *Current Directions in Psychological Science, 15*(2), 54–58. https://doi.org/10.1111/j.0963-7214.2006.00406.x

Deci, E. L., Koestner, R., & Ryan, R. M. (1999). A meta-analytic review of experiments examining the effects of extrinsic rewards on intrinsic motivation. *Psychological Bulletin, 125*(6), 627.

Deci, E. L., & Ryan, R. M. (2000). The "what" and "why" of goal pursuits: Human needs and the self-determination of behavior. *Psychological Inquiry, 11*(4), 227–268.

DellaVigna, S., List, J. A., & Malmendier, U. (2012). Testing for altruism and social pressure in charitable giving. *Quarterly Journal of Economics, 127*(1), 1–56.

Duhigg, C. (2012). *The power of habit: Why we do what we do in life and business.* Random House.

Dunn, E. W., Aknin, L. B., & Norton, M. I. (2008). Spending money on others promotes happiness. *Science, 319*(5870), 1687–1688.

Durkheim, É. (1995). *The elementary forms of religious life* (K. E. Fields, Trans.). Free Press. (Original work published 1912)

Eisenberger, Naomi I., Matthew D. Lieberman, and Kipling D. Williams. 2003. "Does Rejection Hurt? An fMRI Study of Social Exclusion." Science *302*(5643): 290–92. https://doi.org/10.1126/science.1089134.

Everitt, B. J., & Robbins, T. W. (2005). Neural systems of reinforcement for drug addiction: From actions to habits to compulsion. *Nature Neuroscience, 8*(11), 1481–1489. https://doi.org/10.1038/nn1579

Falk, A., & Fischbacher, U. (2006). A theory of reciprocity. *Games and Economic Behavior, 54*(2), 293–315.

Falk, E. B., Berkman, E. T., Mann, T., Harrison, B., & Lieberman, M. D. (2010). Predicting persuasion-induced behavior change from the brain. *Journal of Neuroscience, 30*(25), 8421–8424. https://doi.org/10.1523/jneurosci.0063-10.2010

Ferguson, M. J., Carter, E. C., Norris, C. J., & Van Bavel, J. J. (2023). Warming up cool cooperators. *Nature Human Behaviour, 7*, 1917–1932. https://doi.org/10.1038/s41562-023-01694-3

Fidelity Charitable. (2014). Time and money: The role of volunteering in philanthropy. https://www.fidelitycharitable.org/content/dam/fc-public/docs/insights/time-and-money-volunteering-report.pdf

Fields, R. D. (2008). White matter in learning, cognition and psychiatric disorders. *Trends in Neurosciences, 31*(7), 361–370.

Finkelstein, M. A. (2010). Individualism/collectivism: Implications for the volunteer process. *Social Behavior and Personality: An International Journal, 38*(4), 445–452.

Fowler, J. H., & Christakis, N. A. (2010). Cooperative behavior cascades in human social networks. *Proceedings of the National Academy of Sciences of the United States of America, 107*(12), 5334–5338. https://doi.org/10.1073/pnas.0913149107

Freedman, J. L., & Fraser, S. C. (1966). Compliance without pressure: The foot-in-the-door technique. *Journal of Personality and Social Psychology, 4*(2), 195.

Genevsky, A., Vastfjall, D., Slovic, P., & Knutson, B. (2013). Neural underpinnings of the identifiable victim effect: Affect shifts preferences for giving. *Journal of Neuroscience, 33*(43), 17188–17196.

Genevsky, A., Yoon, C., & Knutson, B. (2017). When brain beats behavior: Neuroforecasting crowdfunding outcomes. *Journal of Neuroscience, 37*(36), 8625–8634.

Gneezy, U., Keenan, E. A., & Gneezy, A. (2014). Avoiding overhead aversion in charity. *Science, 346*(6209), 632–635.

Graybiel, A. M. (1998). The basal ganglia and chunking of action repertoires. *Neurobiology of Learning and Memory, 70*(1–2), 119–136.

223

Graybiel, A. M. (2008). Habits, rituals, and the evaluative brain. *Annual Review of Neuroscience, 31*(1), 359–387. https://doi.org/10.1146/annurev.neuro.29.051605.112851

Green, M. C., & Brock, T. C. (2000). The role of transportation in the persuasiveness of public narratives. *Journal of Personality and Social Psychology, 79*(5), 701.

Grönlund, H., Holmes, K., Kang, C., Cnaan, R. A., Handy, F., Brudney, J. L., ... Zrinščak, S. (2011). Cultural values and volunteering: A cross-cultural comparison of students' motivation to volunteer in 13 countries. *Journal of Academic Ethics, 9*, 87–106.

Gugenishvili, I., & Nyström, A.-G. (2023). Virtual reality and charitable giving – The role of space, presence, and attention. In *32nd European Conference of the International Telecommunications Society (ITS): Realising the digital decade in the European Union – Easier said than done?*, Madrid, Spain, June 19–20,. International Telecommunications Society (ITS). https://www.econstor.eu/handle/10419/276663

Guo, P. J., Kim, J., & Rubin, R. (2014). How video production affects student engagement. *Proceedings of the First ACM Conference on Learning @ Scale Conference* (L@S '14).

Harbaugh, W. T., Mayr, U., & Burghart, D. R. (2007). Neural responses to taxation and voluntary giving reveal motives for charitable donations. *Science, 316*(5831), 1622–1625.

Hasson, U., Silbert, L. J., & Stephens, G. J., (2010). Speaker–listener neural coupling underlies successful communication. *Proceedings of the National Academy of Sciences, 107*(32), 14425–14430.

Herrera, F., Bailenson, J., Weisz, E., Ogle, E., & Zaki, J. (2018). Building long-term empathy: A large-scale comparison of traditional and virtual reality perspective-taking. *PLOS One, 13*(10), e0204494. https://doi.org/10.1371/journal.pone.0204494

Iacoboni, M. 2008. *Mirroring people: The new science of how we connect with others*. Farrar, Straus and Giroux.

Indiana University Lilly Family School of Philanthropy. (2025). The next generation of philanthropy. https://doi.org/10.7912/6K69-9W38

Iyengar, S. S., & Lepper, M. R. (2000). When choice is demotivating: Can one desire too much of a good thing? *Journal of Personality and Social Psychology, 79*(6), 995–1006. https://doi.org/10.1037/0022-3514.79.6.995

Izuma, K., Saito, D. N., & Sadato, N. (2008). Processing of social and monetary rewards in the human striatum. *Neuron, 58*(2), 284–294.

James III, R. N., & O'Boyle, M. W. (2014). Charitable estate planning as visualized autobiography: An fMRI study of its neural correlates. *Nonprofit and Voluntary Sector Quarterly, 43*(2), 355–373.

Jiang, Y., Greene, J. D., & Krosch, A. R. (2019). Psychological togetherness increases compliance in joint decision-making. *Social Psychological and Personality Science, 10*(1), 78–87. https://doi.org/10.1177/1948550617742185

Johnson, E. J., & Goldstein, D. (2003). Do defaults save lives? *Science, 302*(5649), 1338–1339.

Jones, P. M. (2018). *Exactly what to say: The magic words for influence and impact.* Page Two.

Kahneman, D. (1979). Prospect theory: An analysis of decisions under risk. *Econometrica, 47,* 278.

Kahneman, D. (2011). *Thinking, fast and slow.* Farrar, Straus and Giroux.

Kahneman, D., & Tversky, A. (1979). Prospect theory: An analysis of decision under risk. *Econometrica, 47*(2), 263–292. https://doi.org/10.2307/1914185

Kahneman, D., & Tversky, A. (2000). Experienced utility and objective happiness: A moment-based approach. *Choices, values and frames* (pp. 673–692). Cambridge University Press and the Russell Sage Foundation.

Karlan, D., & List, J. A. (2007). Does price matter in charitable giving? Field evidence from a natural experiment. *American Economic Review, 97*(5), 1774–1793.

Kedia, G., Mussweiler, T., & Linden, D. E. (2014). Brain mechanisms of social comparison and their influence on the reward system. *Neuroreport, 25*(16), 1255–1265.

Kessler, J. B., & Milkman, K. L. (2016). Identity in charitable giving. *Management Science, 64*(2), 845–859. https://doi.org/10.1287/mnsc.2016.2582

Kim, J., & Morgül, K. (2017). Long-term consequences of youth volunteering: Voluntary versus involuntary service. *Social Science Research, 67,* 160–175. https://doi.org/10.1016/j.ssresearch.2017.05.002

Kinreich, S., Djalovski, A., Kraus, L., Louzoun, Y., & Feldman, R. (2017). Brain-to-brain synchrony during naturalistic social interactions. *Scientific Reports, 7*(1), 17060.

Korndörfer, M., Egloff, B., & Schmukle, S. C. (2015). A large scale test of the effect of social class on prosocial behavior. *PloS One, 10*(7), e0133193.

Koshy, C., & Chappell, N. (2024). Donor perceptions of AI: Key findings. Retrieved June 12, 2025, from https://www.cheriankoshy.com/aistudy/

Krahé, B., Möller, I., Huesmann, L. R., Kirwil, L., Felber, J., & Berger, A. (2011). Desensitization to media violence: Links with habitual media violence exposure, aggressive cognitions, and aggressive behavior. *Journal of Personality and Social Psychology, 100*(4), 630–646. https://doi.org/10.1037/a0021711

Kwon, S.-J., van Hoorn, J., Do, K. T., Burroughs, M., & Telzer, E. H. (2023). Neural representation of donating time and money. *The Journal of Neuroscience, 43*(36), 6297–6305. https://doi.org/10.1523/JNEUROSCI.0480-23.2023

Lacetera, N., Macis, M., & Mele, A. (2016). Viral altruism? Charitable giving and social contagion in online networks. *Sociological Science, 3,* 234–270. https://doi.org/10.15195/v3.a12

Laskin, B. (2013). Thoughts of a bequest gift light up the brain! *PG Calc Blog,* June 14. Retrieved from https://blog.pgcalc.com.

Liu, W., & Aaker, J. (2008). The happiness of giving: The time-ask effect. *Journal of Consumer Research, 35*(3), 543–557.

Luks, A. (1991). *The healing power of doing good: The health and spiritual benefits of helping others.* Fawcett.

MacQuillin, I., & Sargeant, A. (2019). The ethics of asking: The role of donor interests in fundraising. *Journal of Philanthropy and Marketing, 24*(2), e1654. https://doi.org/10.1002/nvsm.1654

Mark, G. (2023). *Attention span: A groundbreaking way to restore balance, happiness and productivity.* Hanover Square Press.

Marsh, A. A., Stoycos, S. A., Brethel-Haurwitz, K. M., Robinson, P., VanMeter, J. W., & Cardinale, E. M. (2014). Neural and cognitive characteristics of extraordinary altruists. *Proceedings of the National Academy of Sciences, 111*(42), 15036–15041. https://doi.org/10.1073/pnas.1408440111

Martingano, A. J., Hererra, F., & Konrath, S. (2021). Virtual reality improves emotional but not cognitive empathy: A meta-analysis. *Technology, Mind, and Behavior, 2*(1). https://doi.org/10.1037/tmb0000034

Mayer, R. E. (2009). *Multimedia learning* (2nd ed.). Cambridge University Press.

McGaugh, J. L. (2004). The amygdala modulates the consolidation of memories of emotionally arousing experiences. *Annual Review of Neuroscience, 27*(1), 1–28.

McSpadden, K. (2015, May 14). You now have a shorter attention span than a goldfish. *TIME.* https://time.com/3858309/attention-spans-goldfish/

Meehan, M., Insko, B., Whitton, M., & Brooks Jr., F. P. (2002). Physiological measures of presence in stressful virtual environments. *ACM Transactions on Graphics (TOG), 21*(3), 645–652.

Meer, J. (2011). Brother, can you spare a dime? Peer pressure in charitable solicitation. *Journal of Public Economics, 95*(7–8), 926–941. https://doi.org/10.1016/j.jpubeco.2010.11.026

Melumad, S., & Pham, M. T. (2020). The smartphone as a pacifying technology. *Journal of Consumer Research, 47*(2), 237–255. https://doi.org/10.1093/jcr/ucaa005

Meshi, D., Tamir, D. I., & Heekeren, H. R. (2015). The emerging neuroscience of social media. *Trends in Cognitive Sciences, 19*(12), 771–782. https://doi.org/10.1016/j.tics.2015.09.004

Miller, G. A. (1956). The magical number seven, plus or minus two: Some limits on our capacity for processing information. *Psychological Review, 63*(2), 81–97. https://doi.org/10.1037/h0043158

Mogilner, C. (2010). The pursuit of happiness: Time, money, and social connection. *Psychological Science, 21*(9), 1348–1354.

Molenberghs, P., Bosworth, R., Nott, Z., Louis, W. R., Smith, J. R., Amiot, C. E., Vohs, K. D., & Decety, J. (2014). The influence of group membership and individual differences in psychopathy and perspective taking on neural responses when punishing and rewarding others. *Human Brain Mapping, 35*(10), 4989–4999. https://doi.org/10.1002/hbm.22527

Moll, J., Krueger, F., Zahn, R., Pardini, M., de Oliveira-Souza, R., & Grafman, J. (2006). Human fronto–mesolimbic networks guide decisions about charitable donation. *Proceedings of the National Academy of Sciences, 103*(42), 15623–15628.

Morelli, S. A., Sacchet, M. D., & Zaki, J. (2015). Common and distinct neural correlates of personal and vicarious reward: A quantitative meta-analysis. *NeuroImage, 112,* 244–253. https://doi.org/10.1016/j.neuroimage.2014.12.056

Niedenthal, P. M. (2007). Embodying emotion. *Science, 316*(5827), 1002–1005.

Norton, M. I., Mochon, D., & Ariely, D. (2012). The IKEA effect: When labor leads to love. *Journal of Consumer Psychology, 22*(3), 453–460. https://doi.org/10.1016/j.jcps.2011.08.002

Ophir, E., Nass, C., & Wagner, A. D. (2009). Cognitive control in media multitaskers. *Proceedings of the National Academy of Sciences of the United States of America, 106*(37), 15583–15587. https://doi.org/10.1073/pnas.0903620106

Oppenheimer, D. M., & Olivola, C. Y. (Eds.). (2011). *The science of giving: Experimental approaches to the study of charity.* Psychology Press.

Oyserman, D. (2009). Identity-based motivation: Implications for action-readiness, procedural-readiness, and consumer behavior. *Journal of Consumer Psychology, 19*(3), 250–260. https://doi.org/10.1016/j.jcps.2009.05.008

Piff, P. K., Kraus, M. W., Côté, S., Cheng, B. H., & Keltner, D. (2010). Having less, giving more: The influence of social class on prosocial behavior. *Journal of Personality and Social Psychology, 99*(5), 771.

Post, S. G. (2014). Altruism, happiness, and health: It's good to be good. *International Journal of Behavioral Medicine, 12*(2), 66–76. https://doi.org/10.1126/science.1136930

Rilling, J., Gutman, D., Zeh, T., Pagnoni, G., Berns, G., & Kilts, C. (2002). A neural basis for social cooperation. *Neuron, 35*(2), 395–405. https://doi.org/10.1016/s0896-6273(02)00755-9

Sargeant, A. (1999). Charitable giving: Towards a model of donor behaviour. *Journal of Marketing Management, 15*(4), 215–238. https://doi.org/10.1362/026725799784870351

Sargeant, A., & Lee, S. (2004). Donor trust and relationship commitment in the UK charity sector: The impact on behavior. *Nonprofit and Voluntary Sector Quarterly, 33*(2), 185–202.

Sargeant, A., & Shang, J. (2011). Bequest giving: Revisiting donor motivation with dimensional qualitative research. *Psychology & Marketing, 28*(10), 980–997. https://doi.org/10.1002/mar.20424

Sargeant, A., & Woodliffe, L. (2007). Building donor loyalty: The antecedents and role of commitment in the context of charity giving. *Journal of Nonprofit & Public Sector Marketing, 18*(2), 47–68.

Schank, R. C., & Abelson, R. P. (1995). Knowledge and memory: The real story. In R. S. Wyer Jr. (Ed.), *Knowledge and memory: The real story* (pp. 1–85). Lawrence Erlbaum.

Schulreich, S., Tusche, A., Kanske, P., & Schwabe, L. (2022). Altruism under stress: Cortisol negatively predicts charitable giving and neural value representations depending on mentalizing capacity. *Journal of Neuroscience, 42*(16), 3445–3460. https://doi.org/10.1523/JNEUROSCI.1870-21.2022

Shang, J., & Croson, R. (2009). A field experiment in charitable contribution: The impact of social information on the voluntary provision of public goods. *Economic Journal, 119*(540), 1422–1439.

Shang, J., Reed, A., & Croson, R. T. A. (2008). Identity congruency effects on donations. *Journal of Marketing Research, 45*(3), 351–361. https://doi.org/10.1509/jmkr.45.3.351

Shang, J., & Sargeant, A. (2024). *Meaningful philanthropy: The person behind the giving.* Policy Press.

Sharot, T., De Martino, B., & Dolan, R. J. (2009). How choice reveals and shapes expected hedonic outcome. *Journal of Neuroscience, 29*(12), 3760–3765. https://doi.org/10.1523/JNEUROSCI.4972-08.2009

Sherman, L. E., Hernandez, L. M., Greenfield, P. M., & Dapretto, M. (2018). What the brain "likes": neural correlates of providing feedback on social media. *Social Cognitive and Affective Neuroscience, 13*(7), 699–707. https://doi.org/10.1093/scan/nsy051

Sherman, L. E., Payton, A. A., Hernandez, L. M., Greenfield, P. M., & Dapretto, M. (2016). The power of the "like" in adolescence: Effects of peer influence on neural and behavioral responses to social media. *Psychological Science, 27*(7), 1027–1035.

Shiv, B., & Fedorikhin, A. (1999). Heart and mind in conflict: The interplay of affect and cognition in consumer decision making. *Journal of Consumer Research, 26*(3), 278–292. https://doi.org/10.1086/209563

Singer, T., Seymour, B., O'doherty, J., Kaube, H., Dolan, R. J., & Frith, C. D. (2004). Empathy for pain involves the affective but not sensory components of pain. *Science, 303*(5661), 1157–1162.

Sisco, M. R., & Weber, E. U. (2019). Examining charitable giving in real-world online donations. *Nature Communications, 10*, 3968. https://doi .org/10.1038/s41467-019-11705-z

Slovic, P., Västfjäll, D., Erlandsson, A., & Gregory, R. (2017). Iconic photographs and the ebb and flow of empathic response to humanitarian disasters. *Proceedings of the National Academy of Sciences, 114*(4), 640–644. https://doi.org/10.1073/pnas.1613977114

Small, D. A., Loewenstein, G., & Slovic, P. (2007). Sympathy and callousness: The impact of deliberative thought on donations to identifiable and statistical victims. *Organizational Behavior and Human Decision Processes, 102*(2), 143–153. https://doi.org/10.1016/j.obhdp.2006.01.005

Small, D. A., Loewenstein, G., & Slovic, P. (2013). Sympathy and callousness: The impact of deliberative thought on donations to identifiable and statistical victims. In P. Slovic, *The Feeling of Risk* (pp. 51–68). Routledge.

Smith, K. S., & Graybiel, A. M. (2016). Habit formation. *Dialogues in Clinical Neuroscience, 18*(1), 33–43. https://doi.org/10.31887/DCNS.2016.18.1/ ksmith

Stein, B. E., & Stanford, T. R. (2008). Multisensory integration: Current issues from the perspective of the single neuron. *Nature Reviews Neuroscience, 9*(4), 255–266. https://doi.org/10.1038/nrn2331

Stephens, G. J., Silbert, L. J., & Hasson, U. (2010). Speaker–listener neural coupling underlies successful communication. *Proceedings of the*

National Academy of Sciences of the United States of America, 107(32), 14425–14430.

Sweller, J. (1988). Cognitive load during problem solving: Effects on learning. *Cognitive Science, 12*(2), 257–285. https://doi.org/10.1016/0364-0213(88)90023-7

Tajfel, H., & Turner, J. C. (1979). An integrative theory of intergroup conflict. In W. G. Austin, & S. Worchel (Eds.), *The social psychology of intergroup relations* (pp. 33–37). Brooks/Cole.

Tamir, D. I., & Mitchell, J. P. (2012). Disclosing information about the self is intrinsically rewarding. *Proceedings of the National Academy of Sciences of the United States of America, 109*(21), 8038–8043. https://doi.org/10.1073/pnas.1202129109

Taniguchi, H. (2013). The influence of generalized trust on volunteering in Japan. *Nonprofit and Voluntary Sector Quarterly, 42*(1), 127–147.

Telzer, E. H., Masten, C. L., Berkman, E. T., Lieberman, M. D., & Fuligni, A. J. (2010). Gaining while giving: An fMRI study of the rewards of family assistance among White and Latino youth. *Social Neuroscience, 5*(5–6), 508–518. https://doi.org/10.1080/17470911003687913

Thaler, R. H., & Sunstein, C. R. (2008). *Nudge: Improving decisions about health, wealth, and happiness.* Yale University Press.

Valdesolo, P., Ouyang, J., & DeSteno, D. (2010). The rhythm of joint action: Synchrony promotes cooperative ability. *Journal of Experimental Social Psychology, 46*(4), 693–695. https://doi.org/10.1016/j.jesp.2010.03.004

van Loon, A., Bailenson, J., Zaki, J., Bostick, J., & Willer, R. (2018). Virtual reality perspective-taking increases cognitive empathy for specific others. *PLOS One, 13*(8), e0202442. https://doi.org/10.1371/journal.pone.0202442

Ward, A. F., Duke, K., Gneezy, A., & Bos, M. W. (2017). Brain drain: The mere presence of one's own smartphone reduces available cognitive capacity. *Journal of the Association for Consumer Research, 2*(2), 140–154. https://doi.org/10.1086/691462

Warneken, F., & Tomasello, M. (2007). Helping and cooperation at 14 months of age. *Infancy, 11*(3), 271–294. https://doi.org/10.1111/j.1532-7078.2007.tb00227.x

Whillans, A. V., & Dunn, E. W. (2018). People who choose time over money are happier. *Social Psychological and Personality Science, 9*(4), 457–466. https://doi.org/10.1177/1948550617705889

Williams, L. E., Stein, R., & Galguera, L. (2014). The distinct affective consequences of psychological distance and construal level. *Journal of Consumer Research, 40*(6), 1123–1138. https://doi.org/10.1086/674212

Wood, W., & Neal, D. T. (2007). A new look at habits and the habit-goal interface. *Psychological Review, 114*(4), 843.

Ye, Y., Jiang, P., & Zhang, W. (2022). The neural and psychological processes of peer-influenced online donation decision: An Event-related potential study. *Frontiers in Psychology, 13*, 899233. https://doi.org/10.3389/fpsyg.2022.899233

Zagefka, H., & James, T. (2015). The psychology of charitable donations to disaster victims and beyond. *Social Issues and Policy Review, 9*(1), 155–192. https://doi.org/10.1111/sipr.12013

Zak, P. J. (2015). Why inspiring stories make us react: The neuroscience of narrative. *Cerebrum: The Dana Forum on Brain Science*, February 2015, 2.

Zak, P. J., Barraza, J. A., McCullough, M. E., & Ahmadi, S. (2011). Oxytocin infusion increases charitable donations regardless of monetary resource. *Hormonal Behavior, 60*(2), 148–160. https://pubmed.ncbi.nlm.nih.gov/21596046/

Zak, P. J., Stanton, A. A., & Ahmadi, S. (2007). Oxytocin increases generosity in humans. *PloS One, 2*(11), e1128.

Zhao, H., Xu, Y., Li, L., Liu, J., & Cui, F. (2024). The neural mechanisms of identifiable victim effect in prosocial decision-making. *Human Brain Mapping, 45*(2), e26609. https://doi.org/10.1002/hbm.26609

Acknowledgments

Writing this book has been one of the most rewarding and revealing experiences of my professional life and I didn't do it alone. Far from it.

First, to my family: thank you for your unwavering love and patience through countless late nights, early mornings, and missed weekends. To my wife, Betsy, who has always believed in the work even when the words weren't coming, and to my kids, John, James, and Elizabeth, who each made capital campaign pledges last year. Thank you for reminding me every day what joy, generosity, and curiosity really look like.

To Pam Cady Wycoff, every skill I've honed, every question I've chased, every meaningful connection, I can trace them all back to you. If anything in this book works, it's your fault! That I was once among your difficult students only proves how miraculous your teaching truly is.

To my colleagues at **Kindsight**, thank you for championing innovation while holding fast to the humanity at the heart of what we do. You prove that technology and empathy can—and must—coexist in service of good.

To the organizations I've had the privilege to serve and the people I've had the privilege of serving with—across health care, education, the arts, workforce development, and human services—thank you for entrusting me with your missions and your donors.

Each experience has sharpened my thinking and deepened my conviction that generosity is not something we extract but something we elevate.

To the friends and thought partners in this sector who challenged my thinking, asked better questions, and reminded me why this work matters, thank you. You know who you are. Your generosity of spirit, like the donors we serve, is the real engine behind this work.

To the fundraisers, board members, and nonprofit leaders around the world whom I've had the privilege of working with and learning from, thank you for being both the proving ground and the inspiration for these ideas. Your challenges, insights, and courage shaped the thinking behind this book long before the first word was written.

To the **AFP Global Board**, where I'm honored to serve alongside wise and mission-driven colleagues—thank you for your leadership and for your commitment to shaping a better future for our sector. You inspire me every day.

To the **Q3LC community**, and especially to **Marc and Emily Pitman**, thank you for your encouragement, your wisdom, and your example of grounded, values-based leadership. The clarity and confidence this process required were forged in the crucible of those conversations and reflections.

To the **HEROIC Public Speaking team**, thank you for helping me find the shape and spine of these ideas, especially **Amy and Michael Port, and AJ Harper**, who pushed me to speak and write with greater courage and conviction. You helped me say what I needed to say, on the page and on the stage.

To **Brand Builders Group**, thank you for giving me a platform to stand on and a strategy to grow from. **AJ and Rory Vaden, Ben Kolarcik, and Elizabeth Stephens**, your *years* of insight, encouragement, and belief in me and the impact of these ideas has meant more than you know. You helped me build something lasting, not just visible.

To **Phil M. Jones** and the *Exactly What to Say* team: your magic words helped me find better ones of my own. Becoming a Certified Guide wasn't just a credential, it was a deeper commitment to service through language, clarity, and compassion.

To **Dr. Howard Moskowitz**, thank you for introducing me to the power of mind genomics and for showing me that science—done quickly, simply, and creatively—can change how we understand generosity. Your mentorship shaped the heart of this book's inquiry and its practical application. I'm grateful to stand on the shoulders of your decades of insight and innovation.

To the team at **Wiley**, thank you for believing in this book and in this moment. Your care, rigor, and partnership turned this from a manuscript into a message I'm proud to share. Special thanks to my editors and publishing team for guiding this process with wisdom and heart.

To the **friends who are family**, thank you for the laughter, the late-night calls, the pep talks, the prayers, and the presence. You remind me of who I am and why this work matters.

And finally, to every reader who picks up this book with the hope of becoming a better fundraiser, a better leader, or simply a better steward of generosity: thank you. This book was written with you and for you. May it give language to what you've long felt, courage for the conversations ahead, and clarity in the work that still lies before us.

About the Author

Cherian Koshy is a globally recognized keynote speaker, strategist, and entrepreneur with more than 25 years of experience advancing fundraising, leadership, and innovation across the social impact sector. He has led high-performing teams in health care, education, the arts, and human services, raising hundreds of millions of dollars and driving transformational growth in organizations at every size to scale.

A visionary entrepreneur, Cherian is the founder of NonprofitOS (now, *engage*)—an artificial intelligence (AI)-powered platform that revolutionized nonprofit efficiency and strategy. Following its successful acquisition, he now serves as vice president at Kindsight, helping mission-driven organizations harness technology to create ethical, human-centered donor engagement.

Cherian holds the Certified Fund Raising Executive (CFRE) and Chartered Advisor in Philanthropy (CAP®) designations and is certified in behavioral science from Harvard Business School and in the ethics of AI from the London School of Economics. He is a Q3LC Certified Leader, an *Exactly What to Say* Certified Guide, and a member of the Rogare Council and the advisory council of Fundraising. AI, advancing critical thinking in fundraising practice internationally.

A LinkedIn Top Voice and frequent contributor to *Forbes*, *Advancing Philanthropy*, *The Chronicle of Philanthropy*, and *Nonprofit Pro*, he serves on the executive committee of the global board of the Association of Fundraising Professionals, the board of The Giving Institute, and is an adjunct faculty member at The Fund Raising School at Indiana University Lilly Family School of Philanthropy.

Cherian is a recipient of the Iowa Governor's Volunteer Award, a Kentucky Colonel, and a trusted voice on the future of philanthropy. In just the last five years, Cherian has trained thousands of nonprofit professionals from five continents and led more than three hundred workshops, conference presentations, webinars, and keynotes. *Neurogiving* is his debut book—an essential guide to designing donor experiences grounded in science, shaped by empathy, and built for the future.

Index

247

Index